S. MCGUIRE

The Silver Bull Market

The Silver Bull Market

Investing in the Other Gold

Shayne McGuire

WILEY

Library of Congress Cataloging-in-Publication Data:

McGuire, Shayne, 1966-
    The silver bull market : investing in the other gold / Shayne McGuire.
        pages cm
    Includes bibliographical references and index.
    ISBN 978-1-118-38369-8 (cloth); ISBN 978-1-118-42175-8 (ebk);
    ISBN 978-1-118-61514-0 (ebk); ISBN 978-1-118-41754-6 (ebk)
    1. Silver. 2. Precious metals. 3. Metals as an investment. I. Title.
    HG301.M34 2013
    332.63'28–dc23

                                                                    2012048957

Printed in the United States of America

10 9 8 7 6 5 4 3 2 1

For Winnie

Contents

Preface

F inancial market cycles, bookmarked by the booms and the busts, are often illustrated by magazine headlines like "The Death of Equities," which appeared at one of the best times ever to buy stocks (the summer of 1979), or hyperbolic book titles like *Dow 36,000* (1999), which preceded a decade-long period of stock market stagnation. It is always difficult to point to a bull market in a book since its author runs the risk of having the text become the poster child for the end of the run.

My view on silver—that it is likely to outperform gold in the present environment—is not new, as I expressed it openly in both my books on gold.[1] But it is important to point out that this is in reference to silver as an investment for the years immediately ahead, not that silver is somehow superior to gold. Gold is, in my view, the most respected form of long-term wealth preservation in the millennial history of finance and should be a part, however small, of every diversified investment portfolio. Though silver is more highly correlated with gold than anything else, I believe the market has yet to reach a decision regarding the white metal's proper position in the investment arena.

Gold is slowly being reincorporated into mainstream finance following what was, historically speaking, a very brief absence. Since gold and silver moved together for over 3,000 years (separated in value by a spread solely reflecting gold's greater rarity), I think it is rational to assume that, given their similar nature, the metals will continue to move together as they have done in this new century.

Considering the white metal's history of investment disappointments years ago and that its price is more volatile than gold's, most investors simply ignore silver completely. When the metal became part of the fund I manage*, my colleagues and I soon discovered that our pension fund, Teacher Retirement System of Texas, had become the largest nonbank holder of silver in the world. For a pension fund with a penchant for extreme risk management, this seemed bizarre considering the minor scale of the investment. Though our fund is one of the world's largest with over $110 billion under management, the silver investment represented one-tenth of 1 percent of our total assets—a small fraction of the value of our shares of Apple Computer, a single security.

If no other major investment fund in the world owns a significant stake in one of the best-performing assets of this new century, I thought that it made sense to write a book about silver. I hope you, the reader, find this one useful.

*This is public information available on Bloomberg.

Acknowledgments

As with my other books on precious metals, I was helped tremendously by family, colleagues, and friends, and I need to thank them all. As with my previous book, *Hard Money,* my deepest thanks go to John DeMichele, a colleague and member of the GBI Gold Fund team who contributed to writing this book and enriching its content with his ever-deepening knowledge of the precious metals world. At Teacher Retirement System of Texas, in launching the first dedicated gold fund in the U.S. pension system as well as my writing about precious metals I have long been encouraged and supported by Mohan Balachandran, Chi Chai and Britt Harris, who I would like to thank most warmly. I also need to mention my colleague and good friend, Patrick Cosgrove, an expert on European equities, as well as another friend and colleague on the Gold Fund, Tom Cammack. Through multiple conversations about precious metals in our daily interaction in fund management, these six people have each knowingly or unknowingly provided many important ideas developed in this and my other books.

Writing this book would have been impossible without the support of Michael DiRienzo, executive director of The Silver Institute, who always maintained an open door for any and all of my queries and helped provide indispensable statistical information about the global silver market.

I have also been fortunate to have access to some of the most brilliant people in the precious metals investment world: Tom Kaplan, one of the world's boldest gold investors, and Eric Sprott, one of the boldest silver investors; gold fund managers with impressive long-term track records, such as Caesar Bryan, Robert Cohen, Joe Foster, and John Hathaway, each of whom inadvertently provided ideas for this and (some) for other books, as well; Zak Dhabilia, now a fund manager but formerly the gold guru at Goldman Sachs, as well as Russell Stern, a commodities expert still at the firm; Jason Toussaint and Juan Carlos Artigas at the World Gold Council, two of the world's experts on the gold market; as well as other authorities in the precious metals investment world, like Jeffrey Christian, who runs the CPM Group; Jonathan Spall, Barclays' precious metals expert; and brilliant precious metals analysts: Edel Tully, precious metals strategist at UBS; John LaForge, the Global Commodity Strategist at Ned Davis Research; John Bridges at J.P. Morgan; and David Haughton, Andrew Kaip, and John Kayes at BMO Capital Markets; in the physical precious metals investment world, I have found no greater authorities anywhere than Terry Hanlon, who runs the Metals Division at Dillon Gage in Dallas, and Ryan Denby, who heads Austin Rare Coins & Bullion. Michael Byrd, founder of Austin Rare Coins, also provided important suggestions for this book. It has also been my fortune to share a friendship with Hugo Salinas, a fellow author of books about silver, the only activist in the world actually promoting the return to hard money in Mexico. His bill is in the Mexican Congress at this time.

As always, this book would have been impossible without the constant encouragement of my wife, Alejandra (Winnie), and the understanding of my two children. My mother's unwavering support and loving help with her grandchildren were indispensable and, last but not least, I have always counted on my father's expert editorial advice and good judgement to guide my pen.

Introduction

Coming to Terms with an Unfamiliar Investment, One of the World's Oldest

There is a certain absurdity, as contemporary eyes see it, in the idea of preserving wealth in precious metals. "Okay, our leaders might eventually drive us off a fiscal cliff, the economy is barely moving, the European crisis is getting worse and the ancient Mayans predicted 2012 was the beginning of the end. I'm thinking it's time to go out and buy some polished rocks."

This is what investing in precious metals sounds like to a great many rational adults today. In fact, that is how it appears to some of the brightest financial minds of our time, like Warren Buffett, the most successful stock market investor in history.[1] His disdainful view on gold as an investment has not changed since he said this at Harvard in 1998:

> Gold gets dug out of the ground in Africa, or someplace. Then we melt it down, dig another hole, bury it again and pay people

to stand around guarding it. It has no utility. Anyone watching from Mars would be scratching their head.[2]

Buffett has a very different view about silver, gold's sister metal, since he bought 130 million ounces of the metal—one-fifth of total world production—the year before he derided gold at Harvard. But this does not detract from his main point about the *concept* of precious metals investment, which is clear and cogent: How can investing in something—an asset class, as financial professionals call it—that offers no dividends (like stocks), interest (like bonds), or rental income (like real estate) make any sense?

Investing implies putting money—cash—at risk over a period of time with the expectation of earning a positive return. Historically, investment risk has been lower for bonds, especially those issued by the U.S. government. Unless there is a financial crisis or severe recession, most corporate and government bonds deliver interest payments and return of principal, as promised. Investing in a given stock is riskier as this always carries the possibility, however remote, of losing 100 percent of dollars invested; and risks, as well as potential rewards, can be much higher for those opening a restaurant or starting a computer company named after a fruit. But all these investments—buying bonds or stocks or launching new companies—carry with them the expectation of future cash flows: One can make calculations on a spreadsheet or sit down at the kitchen table with pencil and paper to calculate and project how money will be made.

And herein lies the essential absurdity that many individuals, particularly financial professionals, see in buying gold or silver: The metals are inert, nonproductive elements that produce no cash flow. For a precious metals investment to make sense, an investor needs to believe that factors completely outside his or her control will drive the price of gold or silver higher or that the metals' value will be preserved (presumably as that of other investments fall). "Show me how to grow my money" was once a statement hard to respond to with a metallic disk and a serious face, particularly considering the fate of investors in gold and silver during the 1980s and 1990s financial bull market, when metallic values languished while stock and bond market trillions were generated. Furthermore, precious metals have also long been associated with financial catastrophes, and those expecting economic Armageddon—and many of us know some who have been waiting a great many years for an apocalyptic event—have a certain affinity to gold and silver. "If I'm not expecting the end of the world, why should I invest in them?" one might ask. Said billionaire Charlie Munger in 2012: "Civilized people don't buy gold."[3]

Civilized people, by which Mr. Munger surely meant rational, well-informed investors, buy things they understand and believe in. This *trust* is what makes them surrender their cash, driven by a belief in a positive, potentially high return on investment in what they are buying: The trust must compensate them for risk. For example, considering Apple's history of success, most investors in what is now the world's largest company believe they are being well compensated for the possibility that its share price could decline in the future. As such, it is difficult to explain why gold and silver—which offer no direct cash flow, apparently *no compensation for risk*—have provided the highest return on investment over the last decade of any major asset class. Silver has risen an average 19 percent and gold 18 percent per year over the past 10 years, as you can see in Figure I.1.

Perhaps most notably, gold and silver performed extremely well in comparison with other investments during 2008, the year of the worst global financial crisis in four generations. During a year in which the stock market collapsed, along with numerous of the world's largest financial institutions—including some that had even survived the Great Depression—gold is one of the select few investments that actually increased in value; silver, though down 23 percent for the year, outperformed all stock markets and major commodities by a wide margin during that year. (See the 2008 column in Figure I.1.) Furthermore, from its lowest levels in 2008, gold has risen 140 percent and silver 260 percent as I write this sentence in October of 2012. Gold and silver remain in a bull market. (See Figure I.2.)

What explains the rise of ancient forms of financial wealth above virtually all others over the last decade, particularly during the periods of severe economic adversity we have experienced?

Rank	2011	2010	Annual 2009	2008	2007	5-Year	Annualized 10-Year	20-Year
1	Long Treasury 29.9%	Silver 83.2%	EM Equity 78.5%	Long Treasury 24.0%	EM Equity 39.8%	Gold 19.2%	Silver 19.0%	Private Equity 17.1%
2	Real Estate 17.2%	Gold 29.5%	High Yield 58.2%	Japanese Yen 23.3%	Commodities 32.7%	Silver 17.5%	Gold 17.6%	REITs 11.3%
3	U.S. I/L 13.6%	REITs 28.5%	Silver 48.2%	Gold 5.8%	Gold 31.0%	Long Treasury 11.2%	EM Equity 14.3%	Silver 10.1%
4	Private Equity 11.6%	U.S. Small 26.9%	U.S. Growth 37.2%	Real Estate 2.3%	Private Equity 21.1%	Japanese Yen 9.9%	Private Equity 11.5%	U.S. Value 9.1%
5	Gold 10.1%	EM Equity 18.9%	EAFE + CAN 33.7%	U.S. I/L -2.4%	Real Estate 17.1%	U.S. I/L 7.6%	REITs 10.3%	U.S. Small 9.0%
6	REITs 8.7%	U.S. Growth 16.7%	REITs 28.6%	Euro -4.2%	Silver 14.6%	High Yield 6.9%	High Yield 10.2%	Long Treasury 8.9%
7	Japanese Yen 5.5%	Private Equity 16.2%	U.S. Large 28.4%	Silver -23.0%	U.S. Growth 11.8%	Private Equity 2.5%	Long Treasury 8.9%	U.S. Large 8.5%
8	High Yield 5.0%	U.S. Large 16.1%	U.S. Small 27.2%	Private Equity -25.1%	U.S. I/L 11.6%	U.S. Growth 0.9%	U.S. I/L 8.0%	EM Equity 8.2%
9	U.S. Growth 2.6%	U.S. Value 15.5%	Gold 24.4%	High Yield -26.2%	EAFE + CAN 11.6%	REITs -0.2%	U.S. Small 7.0%	High Yield 8.1%
10	U.S. Large 1.5%	High Yield 15.1%	U.S. Value 19.7%	U.S. Small -33.8%	Euro 10.5%	EM Equity -0.8%	U.S. Growth 6.0%	Gold 8.0%
11	U.S. Value 0.4%	Japanese Yen 14.7%	Commodities 13.5%	U.S. Value -36.8%	Long Treasury 9.8%	Euro -0.9%	U.S. Large 5.7%	U.S. Growth 7.5%
12	Commodities -1.2%	Long Treasury 9.4%	U.S. I/L 11.4%	U.S. Large -37.6%	Japanese Yen 6.5%	U.S. Small -1.1%	EAFE + CAN 5.5%	Real Estate 6.4%
13	Euro -3.2%	Commodities 9.0%	Private Equity 10.5%	REITs -38.0%	U.S. Large 5.8%	U.S. Large -1.4%	Real Estate 5.4%	EAFE + CAN 5.6%
14	U.S. Small -4.2%	EAFE + CAN 8.9%	Euro 2.5%	U.S. Growth -38.4%	High Yield 1.9%	Real Estate -2.3%	U.S. Value 5.3%	U.S. I/L 5.3%
15	Silver -9.9%	U.S. I/L 6.3%	Japanese Yen -2.6%	EAFE + CAN -43.6%	U.S. Value -0.2%	U.S. Value -3.8%	Japanese Yen 4.1%	Commodities 3.1%
16	EAFE + CAN -12.2%	Real Estate 6.0%	Long Treasury -12.9%	Commodities -46.5%	U.S. Small -1.6%	Commodities -4.0%	Commodities 3.4%	Japanese Yen 2.3%
17	EM Equity -18.4%	Euro -6.5%	Real Estate -35.7%	EM Equity -53.3%	REITs -16.8%	EAFE + CAN -6.2%	Euro 2.5%	Euro -0.4%

Figure I.1 Annualized Return on Investment of Major Investment Asset Classes

SOURCE: Teacher Retirement System of Texas, Bloomberg.

NOTE: Private Equity and Real Estate returns are quarter lagged, JPY and EUR are expressed in their purchase power of USD.
All Domestic Equities modeled by Russell Indexes, All international Equities and REITs modeled by MSCI Indexes.
REITs—Real Estate Investment Trusts; U.S. I/L—U.S. Inflation Linked Bonds; EAFE + CAN—Developed Market Stocks Non-U.S.; EM Equity—Emerging
Markets Stocks. U.S. Value—U.S. Value Stocks; U.S. Growth—U.S. Growth Stocks; U.S. Small—U.S. Small Cap Stocks; U.S. Large—U.S. Large Cap Stocks;
Euro—Euro Currency.

★★★Through June 30, 2012

4

Figure I.2 Performance of Silver, Gold, U.S. Stocks, and Commodities since November 20, 2008 (indexed at 100)

Source: Bloomberg.

Inflation Is Coming and the Financial World Knows It

A government expenditure has the same impact on the economy whether the expenditure is financed through current taxation or deferred taxation (debt). Moreover, any debt incurred by the government can be paid off either through future direct taxation or through inflation (that is, by decreasing the real value of the currency in which the debt is to be repaid). Inflation is thus a form of indirect—but very real—taxation.

**—Laurence Siegel, Director of Research,
CFA Institute Research Foundation[4]**

I think most financial professionals would say, quite simply, that many investors have been accumulating gold—and the more volatile silver, which is highly correlated to its sister metal—out of concern that inflation will likely be significantly higher in the years ahead. Precious metals—most often star financial performers during times of rising inflation—are a subset of so-called real assets, which are formally defined as assets whose value is independent of variations in the value of money. Translation: Real assets provide some degree of financial protection from inflation, as they remain fixed in quantity and become scarcer as the amount of money being printed grows. Another way of thinking about real assets—if you agree with the logic of Mr. Siegel's preceding words—is that they are legal forms of tax evasion. And there is much that is blowing from the future to evade.

Global government debt and deficits have been surging for a number of years. In fiscal 2012—for the fourth year in a row—at least 25 cents of every dollar the U.S. government spent was borrowed. The fiscal cliff threatening the U.S. economy is also steep in Japan and the United Kingdom, not to mention a number of European countries, including large economies like France and Italy. If the troubled Eurozone is to avoid falling apart as an economic unit, most economists would acknowledge that the contingent liabilities of Germany, historically a frugal nation, will need to rise in fiscal harmony with its neighbors.

Given the dimension of the leverage problem, adopting austerity—drastic reductions in public spending—has brought severe consequences to countries like Greece and Spain. "You can grow out of excessive debt, but you cannot *shrink* out of excessive debt," observed investor George Soros in April 2012, referring to the European dilemma.[5] But considering the world's present sluggish economy, the politically convenient notion that we can somehow grow our way out of debt is now beyond empirical reality. And yet the global debt quagmire remains and federal liabilities continue to increase. Little has changed since the Bank of International Settlements, widely regarded as an authority among central bankers, made this assessment in 2010:

> Our projections of public debt ratios lead us to conclude that the path pursued by fiscal authorities in a number of industrial countries is unsustainable. Drastic measures are necessary to check the rapid growth of current and future liabilities of

governments and reduce their adverse consequences for long-term growth and monetary stability.[6]

Stated with less institutional formality and caution, Bill Gross, the managing director of PIMCO, the world's largest bond fund management company, said this about the United States' situation in October of 2012:

> Unless we begin to close [the fiscal gap of the U.S. federal government], then the inevitable result will be that our debt-to-gross domestic product ratio will continue to rise, the Fed would print money to pay for the deficiency, inflation would follow and the dollar would inevitably decline. . . . Bonds would be burned to a crisp and stocks would certainly be singed; only gold and real assets would thrive.[7]

Economists understand that there is an additional unstated dimension to the U.S. fiscal predicament Mr. Gross described: Attempting to close the gap could drive us *over* the fiscal cliff. Laying off thousands of government workers is a possibility, though it would have a minor effect on the gargantuan deficit and would immediately imperil a number of high-level political careers. On the other hand, in the present slow-growing economy, raising taxes to close the fiscal gap could quickly drive the economy into recession, as well, as it might actually *reduce* tax revenue and widen the gap further. Going in the opposite direction—actually having our leaders *spend more*, as some have suggested is needed—could ignite unexpected inflation as the Federal Reserve would likely have to absorb a growing portion of the government's new bond supply with freshly printed money.[8]

In this Catch-22 situation, something has to give, and a growing number of financial professionals believe that the tax man—whether the actual IRS or inflation (the virtual tax man)—is coming and they (and their clients) are getting prepared. They are buying real assets.

Real assets tend to perform far better than stocks and bonds, the dominant assets in present financial portfolios, during inflationary periods. But they also tend to outperform during periods that *precede* an acceleration of price levels in the economy, which invariably are times of surging government borrowing and spending. Although there are numerous investments regarded as real assets, the primary ones are commodities, precious metals, and real estate—assets whose supply is fixed, at least over the short term. But inflationary periods often cloud the country's growth outlook and economically sensitive real assets—like copper and crude oil—are usually eclipsed in price performance by the rarest, most desirable ones. We are already seeing this today.

While the U.S. housing market is still struggling to get back on its feet, consider events in a corner of the real assets space, the ultra-luxury real estate market. After former Citigroup Chairman Sanford Weill got a record $88 million for his condo at 15 Central Park West in 2012, as of this writing other properties at the address were listed at an average 192 percent premium to what owners paid just five years before. Despite the weak economy, the sellers' expectations are realistic: "When the demand is intense, that's when you get these crazy prices," commented a real estate analyst.[9]

Those crazy rich guys. Or are they? As if we were living in the booming late 1990s, in August 2012 a rare 1968 Ford GT40 expected to fetch $8 million in a sale of investment-quality cars went for $11 million, the highest ever for a U.S. automobile. At the same event, a cream-colored 1955 Ferrari 410 S Berlinetta sold for $8.25 million. "Two years ago this 410 S would probably have sold for less than $5 million," said the founder of the Historic Automobile Group International.[10] There are similar headlines in the international art world: In October 2012, a painting by Indonesian artist Lee Man Fong sold for three times what had been expected, a new record for Southeast Asian art. During the same month, a pair of 1941 Sun Yat-sen Chinese stamps sold for $709,000, by far a world auction record.[11] The same can be observed in the market for ultra-rare collectible coins of the million-dollar-plus variety. But these acquisitions are a select corner of the real asset investment arena, a world in which millionaire and billionaire buyers might expect these trophies to sit in their families for a generation or two as part of their family wealth.

As for real assets in the *real* investment world, the world in which both average individual investors and fiduciaries at large institutions participate, the investment horizon is complex. History has shown that both commodities and real estate tend to benefit from present conditions of extremely low borrowing costs and continuing easy monetary conditions: It would be difficult to find a historical situation in which money printing accelerated and commodity and property prices did not benefit. But commodities have already enjoyed an impressive boom over the last decade, eclipsing the stock market in performance while the global economy has slowed significantly.

The world's institutional investors have already made significant investments in the commodity space, which a great number of specialized funds actively trade in. The economy of China, the largest consumer of major commodities today, is beginning to show notable signs of slowing. Meanwhile, the real estate market's boom and severe bust have left some investors wondering about the wisdom of returning to this market, at least for the time being. Fortunately, the U.S. residential real estate market is beginning to recover as I write these lines and there are some tentative signs that China could be turning the corner. But let us consider the outlook for a minor league player in the real asset space.

Drivers of the Silver Bull Market

Over the last two generations, silver has widely been regarded as gold's shadow investment. Though gold has captured the financial headlines since 1971, when its price was freed from the $35-an-ounce price the U.S. government had maintained for decades, silver surged in tandem with the costlier metal during the 1970s. Both entered and remained in a bear market during the 1980s and '90s. And together silver and gold have risen in the present bull market, which began roughly when the 1990s stock market boom ended and the new century began.

Despite their similar price movements, silver has remained in gold's shadow as an investment for significant reasons, some of which are historical. Silver lost its monetary gleam in the nineteenth century as major economies left bimetallic systems, in which gold and silver both served as money, and replaced them with what became the international gold standard. Such it was with the United States, which abandoned silver formally in 1873 although the trend had begun years earlier.[13] China was the last major economy to leave its pure silver standard in 1934, a late chapter in a protracted monetary trend that enhanced the value of gold and eventually reduced silver to small change use.

Thirteen Drivers of Silver in Today's Financial World
These are, in my opinion, important drivers of silver's bull market today. If you find them convincing, please read Chapter 6: Always Keep in Mind the Risks of Investing in Silver.

1. **Silver, a hybrid precious/industrial metal, is a commodity play on global technological advancement.** Silver was once highly dependent on the film photography industry, which collapsed into insignificance with the rise of the digital camera, a major reason for the metal's weak price in the 1990s. Today silver's industrial demand is driven by brazing alloys and solders, growing electronic demand (smart phones, tablets, plasma panels and increasingly by new applications like silk-screened circuit paths and radio frequency ID tags), photovoltaics (solar panels) and new medical applications: silver is both biocidal and highly conductive. (See Chapter 3.)

2. **Silver moves with gold.** Though the metal exhibits more price volatility than gold as an investment asset, silver has been correlated more closely with gold than with anything else for two generations. Despite sometimes violent market swings, silver has kept pace with gold and has even outperformed it over the past decade. This is a return to normality, in my opinion, as the sister metals moved in tandem for thousands of years, notwithstanding the historical interruption between the 1870s and the 1930s, caused by adoptions of the Gold Standard. (See Part II about silver's history.)

3. **As an investment metal, silver is more precious, less industrial.** Silver is significantly more highly correlated with gold than with industrial metals, like copper, which means that the market regards it as more of a safe-haven precious metal than an economically sensitive industrial one. This was seen during the 2008 crisis: though silver declined, it outperformed collapsing stock markets and commodities by a wide margin. The exception was gold, which rose in that year. (See Chapter 3.)

4. **Silver is rarer than gold in the investment world today.** Total aboveground silver in all forms is worth approximately $800 billion, about one-tenth the value of the world's gold. Although there are 5 times more ounces of silver in the world, because gold is more than 50 times more expensive than its sister metal per ounce, the silver market is effectively much smaller. Silver is becoming rarer each year due to annual unrecoverable loss of tons of silver in industrial activities. Throughout history, tens of billions of ounces of silver have been used up in industrial production. Compare this fact with gold, the vast majority of which remains with us today. (See Chapter 3.)

5. **Silver is a premier real asset for inflationary times.** Sister metals gold and silver often outperform other real assets during periods of significant monetary expansion (they each surged over 2,000 percent in the 1970s) because they have a relatively small fixed supply, are nonperishable, liquid (as investments), easily storable, and historically recognized as alternatives to government-issued cash. Over the last decade, one of dramatic monetary experimentation, silver has outperformed all real assets (real estate, commodities— even gold) by a wide margin, not to mention the stock and bond markets. It also surged during the inflationary 1960s and 1970s. However, all real assets (houses, commodities, precious metals) have investment trade-offs, and silver's risks are important to consider. (See this Introduction, and Chapter 6.)

6. **Government today is silver's friend: Amidst global fiscal excess, unprecedented and extreme use of monetary tools is the only major policy our leaders have.** To help the economy recover from the 2008 economic downturn, the worst since the Great Depression, global leaders assumed more debt than ever to reignite the economy (with credit). With bloated balance sheets, expansionary fiscal policy options at present are limited and increased central bank money-printing, which is already being used around the world as a major policy

(continued)

(continued)

tool, will be vital when the next recession arrives. (See this Introduction, and Chapter 2.)

7. **Large investment fund ownership of silver is in its infancy.** Although the metal has been one of the winning investments of this new century, pension funds, insurance companies, and other large institutions managing tens of trillions in assets have largely ignored silver as a viable investment (for important reasons discussed in this book). Gold very recently was reincorporated into the financial system as the viable, respected financial asset it once was. In the scramble for scarce global real assets, institutional investors are likely to begin considering the investment merits of silver, which is highly correlated with gold. (See this Introduction.)

8. **The gold–silver ratio, a 3,000–year–old exchange rate, is out of historical balance.** While gold is 8 times scarcer than silver (in terms of total ounces produced annually), its price is more than 50 times higher than silver's. For 3,000 years in which the exchange rate could be observed, gold was 9 to 16 times more expensive, making today's level historically extreme. Now that many of the factors distorting the ratio have disappeared, it seems logical that the market exchange rate between the two should begin to approximate the difference in scarcity of each metal, which points to silver being significantly undervalued. (See Chapter 5.)

9. **Like gold, silver is an antibond and nonstock, one of the few investment vehicles allowing a person to completely remove wealth from the financial system.** Traditional financial assets represent claims on other entities. To preserve their value, bonds require that a government or company make interest and principal payments; stocks require dividend payments and/or that management deliver on earnings expectations; derivatives of many kinds can require financial faith at multiple levels; and ultimately, the financial system itself relies on *trust* that world economic

leaders will keep markets functioning properly by meeting their ever-expanding financial commitments. Gold and silver, inert metals recognized for thousands of years as stores of wealth whose nature cannot be altered by human error, have value outside the financial system. (See this Introduction and next point.)

10. **The global scarcity of safe assets that are not someone else's liability.** According to the International Monetary Fund, of the world's potentially safe investment assets, 89 percent are bonds of some kind—that is to say, someone else's debt.[12] For those believing that ultimate financial safety should not involve lending money to a company or government (buying a bond), there is only gold, the other 11 percent. But given the scarcity of gold and other real assets that are not economically sensitive (as real estate and major commodities are), silver is increasingly being regarded as a viable alternative to gold, which it was for most of human civilization.

11. **Anyone anywhere can buy silver.** Silver is an investment that can be made in any country by virtually any person—even in countries where there is no stock exchange, where even apple, the fruit, is hard to find. An ounce of gold, presently worth in excess of $1,600, is an investment unreachable to most people in the world, and represents a difficult financial decision even for middle class families in the United States. A $40 silver coin is something that can be bought by a great many people almost on a whim, a minor investment decision that chips away at globally scarce supply. If expectations for future inflation begin to rise— a concept that virtually any working adult understands— silver's well-known positive sensitivity to higher prices in the economy and its very accessibility could make it an important asset for many. (See Introduction.)

12. **The 1980s and 1990s bear market for precious metals had powerful drivers that no longer exist.** Extreme confidence in the U.S. dollar and Treasury bonds made

(*continued*)

(*continued*)

central banks dump an average 10 million ounces of gold for each of 20 years ending in 2008, most likely an unrepeatable event. This pushed gold from being close to 50 percent of global central bank reserves in 1980 to an all-time low of 14 percent in 2012. Heavily weighted in dollar, euro, and yen reserves and fixed income securities, a number of central banks are diversifying back into gold. In the wake of an aborted silver market manipulation plan that caused the metal's price to collapse in 1980, the metal was pushed down mostly by the collapse of film photography, the largest source of demand for the metal. But film photography is in silver's past, a very small part of demand today, and investment demand has become the key driver. That the two richest families in the world conspired to manipulate silver and inadvertently caused a crash was surely a singular moment in history.

13. Silver is an important investment asset in Asia, where demand has remained strong throughout history. Throughout Asia, but mostly in populous India and China silver, like gold, is a key investment asset worn and stored as a wealth instrument by a great many people. Every year, generally late in the summer and into the fall, the silver and gold markets are deeply influenced by a major financial event—the Indian wedding season, which draws a substantial portion of the world's precious metals as part of an enduring millennial tradition.

The metals' separation became most extreme during the worst years of the Great Depression: In 1933 while the price of silver was plunging alongside other commodities, gold buying became so intense that the U.S. government was eventually forced to make its ownership illegal. Ironically, over the following two years silver's price would triple—caused, in a manner that rhymes with present events, by the government's attempt to artificially boost economic demand. And in time silver would begin a protracted price rally driven by surging industrial use of the metal. During the 1960s, this demand became so intense that the U.S. Mint was forced to remove silver from American coinage due to the metal's surging price. And despite the hit to silver demand that the decline of film and rise of digital photography represented in the 1990s, Warren Buffett decided in 1997 to make a large investment in gold's sister metal. Not long afterward, silver would begin another strong price rally, one that has endured.

But silver has also been gold's shadow investment for a negative reason: Its price movements have been far more volatile than gold's over the years. When the two richest families of the world tried to corner the relatively small silver market in the late 1970s and trading authorities intervened to prevent it, the price of silver fell 50 percent in a single day, March 27, 1980, an event not forgotten by many senior investors. And, due to its smaller market, silver remains more volatile than gold, and on any given day, its price can rise or fall three times as much as that of its sister metal. Historically, silver—the restless metal, as one precious metals historian called it—has not been an investment for the faint-hearted. And despite its strong performance over the past decade, it has never been an asset that financial professionals have felt comfortable recommending with confidence.

In the present environment of global economic uncertainty, irrationality pervades a great many conversations about silver, which has made it an investment many simply avoid altogether. The metal is somehow a magnet for monetary conspiracy theories of the most bizarre nature. Being manager of a precious metals fund and author of two books on the subject, I have had a great many chats about silver and many start like this: "Well, if I put *all* my money in silver. . . . " Doing such a thing would not be sensible for a person of average wealth, just as concentrating entirely in tech stocks, beachfront real estate or any number of other assets, would not be wise. It is also unreasonable to regard silver simply as a "junk metal" when comparing it with gold. Perhaps it is a matter of semantics, but I think any metal that is made into investment coins by mints of the world's largest economies, including the United States Mint; is held by the ton in bank vaults in Geneva, Paris, London, and New York; and sells for more than $25 per ounce cannot be junk.

Yet silver is not gold.

Although the white metal has been in a bull market for some time, silver remains in gold's shadow. While gold has more than doubled in price since the peak of $850 it reached in 1980, as of this writing silver remains well below the all-time high near $50 it reached in that year.

Amidst surging government debt that makes up the so-called risk-free bonds the investment world requires for ultimate financial safety, gold may be emerging in time to challenge the U.S. Treasury bond as the safest investment on the planet, as it was once regarded. This is not the case today, as gold still trades like and is widely regarded as a "risk asset": Although gold has outperformed stocks and bonds for over a decade, during severe "risk-off" days when financial markets are falling sharply, gold frequently declines while U.S. Treasury bonds rally. But recently Ray Dalio, the founder and managing director of Bridgewater, the world's largest and most respected hedge fund, called gold "the new cash," a bold statement that rings true amidst present fiscal challenges and questions regarding U.S. government solvency.

Gold is once again being widely regarded as a mainstream investment, and yet silver remains a volatile, uninvestable asset in most fiduciaries' eyes. Unless we were to return to the monetary system that existed 200 years ago, silver cannot equal gold as an investment and core portfolio asset representing a substantial portion of wealth.[14] Gold is, quite simply, the most respected form of long-term wealth preservation in the millennial history of finance. It is an asset that to this day—a time in which trillions in financial assets can be electronically mobilized globally in seconds—central banks acquire in physical form to deposit in their vaults as a national asset. But this does not mean that silver, gold's shadow, cannot continue rising alongside—or even outperform—its sister metal as an investment in the coming years. Considering present financial conditions, and the scramble to acquire inflation-protection investment assets, I believe there are a number of major drivers that will keep silver in a bull market.

Silver Is the Most Accessible Real Asset in the Investment World

Perhaps the most important driver of silver for the years ahead is really the simplest one: Anyone, anywhere, can buy it. It is affordable in small quantities and is widely accessible, even to the world's poorest people. An ounce of silver, a coin, is something a person can purchase for less than $40 outside a formal investment arena. A gold coin of the same weight requires writing a check for more than $1,600, an experience unreachable to the vast majority of persons in the world. For many that's the down payment on a car. For an average household in the United States, or that of any of the other prosperous countries in the world, buying gold generally represents a very significant financial decision, one to be made perhaps after careful deliberation. Buying an ounce of silver can be done on a whim, being a minor investment. "Rolling the dice" on silver, if the purchase is modest, is not really rolling the dice at all: It could represent a minuscule, barely perceptible portion of a middle class family's wealth, the difference between having the family eat out or save $40 by dining at home.

Perhaps this simple, rather obvious observation partially explains why poor man's gold, as silver is often called, has been a better investment than its more expensive sister metal in this new century: More people can buy a metal that aboveground is not too far from the rarity of gold. In fact, the silver investment market is significantly smaller than the gold market. Silver has risen from $5 to over $30 an ounce during one of the most turbulent financial periods ever. But aside from the metal's affordability, consider its accessibility.

After a pause lasting more than half a century, the U.S. Mint and virtually all other mints only started to produce silver coins in the 1980s and 1990s. (See Chapter 15 on investment coins.) So the popular investment silver coins that are now widely available in the United States and several other developed countries are really a novelty: Before 1986 (when the metal was still in a deep bear market), the U.S. Mint had not produced any wide circulation silver coins since 1935, when the last Peace silver dollars were minted.[15] Today, as you can see in Chapter 15, there is a wide range of very high quality investment coins available around the world. And purchasing them online is extremely easy, far easier than finding a reputable coin shop, and something that can be done 24/7: A coin investor can make a physical precious metals purchase on the Internet at any time of day and lock in the price immediately, a very modern transaction unavailable to stock investors who must trade during market hours.

But think about the people who cannot invest in stocks and bonds, or those living in countries that don't even have a stock or bond market to speak of. Investing in shares of Apple is an experience reachable to a minority of people in the world—those affluent enough to actually buy and sell shares or institutions, like pension funds, who invest for their beneficiaries. Certainly far more than half of adults on the planet do not and cannot invest in the stock market and yet all have access to silver. Silver in its multiple forms (coins, jewelry, medals, flatware and others) is available literally in all countries and for persons at virtually all levels of income. The metal, the second oldest form of money, is bought and sold in the most remote communities where even apple, the fruit, is unavailable.

If there was a good reason to do so—say, a fear of future inflation, a concept even the poorest of the poor understand—literally any person could buy silver. So could any financial institution, but few investment funds have any silver investment to speak of.

The Reincorporation of Precious Metals into Mainstream Finance Is at a Very Early Stage

One of the most important drivers for silver as an investment is, ironically, that it does not matter in the financial system today.[16] Although investments in alternative assets, like real estate and commodities (including gold and silver[17]) have increased, today the overwhelming majority of the world's financial wealth is invested in stocks and bonds, which before the 2008 crisis had seen the best financial times in U.S. history. The 24-year period that ended in 2006 represents the most fantastic boom in stock and bond market investment returns in the past 200 years, counting from when Thomas Jefferson was president in his first administration.[18] The years since 2006 have been an amazing coda for the bond market, with returns unimaginable before the advent of Fed-driven zero percent interest rates. Considering the tremendous returns the stock and bond markets have provided over the last generation, it is no surprise to find that today pension funds hold 87 percent of their assets in equities and bonds.[19]

While a number of individuals, hedge funds and small funds have been investing in silver, either via financial markets or in physical form, silver has essentially no importance in the institutional investment world: Pension funds, insurance companies, endowments, and sovereign wealth funds—which manage tens of trillions of the world's wealth—hold virtually zero silver as a percentage of total assets. This is mostly explained by the small size of the silver market. Last year the physical silver absorbed by all the world's investors on all markets was worth approximately $10 billion, an amount equivalent to the shares traded in Apple

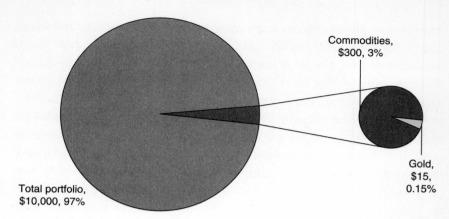

Commodities,
$300, 3%

Gold,
$15,
0.15%

Total portfolio,
$10,000, 97%

Figure I.3 Percentage Holding in Gold at a Typical Pension Fund (in $ millions)
SOURCE: Teacher Retirement System of Texas.

Computer, a single security, in one day. Although substantially more than that trades on the futures market in silver, widely regarded as paper silver, less than 3 percent of futures contracts are ever converted into the actual metal, making much of this activity essentially virtual.

The chart in Figure I.3, which I first presented in my previous book about gold but which has been widely circulated on the Internet, will help illustrate the point that silver investment in the world is negligible.

Pension funds, which today manage $31 trillion in global assets, typically hold less than 0.30 percent of assets in gold, which is to say, virtually nothing.[20] But gold is an asset class that the investment world has finally come to terms with, one that is widely respected as something that should hold a certain position in well-diversified portfolios. Silver, despite being more correlated to gold than anything else (as discussed further on), is in a completely different situation: Holdings in the white metal most likely are less than 0.05 percent of total assets at any pension fund, if they own any at all. Consider this fact: After my pension fund invested less than one-tenth of 1 percent of total assets in silver in recent years, Teacher Retirement System of Texas became the largest nonbank silver holder in the world.[21] Big money has not invested in the silver market, which has mostly advanced driven by individual investors, family funds, and hedge funds.

To argue that the world's investors collectively are about to move substantial investments out of stocks and bonds—say, more than

5 percent—and into precious metals would be absurd. Stocks and bonds have earned their place as dominant assets on institutional balance sheets because they have offered better risk-adjusted returns over time. Gold and silver are nonyielding assets that may not outperform traditional investments over the long run,[22] notwithstanding the present investment drive into real assets. But consider the historical starting point from which I am making the assertion that the investment world holds almost no silver in its portfolios: Stocks and bonds recently concluded the best generational investment returns in two centuries. And although silver has been outperforming traditional financial asset classes for over a decade, inflation has not even started to rise. And yet the conditions that historically have led to inflationary surges that benefit real assets like gold and silver are striking:

- We cannot grow our way out of massive debt, and yet leaders continue resorting to deficit spending to keep their economies growing. Governments, most notably those of the United States, Japan, the UK, and Southern Europe are heavily indebted and carry unsustainable deficits, while their economies are barely growing (or in recession). Consider the situation in Europe, where stock markets rallied sharply in late 2012 when it became clear that troubled Spain eventually will be allowed (*and encouraged*) to borrow even more from other European nations. It is important to keep in mind that all documented cases of hyper-inflation (which are fortunately rare events) were preceded by government deficits that got out of control. (See Chapter 2.)
- Central banks are actively and openly implementing aggressive inflationary policies. Widely regarded today as "currency wars," global central banks are printing money to maintain weak domestic currencies in an effort to promote economic growth. Gold and silver surged in the 1970s, when central banks were actively trying to *suppress* inflation. They were unsuccessful until the Federal Reserve drove the Fed Funds rate above *20 percent*. What can be expected now that global monetary authorities are doing the inverse—*promoting* inflation with the Fed Funds rate starting at zero?

Consider the comments made by Fed Chairman Ben Bernanke in October of 2012:

We are trying to create more employment. We are trying to meet our maximum employment mandate, so that is our objective. Our tools involve, I mean the tools we have, involve affecting financial asset prices and those are the tools of monetary policy.[23]

For the first time, the chairman of the Federal Reserve is effectively stating, on the record, that the institution responsible for defining the value of American money will print currency to create jobs. That such an effort is mathematically challenging to the mind explains why so many financial asset managers, and high net worth individuals in particular, continue scrambling to acquire real assets, proven inflation-protection vehicles. They are trying to insulate their wealth from government error. Paying over $10 million for a unique car may seem extreme today, but wise in the future if the value of that money has fallen dramatically while the vehicle remains unchanged.

For many investors who are seeking to increase investments in real assets, gold is the simplest choice in the present environment. I have called the rediscovery of gold by the professional asset management world the *gold reincorporation trade*. Commodity specialists, who have been predicting a decline of (nonproductive) gold prices for years, have not considered the reality that gold, which provides time-proven diversification benefits to portfolios, is gradually taking a position alongside traditional financial assets, like stocks and bonds. Drawing on a limited supply of gold (mining production increases supply annually by less than 2 percent) forces increased demand to result in higher prices. If, as I expect, pension funds, insurance companies, endowments, and sovereign wealth funds begin to consider silver—many for the first time—as a viable real asset to take more seriously, the metal's rally is likely to intensify because its supply is so limited (see Figure I.4).

Silver Moves Less like an Industrial Metal and More like Gold

Though a precious metal, silver is an important industrial one, as well. Investors drove the metal's price down sharply in 2008 expecting that reduced industrial demand would cause a surge in unsold supply of the metal. This made sense: more than half of total silver demand is industrial,

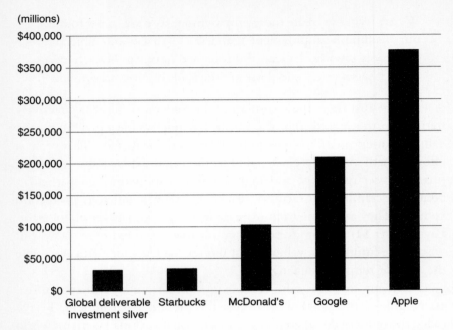

Figure I.4 Deliverable Silver on the Global Market Compared with the Market Value of Four Companies

SOURCE: The Silver Institute, Bloomberg.

as the metal is employed in such things as brazing alloys and solders, electrical application, and electronics, and it is used heavily in the solar panel industry. In recently discovered applications, silver is being used in new battery technology for smart phones, laptops, and tablets, as well as in creams, bandages, and powders in the medical sector. Since the metal inhibits fungal growth, silver is also being used in new ways to disinfect water, and in food packaging and refrigerators. Silver has important industrial applications that have been growing each year.

And yet silver is very different from other industrial commodities. While virtually all of them—most notably copper and crude oil—remain below their price high points of 2008, silver has risen more than 50 percent higher. Despite the multiple uses of silver in industrial processes, in recent years the metal's key price driver has been investment. And over the last decade, silver has traded more closely with gold than with copper, a purely industrial metal. In fact, "Dr. Copper" is regarded by many economists as a key barometer of global economic health. The charts in Figure I.5 show

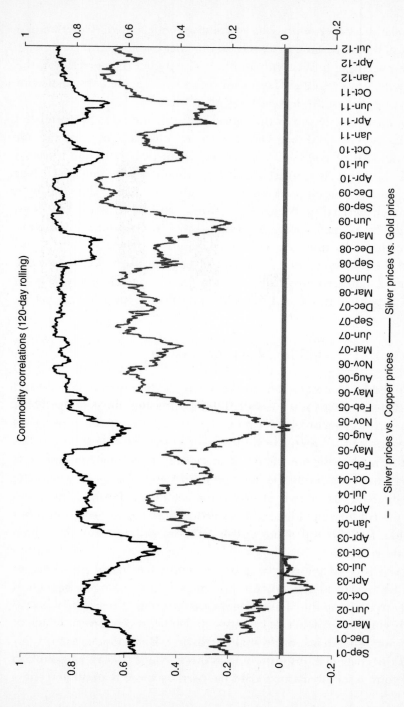

Figure I.5 Correlation of Silver with Gold and with Copper since 2002

Source: Bloomberg.

Commodity correlations (120-day rolling)

- – Silver prices vs. Copper prices   —— Silver prices vs. Gold prices

23

the correlation of silver with gold, and of silver with copper. (Correlation is a statistical metric ranging from zero to one that essentially measures how much a given asset moves with another. The higher the correlation, the more assets move together. For example, snow is highly correlated with temperatures below 30 degrees Fahrenheit.)

The chart clearly shows that silver has been substantially correlated more closely with gold than with copper, even during the very difficult economic crisis of 2008 and early 2009, when real estate and financial markets collapsed. As pointed out above, though its price declined, silver outperformed all stock markets and commodities during the crisis by a wide margin reflecting its closer investment affinity to gold. This is an extremely important point regarding silver's economic sensitivity. Because the next time the economy begins to falter, if copper and gold go their separate ways (as usual), silver most likely will follow the rarer metal. Furthermore, if silver continues to move closely with gold, the less expensive metal will be more accessible to more investors.

The Next Recession

The United States emerged from the severe 2008 recession in 2009 and has been in recovery for a number of years. Although the economy's last growth rate was recorded at a mere 1.3 percent, as of this writing no major economist has mentioned the risk of a return to recession. But this is a fact: It is a historic inevitability that sooner or later the economy will contract. And considering the ongoing European recession, as well as the recent dramatic slowdown in economic activity in Japan, China, and Brazil, the risk that the United States will go into a recession soon is not negligible. Let's go ahead and visualize the upcoming recession, which hopefully is far off.

At the pace of present job growth, which has barely been able to match the growth in new entrants into the workforce, unemployment is unlikely to drop rapidly. There is hope that economic recovery will lead to improving job growth that can drive higher tax revenue with which to reduce our dependence on federal borrowing. But consider the magnitude of the challenge, disheartening as this is. Since the last recession, in merely four years the national debt has risen by more than 50 percent, a rise in leverage not experienced ever in the United States in peacetime. With deficits of over $1 trillion in each of the past four years, about a third of government spending each year is borrowed. Facing the so-called U.S. fiscal cliff—an expected combined $600-billion hit from impending tax increases and spending reductions—to say that the federal government would struggle to spend *even more* to confront an economic slowdown is an understatement. It would not be difficult to argue that the country simply cannot afford to embark on expansionary fiscal policy when the next recession arrives.

But most recessions end or are mitigated by the Fed. When the economy slows and inflationary pressures wane, the Fed begins reducing interest rates, which encourages spending that leads to recovery. However, to combat the last recession, the Fed drove the interest rate it controls to zero for the first time in U.S. history. This has driven interest rates on virtually all forms of borrowing to the lowest rates ever experienced. When the next recession arrives—assuming the economy has not normalized, which is a fair assumption considering the present environment—the Fed will be forced to *intensify* the only policy it can employ: to print money and buy financial assets from investors that will hopefully spend the money on things that help the economy.

Money printing, both in recent years and throughout financial history, invariably leads to higher gold prices. Silver is more highly correlated with gold than anything else, as financial markets have shown over the past 40 years. Though silver is a more volatile investment, higher gold prices most often lead to higher silver prices. Considering that the scale of monetary easing would have to be even deeper in recession than in the sluggishly growing economy we have seen in recent years, it follows that silver is likely to benefit from the next recession.

The Scarcity of Assets That Are Not Someone Else's Liability

Since private gold ownership was made illegal in the United States in 1933, those seeking ultimate financial safety have been presented with this singular recommendation: Buy government bonds. This advice did not change when Americans were allowed to legally own gold again in 1974, since by then the U.S. Treasury bond had come to be widely regarded—and even formally defined in financial academia—as the ultimate "risk-free" asset. And the recommendation, which continues to this day, has been superb: Not only have federal government debentures provided investors with protection from financial adversity, but Treasury bonds in all maturities also have provided outstanding returns for decades, while gold's performance has been inconsistent—despite the metal's strong rally over the past decade, its price fell sharply during the 1980s and '90s. Silver has moved similarly, but with substantially more volatility.

Treasury bonds have rightfully been regarded as risk-free simply because the U.S. government always meets its financial obligations. It cannot—and presumably *will never* default: Even if the U.S. Treasury ran completely out of funds and could not sell bonds on the open market, it could rely on the Federal Reserve to buy them with freshly printed money to prevent a default. One could argue that this has already been occurring. In 2011, more than half of total net Treasury debt issuance was purchased by the Fed,[24] an action that was not disruptive to financial markets because the consequences were not inflationary. And the resulting stability of government borrowing rates provided by the Fed's market-smoothing activity has allowed our leaders to continue adding liabilities to the country's balance sheet—at a trillion-dollar-per-year pace. There have been no serious consequences to these actions and U.S. Treasuries continue to trade like risk-free assets.

But in April 2012, the International Monetary Fund published an important paper that raised questions about the safety of vital investment assets, like U.S. Treasury bonds, that for generations have been regarded as riskless:[25]

> The financial crisis and the heightened concerns about sovereign debt sustainability in many advanced economies have reinforced the notion that no asset can be viewed as truly safe. Recent rating downgrades of sovereigns previously considered to be virtually riskless have reaffirmed that even highly rated assets are subject to risks. The notion of absolute safety—implicit in credit rating agencies' highest ratings and embedded in prudential regulations and institutional investor mandates—can create a false sense of security, and it did prior to the crisis.[26]

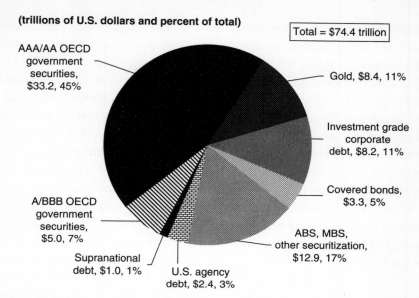

Figure I.6 Potentially Safe Assets in the World
SOURCE: International Monetary Fund.

Safe assets are vital holdings for commercial banks, insurance companies, pension funds, sovereign wealth funds, and central banks. They provide the foundation upon which these institutions, managers of the world's wealth, define their very solvency. In 2008, the largest bank in the world (in terms of total assets), Royal Bank of Scotland, and the largest insurer, AIG, folded and were taken over by government because a substantial part of their assets, which were assumed to be trustworthy, collapsed in value. And there were a number of other financial institutions around the world that folded, as well.

What are safe assets? In its paper, the International Monetary Fund (IMF) provides a chart showing the $74.4 trillion in total "potentially safe assets" available to the world. (See Figure I.6.)

Upon examining this pie chart, a person with little experience in financial markets likely would only be able to understand the terms "debt," "bonds," and "securities" aside from the easy one—gold. With the terms completely understood, the same person would realize that of all slices of this pie the IMF regards as potentially safe, gold is the only asset that is not someone else's liability. As such, it is not surprising that during the 2008 financial crisis—although the metal initially declined in the tidal wave of collapsing commodities—gold ended the year with a higher price, something only seen for the safest of bonds, like Treasuries.

In times of crisis, virtually all traditional financial assets, like stocks and corporate bonds, become risky investments that are sold off in heavy volume. During the credit crisis the world lived through in 2008 and early 2009 financial trust evaporated and investors ran to the only assets they believed could endure any crisis, which at that time were government bonds issued by the world's strongest economies, most notably the United States, Japan, and Germany. This trust allowed these countries to increase their borrowing dramatically. What is ironic about the present financial situation is that notwithstanding surging deficits and federal debt levels among the world's leading economies in recent years, for most financial advisors the safest investment recommendation remains to lend money to the government.

Putting complete trust in government-issued securities, and not gold, as the ultimate financial safe haven is a historical anomaly. The U.S. dollar is today the monetary foundation of the world: More than half of the trillions in global monetary reserves are in dollars or dollar-denominated U.S. fixed income securities. And yet the United States—which by virtue of its financial dominance defines the value of global money—is the world's largest borrower. One hundred years ago, when the United States was rising to become the world's largest creditor, it did so based on "sound monetary policy," the gold standard, which set the foundation for global confidence in the nation's solvency. Back then, when the American balance sheet was in balance, it would have been impossible for the nation's leaders to borrow more than 25 cents out of every dollar it spent, which has been the case for the past four years.

Considering the small size of the market for gold—the only safe financial asset that is not someone else's liability—the rise we have seen in the metal's price is not dramatic. After all, it rose 2,300 percent in the 1970s, when there was no question about the U.S. government's solvency. If more and more investors increasingly begin to question the safety of sovereign bonds, as the IMF has done openly, gold demand should continue to rise.

And for the past two generations, silver has moved with gold.

Part One

THE LOGIC OF OWNING SILVER IN TODAY'S FINANCIAL WORLD

Chapter 1

Silver Moves with Gold, a Vital Asset for These Times

Although silver is a precious metal, most central bankers would never consider investing in silver bars to be put alongside the stacks of gold in a national vault. Though the white metal was used as money for thousands of years (and was the first widely used American money) silver is no longer regarded as a monetary asset comparable to gold as discussed in the history section of this book. Furthermore, while there is a rich literature discussing the investment virtues of gold as an asset providing diversification benefits to an investment portfolio, there is no such financial love for silver, at least at this time in history.

And yet, as the metal's price moves in the marketplace, silver's performance over the past 45 years shows that it is more closely correlated

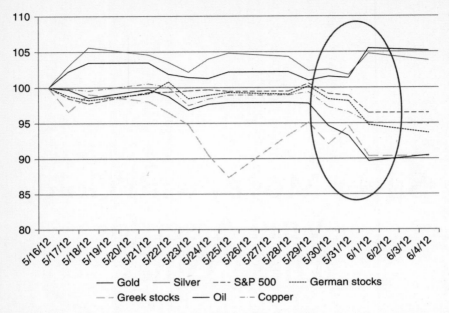

Figure 1.1   Movement of Gold and Silver along with Other Markets from May 16 to June 4, 2012 (Indexed to 100)

SOURCE: Bloomberg.

with gold than with anything else: Silver moves in the same direction as gold over extended periods—and increasingly on the same day. Consider Figure 1.1, which shows financial market movements over a few weeks in the summer of 2012.

This was the day before an important weekend in European history, the week in which French and Greek voters would be allowed to give their first opinion on how government had been managing affairs during the credit crisis. (Verdict: French and Greek leaders had failed.) This particular period a "risk-off" set of trading days in the market, saw stock and industrial and energy commodity prices plunge, and yet silver followed gold up. Figure 1.2 is a chart showing how the metals performed earlier in the year, a time in which gold and silver were down while stocks and other asset classes were up.

Both of these charts show the main point of this chapter, which is that silver is most likely to go where gold goes. Rising investment in silver tends to go hand in hand with rising investment in gold. Let's look at some longer-term charts of gold and silver.

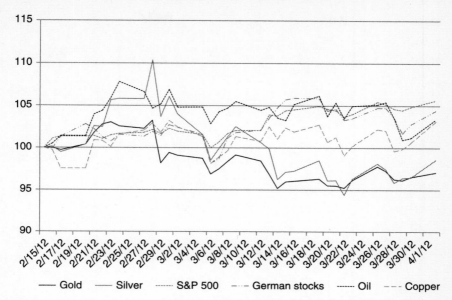

Figure 1.2   The Movement of Gold and Silver along with Other Markets from February 15 through April 2, 2012 (Indexed to 100)
SOURCE: Bloomberg.

The chart in Figure 1.3 shows how gold and silver have traded during the present bull market that started in 2000. (Note that this is merely to show the direction of trading for the metals, as silver has actually outperformed gold in percentage terms.) The chart in Figure 1.4 shows how gold and silver traded during the gold bear market between 1980 and 2000. And the chart in Figure 1.5 shows how these metals performed during the bull market of the 1970s.

Once again, the point is simply that silver is highly correlated with gold. For half a decade, the two metals have been moving in the same direction. If you believe that gold prices are going higher or lower, this should affect the way that you are thinking about silver. But here is another consideration: Silver tends to move in the same direction as gold, *but with greater intensity* and, at times, erratically. For example, if gold rises 2 percent in a given week ($34 at present gold levels), silver could rise 3 to 4 percent ($1.20) or more. But if gold falls 2 percent, silver might fall 3 or 4 percent—or a lot more.

This is important to keep in mind when the metals begin to get hit in the market as this will rattle any silver conviction you may have. In April

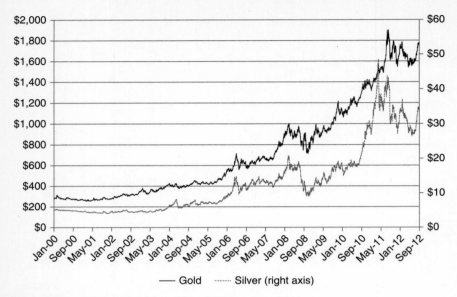

Figure 1.3   The Price of Gold and Silver since 2000

SOURCE: Bloomberg.

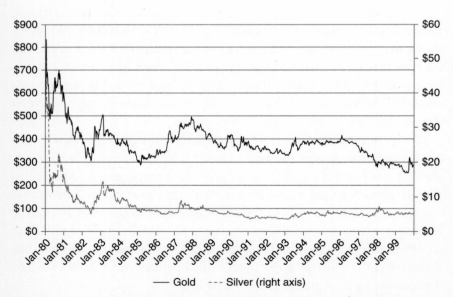

Figure 1.4   The Price of Gold and Silver between 1980 and 2000

SOURCE: Bloomberg.

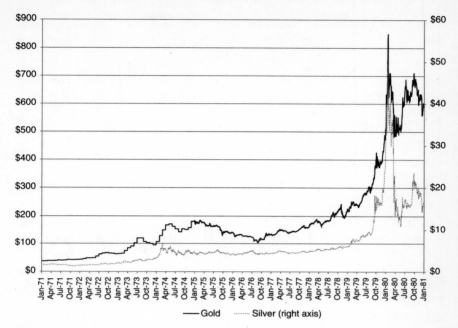

Figure 1.5   The Price of Gold and Silver between 1971 and 1980
SOURCE: Bloomberg.

of 2006, I remember seeing gold and silver begin to wobble. The metals had started the year with a surge—silver had jumped 78 percent by mid-April. Then, on April 20, the price of silver fell like a rock—down 20 percent in a single day. It recovered ground, but only before plunging 35 percent into mid-summer, as you can see in Figure 1.6. Gold declined 20 percent for the same period. Although silver had a strong year in 2006 (up 46 percent), this episode illustrates one of the undeniable and important risks to consider with silver: It is a volatile asset to invest in, and as an investor, you should be prepared for intense price swings.

That being said, there are also days and months of intense volatility to the upside, as seen during several weeks in 2011, when the price of silver rose an impressive 42 percent. (See Figure 1.7.)

A friend working at one of the leading commodities banks in the world openly criticizes silver as a "heart breaker," a metal that surges briefly and gets "suckers" into the trade before declining. Silver, he believes, lacks the financial fortitude of gold and deserves to be ignored as a solid investment. Silver's performance during the 2011 sell-off (which

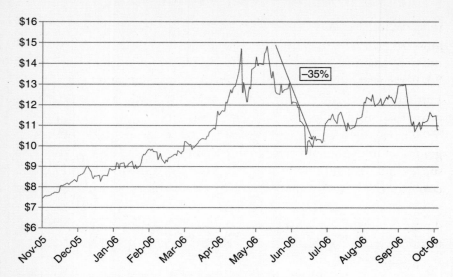

Figure 1.6   The Price of Silver during Part of 2005 and 2006
SOURCE: Bloomberg.

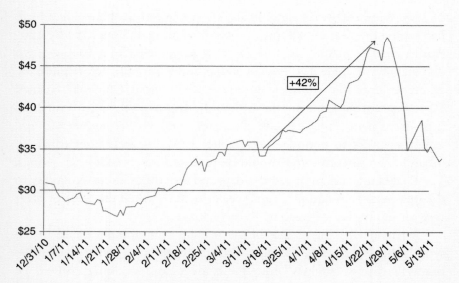

Figure 1.7   The Price of Silver in Early 2011
SOURCE: Bloomberg.

followed the big rally shown in Figure 1.7) would seem to vindicate his view that silver is not to be regarded as a solid investment. And yet he did not deny the truth of this simple statement: "If you knew gold would rise 20 percent, you would expect silver to rise significantly, as well." Furthermore, considering its higher volatility, silver would likely rise more than gold, at least in the short term.

There is no questioning the fact that silver presents more risks than gold as an investment. There are important considerations from both the supply and demand sides. But if you expect that gold will be rising, the correlation to silver that has been observed for half a century should make you confident that silver will probably rise as well. Furthermore, considering that the silver market is smaller (there is less silver for sale than gold in dollar terms), a surge in demand generally leads silver to rise faster than gold.

Chapter 2

Thinking about Future Inflation[*]

T hat silver moves with gold is important considering the latter's historical connection with inflation. While gold can surge in value as an investment over the space of a few years, such as occurred in the 1970s (up 2,300 percent) or the the last decade (450 percent), over the long run the rise has been smoother as gold is simply a proven means of protection from inflation, a way to preserve purchasing power. Some critics of gold often cite brief periods of time, such as the 1980 to 1999 period when gold fell, to show that it has offered poor protection against inflation.[1] But gold's fixed supply ensures its defense against rising prices over extended periods because inflation is, in the words of economics Nobel laureate Milton Friedman, *"always and everywhere a monetary phenomenon."*[2] Since governments (and I'm

---

[*]Much of this chapter is an updated version of my book *Hard Money: Taking Gold to a Higher Investment Level*, which was published in 2010, with permission from John Wiley & Sons.

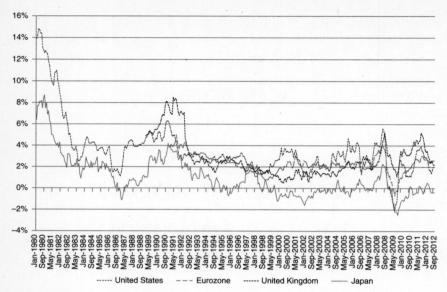

Figure 2.1   Annual Inflation Rates in Major Economies since 1980
SOURCE: Bloomberg.

including central banks as part of them) invariably increase the quantity of money in circulation more rapidly than the supply of gold rises each year—which is very little, typically less than 2 percent—it follows that gold rises in value versus all paper currencies over time: Currency supply outpaces gold supply and the scarcer asset rises in value relative to the more abundant one. Or, put differently, gold's value remains relatively unchanged while the value of paper money falls over time. What proves this monetary fact is that every single paper currency in human history has lost value against gold. There is no exception.

Gold (along with silver) fell out of favor as an investment in the 1980s and 1990s partly because inflation began to decline rapidly from the double-digit levels of the previous decade. (See Figure 2.1.) With inflation under control, the economy began expanding and asset classes like stocks and bonds became attractive once again as interest rates began a steady decline. There was a sense during these prosperous times that the Federal Reserve and other central banks, which guide the level of global interest rates, had completely mastered the price level and that inflation was unlikely to jump by more than one or two percentage points from one year to the next. And while there was ample academic debate over whether inflation was being measured correctly—for example, some thought surging equity, real estate, and other asset prices were not being properly included in Fed inflation metrics—it has been decades since a wave of gold or silver buying was ignited by concerns about inflation. If anything, there have been serious concerns about *de*flation, the threat that prices could fall, as occurred during the Great Depression and more recently in Japan. As you can see in Figure 2.1, inflation rates have been falling for quite some time, and Japan has actually been fighting deflation for decades and continues to do so at present.

Deflation, a rare economic phenomenon (as can be seen in Figure 2.2), occurs when the supply of goods and services in the economy is too large relative to the demand for them and typically surfaces after a war or protracted economic boom, such as the one that recently ended in the United States, as well as the one leading up to the Great Depression. Its occurrence is highly disruptive to the economy because falling prices lead to increased unemployment, which can drive the economy into a

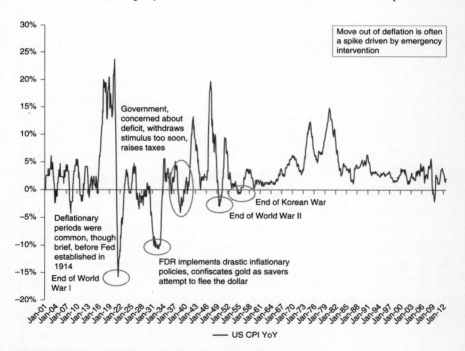

Figure 2.2 U.S. Inflation, 1901 to the Present

SOURCES: Bloomberg, Datastream, Morgan Stanley, Teacher Retirement System of Texas.

downward spiral of contracting demand and eventually a severe recession or even a depression. Before the 1930s, when governments began actively using deficit spending to prevent demand from falling too sharply, economic authorities allowed the supply and demand balance to be restored by the brutal forces of the marketplace: Through the shutting down of businesses and a rise in unemployment, supply would contract until it eventually came into balance with lower demand.

Governments no doubt were concerned about the recurring, though relatively short, recessions and depressions occurring in the United States during the late 1800s and into the early twentieth century, but putting the national balance sheet at risk was unthinkable at the time. Unlike today, deficit spending was seen as the road to economic ruin. During his first inaugural address in 1933, President Franklin Roosevelt, surely expressing the conventional wisdom regarding government finances of his time, said: "Revenue must cover expenditures by one means or another. Any government, like any family, can for one year spend a little more than it earns. But you and I know that a continuation of that habit means the poorhouse."[3] But the president would soon change his mind.

As I discussed at length in my books about gold, the historical axiom that government and family books need to balance was debunked by the dire circumstances of the Great Depression. Regardless of the Depression's causes, which have been debated by economists—including Ben Bernanke, an expert on the topic—for decades, the severe contraction in demand caused the country's worst deflationary crisis on record. The chart in Figure 2.2, which shows the past century of price changes in the United States, gives a sense of the severity of the fall in prices in the 1930s and its deleterious effect on the economy: Unemployment eventually surged to over 25 percent.

One stunning example of the monetary emergency the country was living through is the fact that in parts of the country the price of corn went *negative* for some time: Farmers had to pay a distributor to take it off their hands.[4] It was the brutality of an economic collapse never experienced before that forced leaders to think the unthinkable and consider long-shunned economic ideas, like deficit spending. The deflationary spiral had to end. And thanks to economists like John Maynard Keynes, in time it became acceptable for government to spend more than it received, at least during economic downturns. But in recent decades, virtually all major economies have had substantial deficits, even during

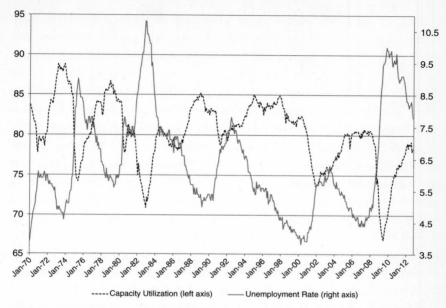

Figure 2.3   U.S. Capacity Utilization and Unemployment Rate, 1970–2012
SOURCE: Bloomberg.

economic expansions. Deficit spending has become a permanent fixture of macroeconomic policy.

Today, deflation is once again a significant threat to several major economies in the world, as excess capacity is evident throughout several sectors. (See Figure 2.3, which shows capacity utilization in the United States.) Unemployment is extremely high in many countries, a factor that hinders price increases across the global economy. Additionally, the sheer level of debt across the world—but primarily in developed economies—at the private and public level acts as a demand suppressant to a significant degree. Furthermore, as seen in Figure 2.1, the inflation rate had already been declining in recent years and we even had a deflationary scare in 2002.

Armed with the historical experience of having fought an intense battle with deflation in the 1930s, in 2008 the U.S. government (via massive deficit spending) and the Federal Reserve (by way of operations that effectively involved money printing) launched their complete fiscal and monetary arsenal upon the financial system in an effort to prevent deflation. The government, as it has done often before, was attempting to replace falling private demand with rising public demand in the economy. And our leaders were successful in preventing full–fledged deflation from occurring: The economy has rebounded. But the price paid was high as the deficit and national debt soared, and the downturn has been so severe that unemployment has risen sharply despite the government's efforts. And so it went with other major economies, like Japan, the United Kingdom, and the European community, all of which have been left with tremendous deficits, debts, and high unemployment.

Now, in financial terms, markets are "priced" for inflation to remain low and perhaps even move into deflation: This is what is expected. And considering the tremendous excess capacity and unemployment levels present in the global economy, the *slack* that economists often refer to, it makes sense to believe that inflation is unlikely to surface anytime soon. This is perhaps the main frustration for economists who see little reason for the continued climb of precious metals in the face of tremendous deflationary forces at play in the economy. ("Isn't gold supposed to be about inflation, and not *de*flation?") But the reason there is a significant risk that inflation could erupt—perhaps violently—in the years ahead is government debt.

Today 7 of the world's 10 largest economies, including the United States, have total debt representing more than 250 percent of gross domestic product. (See Figure 2.4.) The United States' debt ratio is substantially higher than that, and Japan and the United Kingdom have already surged well over 400 percent. Although national debts have been climbing for many years now, the global economy was generally expanding in lockstep. But since the economy fell off a cliff in 2008 and is projected to grow at a modest pace over the next few years, those debts have become alarming as growth is needed for them to be serviced. Furthermore, as Morgan Stanley's chief global strategist put it, "there is no historical precedent" for an economy with debt greater than 250 percent of GDP to avoid financial crisis (or inflation) in its attempt to bring down the colossal debt level.[5] Paying down debt when it has reached such a scale invariably requires a severe recession, as consumption contracts sharply so that savings can be destined toward creditors. And yet, considering the economic catastrophe the world recently lived through, there is little tolerance for economic pain at present. To complicate the situation further, there has been minimal deleveraging in many of the world's major economies up to now, mostly because government deficits and debts have been rising so rapidly.

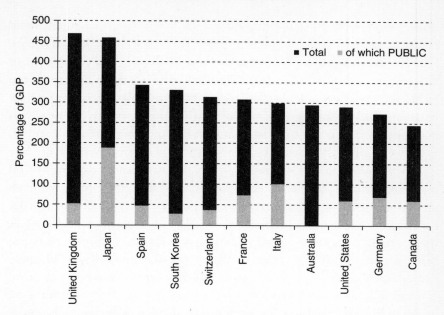

Figure 2.4   Total Debt to GDP for Major Industrialized Countries, 2011
SOURCE: Morgan Stanley.

High government deficits become an inflationary concern because, absent some supply shock (such as a spike in oil prices), historically they have tended to provoke an increase in prices throughout the economy over time. And in several important situations, rising deficits have led to hyperinflation, a situation of severe economic dislocation. Although the path of rising prices can vary from country to country, the logic for why government excess can lead to inflation is straightforward: Rising deficits eventually reach a point at which governmental debt requirements become so large that the bond market is saturated and/or alarmed investors refuse to continue lending to a nation—at least at low interest rates. At that point, unless leaders impose emergency spending reductions, they are forced to print money for spending, and more money in circulation in time leads to a higher inflation rate.

The Risk of Hyperinflation

Although inflation caused by government is known to have occurred as far back as the early days of the Roman Empire, there are only 56 documented cases in economic history of *hyper*inflation, defined as an inflation rate exceeding 50 percent per month. (See Table 2.1.) This list, which took economists Steve Hanke and Nicholas Krus three years to compile, is a product of the most comprehensive work on hyperinflation published up to now. The task was daunting not only due to the scarcity of data in many situations, but because of the "size problem": How can an economist get his or her hands around a monthly inflation rate of 4.19×10^{16}, which is what Hungary experienced in July of 1946?[6]

Hyperinflation is fortunately a rare event because hyperinflation essentially means, in blunt economic terms, game over: The value of savings collapses, financial markets shut down, there are runs on banks, capital flees the country, supermarkets run out of multiple food items, many gas stations shut down, unemployment surges, and severe recessions ensue. With the help of international organizations like the International Monetary Fund, it is possible for a country to recover economic and price stability relatively quickly, but at a new level far lower than existed before: The nation's standard of living has fallen and it takes many years for past affluence to return.

Like Steve Hanke, Peter Bernholz, professor of economics at the University of Basel in Switzerland, is widely regarded as one of the world's leading experts on hyperinflation, and his explanation for why it occurs is unambiguous: "Hyperinflations are caused by government budget deficits."[7] There is no exception: Hyperinflation, meaning the emergence of an economic catastrophe, has *never* occurred without a huge budget deficit. And in each case of hyperinflation, the deficit amounted to more than 20 percent of public expenditures.

One doesn't need a PhD in economics to understand how these nations met their fate, because the cause is so straightforward: The countries listed in Table 2.1 arrived at their terrible predicament essentially because their governments, having exhausted the revenues needed to meet their expenditures, ultimately decided to print money to pay their bills. The surge in money in circulation caused the value of goods, which became scarcer than the rising amount of currency notes and coins, to begin rising rapidly. Inflations then have a tendency to accelerate, Bernholz says, because the public tries to get rid of the depreciating currency, spending it as quickly as possible.[8] Rapidly increasing inflation, not surprisingly, is highly disruptive to the economy as both creditors and

Table 2.1 Hyperinflationary Episodes in World History

Country	Year	Highest Inflation Rate per Month (%)	Country	Year	Highest Inflation Rate per Month (%)
1 Hungary	1945/46	41.9 quatrillion	29 Belarus	1992	159
2 Zimbabwe	2008	79.6 trillion	30 Kyrgyzstan	1992	157
3 Yugoslavia	1992/94	313 million	31 Kazakhstan	1992	141
4 Republika Srpska	1992/94	297 million	32 Austria	1921/22	129
5 Germany	1920/23	29,500	33 Bulgaria	1991	123
6 Greece	1942/45	13,800	34 Azerbaijan	1991/94	118
7 China	1947/49	5,070	35 Uzbekistan	1992	118
8 Free City of Danzig	1922/23	2,440	36 Congo (Zaire)	1991/92	114
9 Armenia	1993/94	438	37 Peru	1988	114
10 Turkmenistan	1992/93	429	38 Taiwan	1948/49	108
11 Taiwan	1945	399	39 Hungary	1923/24	98
12 Peru	1990	397	40 Chile	1973	87
13 Bosnia	1992/93	322	41 Estonia	1992	87
14 France	1795/96	304	42 Angola	1994/97	84
15 China	1943/45	302	43 Brazil	1989/90	82
16 Ukraine	1992/94	285	44 Democratic Republic of Congo	1998	78
17 Poland	1923/24	275	45 Poland	1989/90	77
18 Nicaragua	1986/91	261	46 Armenia	1992	73
19 Congo (Zaire)	1993/94	250	47 Tajikistan	1995	65
20 Russia	1992	245	48 Latvia	1992	64
21 Bulgaria	1997	242	49 Turkmenistan	1995/96	62
22 Moldova	1992/93	240	50 Philippines	1944	60
23 Russia/USSR	1922/24	212	51 Yugoslavia	1989	59
24 Georgia	1993/94	211	52 Germany	1920	57
25 Tajikistan	1992/93	201	53 Kazakhstan	1993	55
26 Georgia	1992	198	54 Lithuania	1992	54
27 Argentina	1989/90	197	55 Belarus	1994	53
28 Bolivia	1984/86	183	56 Taiwan	1947	50

SOURCE: Steve H. Hanke and Nicholas Krus (2013), "World Hyperinflations," in Randall Parker and Robert Whaples (eds.) *The Routledge Handbook of Major Events in Economic History,* London: Routledge Publishing.

businesspeople find it increasingly difficult to provide credit and price goods. And invariably, the consequences for financial markets are severe.

Judging by the graph lines in Figure 2.5, which show surging budget deficits for major economies, one could argue that conditions are present for an eruption of hyperinflation in the United States, the United Kingdom, and Japan, countries that collectively account for almost

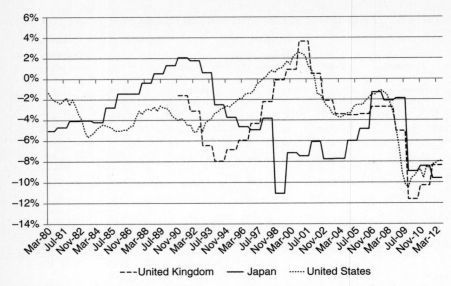

Figure 2.5   U.S., UK, and Japan Budget Deficits as a Percentage of GDP, 1980–2012

SOURCE: Bloomberg.

half of global GDP. Deficits, which had already existed in these countries, shot up dramatically in 2008 as a result of the global financial crisis. Consider that the U.S. government's debt-to-GDP ratio surged a stunning 20 percentage points in a single year. The national debt rose 50 percent in four years. And yet governments have been unable to provide a credible plan for how deficits—not to mention the trillions in debt—will be reduced in the years ahead, particularly considering the demographic challenges each country faces.

Federal outlays to an increasing population of retirees will be *accelerating* over the next decade, particularly in Japan, which implies increasing federal spending. Furthermore, the global sovereign bond market of tens of trillions of dollars, large as it is, was not deep enough to absorb the massive amount of U.S., UK, and Japanese bond issuance, and this has required that central banks absorb a significant portion of issuance: These countries' central banks printed money to buy federal bonds. In 2011, the Federal Reserve purchased 61 percent of the total net bond issuance of the federal government.[9]

That the world's major economies have surging deficits and debt does not mean that hyperinflation is about to erupt. An American real estate crash did not occur in 2003, which is when UCLA Professor John Talbott wrote *The Coming Crash in the Housing Market* (McGraw-Hill Professional), but the conditions for the crash that took three more years in coming were certainly present: Home prices were rocketing far more rapidly than incomes; families were cashing out billions in equity; and regulators, loan officials, and market professionals were ignoring troublesome signs. The conditions were present for a collapse of the housing market, just as today we have massive federal deficits across the world that provide the conditions necessary for hyperinflation to rear its head, at least in some countries. Our leaders are faced with the need to slash expenditures and/or increase tax revenues to prevent an inflationary catastrophe from occurring. But as we wait for governments to form a credible path for the reduction of debts and deficits, it is likely that investment will continue to move into inflationary insurance instruments like gold and silver.

Chapter 3

Silver's Supply and Demand Dynamics

For the silver bull market to persist—and for any bull market to persist, for that matter—one has to believe that demand is likely to be rising faster than supply in the months and years ahead. Or, taking another approach, one has to think that supply is so small that even a relatively minor increase in demand would be sufficient to push the price of silver substantially higher. There are a number of drivers of silver demand that are spoken of in broad terms, like the risk of rising inflation caused by climbing government debt and deficits, which historically have driven precious metals prices sharply higher. But this chapter delves into the actual quantity of demand for silver, the number of total ounces that is met each year by a given supply.

The main point is rather simple: As silver is being increasingly regarded within the financial system as an investment asset appropriate for today's environment, its supply—once the substantial amount of silver that is destined for industrial use is subtracted—is minuscule, literally a negligible part of the sum of financial assets in the world. A relatively small amount of investment dollars moving away from other assets—stocks, bonds, real estate, cash—would be sufficient to cause an even more significant rise in price than what silver has experienced so far. This is a point I made about gold when I wrote two books about the metal: A small shift in investor sentiment, a minor move into gold away from the traditional asset classes that investors have generally felt most comfortable with, would be sufficient to push gold prices higher.

And this is precisely what has been occurring. There is this ubiquitous sense that *everybody is buying gold*, and yet this is simply not true. The increase in gold investment since I began writing *Buy Gold Now* in late 2006 has been of approximately 260 million ounces, worth about $352bn (using average gold prices for each year). This is a small amount for a six-year period during which trillions were invested in global bond, equity and real estate markets. Yet that relatively small increase in gold demand caused the metal's price to triple. And consider that the gold investment market is multiple times larger than the silver investment market.

In my writing about gold and in a number of presentations I've made at investment conferences around the world, I focus on an important theme: the reincorporation of gold into the financial system. Gold is being recognized as an asset class that like stocks, bonds, and real estate has investment attributes that are attractive in certain financial environments (climbing inflation, negative real interest rates, large government deficits) and not so in others (stable inflation and healthy economic growth). The main point is that gold *is* an asset class and not something that should be considered uninvestable for professionally managed globally diversified portfolios, a widely held financial view as recently as 2008.

Gold's reincorporation into the broader financial world has had little impact on the investment arena since the metal in investment form represents less than 1 percent of total global financial assets of approximately $200 trillion. While institutional investors (pension funds, insurance companies, banks, private wealth managers of many stripes) have increased investments in gold, as a percentage of total assets the amount remains extremely small. A point I've made often is that a typical globally diversified pension fund holds less than 0.40 percent of assets in gold, a remarkable fact considering that these institutions manage $31 trillion of the world's wealth. Consider that Teacher Retirement System of Texas, the pension fund I work for, holds a substantially higher percentage in gold than most pension funds in the world. But our investment, at less than 1 percent, is a very small part of the pension fund's total assets.

In this sense gold does not matter, at least for now, in the big financial picture: Gold's importance remains far beneath stocks and bonds in the asset allocation decision-making process for most institutions, which makes sense, to an extent: Gold, a nonyielding asset, is unlikely to outperform stocks and bonds over the long run. But for gold investors the metal's low significance for large funds is less relevant than the fact that gold finally matters again, and the metal's rising price reflects its reincorporation into mainstream finance. The effect on the gold price and the metal's supply and demand dynamics has been dramatic: Investment demand (in terms of volume of gold) has more than tripled in the last decade and the price has risen even higher, this despite gold remaining a minuscule part of the world's total financial investments.

The same thing has happened with silver, but its story is very different because the metal's rise has been caused primarily by different buyers. Silver has risen more sharply than gold in the past 10 years (540 percent compared with 380 percent for gold) and investment demand has surged, but very little of this demand has come from institutions. (Let me put the importance of institutions into perspective: Pension funds, insurance funds, and mutual funds alone manage in excess of $79 trillion, more than four times the size of the U.S. economy. Institutional money is the leviathan of the investment world.) Virtually all silver investment demand has come from specialized funds (mostly focused on commodities) and individuals from around the world. Although major institutional investors may have some (extremely small) exposure to silver via their commodities investments, by and large their investment in gold's sister metal is extremely small. And for silver there are no institutions like the pension fund UTIMCO, which decided to invest a whopping $1 billion in gold bullion, an amount representing 5 percent of their total investments.

There are a number of reasons why gold and silver have been outperforming all other investment asset classes for the last decade. Metals' prices have been driven higher by such factors as increasing Asian purchases, rising needs from industries like electronics, and by climbing global investment demand. But ultimately, supply and demand dynamics determined where the price of each metal would go. The real estate market went bust in the United States and several European nations because the dollar amount of supply surged and eventually overwhelmed climbing demand. But for gold and silver, supply is very small relative to the amount of money sloshing around the world that could be invested in the metals, and supply is severely constrained.

Silver Supply

All the silver ever mined and refined in the world since 4,000 B.C. is estimated at 49.5 billion troy ounces. But after centuries of silver use in industrial production, most notably the decades since the 1920s, only 27.1 billion ounces remain in the world today.[1] Considering the low cost per ounce of silver for many decades, it was not profitable for it to be recycled, the way gold always has been. Consequently, billions of ounces of silver have been permanently destroyed in the medical industry, mirrors, innumerable electrical uses, dentistry, brazing and soldering, photography, and many other industrial processes. These remaining 27 billion ounces are held in the form of bullion, coins and medallions, jewelry, silverware and in an array of art forms as well as in industrial stockpiles. If we valued all that silver at present market prices, it would be worth $800 billion. To put that amount into perspective, all the world's silver is worth one-tenth of all the world's gold.

The total amount of silver supplied to the market in 2011 was 1 billion ounces, which was worth close to $35bn at the average price of that year (see Figure 3.1). It was a record year, with mining production rising 3 percent, and it follows a strong 2010, which saw an 2 percent rise. Silver mining production has increased by 25 percent over the last decade, which is a growth rate in sharp contrast with that of gold, which has barely risen. (See Figure 3.2.) However, though the billion ounces of silver reaching the market each year are almost 8 times the ounces of gold produced, the value of that gold is 7 times greater than the amount of silver. But perhaps more importantly, as mentioned above, much of the silver supplied to the market each year is destroyed permanently in industrial production; only a small fraction is recovered and recycled. However, since gold is so much more valuable per ounce, the vast majority of gold used in industrial production is recycled. More than 96 percent of all the gold ever mined and refined is in the world

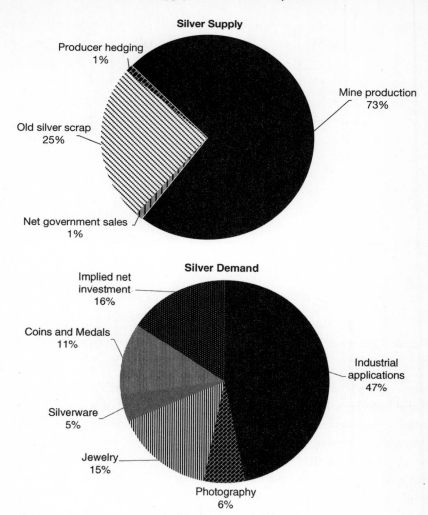

Figure 3.1   Silver Supply and Demand in 2011
SOURCE: The Silver Institute.

today. But more than a third of the world's aboveground silver was used up in industrial production in the decades following World War II. In a 1992 study, the Silver Institute estimated that 49 percent of all the silver ever mined and refined has been consumed.[2]

Most of the new silver supply on the market comes from the mining industry (73 percent) and the rest from scrap (25 percent) and sales made by governments (1 to 2 percent). (See Figure 3.1.) From year to year some

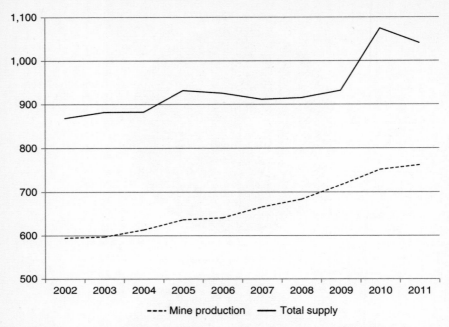

Figure 3.2 Silver Mining Production and Total Supply (millions of ounces)
SOURCE: The Silver Institute.

mining supply can come from producer hedging, which essentially means that miners are selling some of their production ahead of actual delivery to protect themselves from price fluctuations. But producer hedging is generally a very small part of the supply and demand equation. It is worth noting that more than half of silver mined comes as a byproduct in the mining of other metals, like copper. Southern Copper Corporation is the world's 12th largest producer, as you can see in Figure 3.3. That silver is mostly a byproduct metal has notable economic implications: During recessions, when industrial mining activity slows, silver production tends to weaken as well, which constrains silver supply. If copper production declined significantly due to lower metal prices, silver's supply would decline.

Over the years, governments have sold silver on the market both for their own funding needs and to reduce pricing pressure on industrial users when silver deficits have occurred. The U.S. government used to be one of the largest silver holders in the world (as discussed in Chapters 9 and 10) due to large purchases in the 1930s, when the Roosevelt administration

2011 Rank	Country	Output (mm oz)	2011 Rank	Company	Country	Output (mm oz)
1	Mexico	152.8	1	KGHM Polska Miedź S.A.[1]	Poland	40.5
2	Peru	109.8	2	BHP Billiton plc.	Australia	39.0
3	China	103.9	3	Fresnillo plc[2]	Mexio	38.0
4	Australia	55.2	4	Goldcorp Inc.[3]	Canada	28.8
5	Chile	42.1	5	Pan American Silver Corp.[2]	Canada	21.9
6	Poland	40.8	6	Volcan Cia. Minera S.A.A.[3,4]	Peru	21.1
7	Russia	40.0	7	Polymetal International plc.	Russia	19.9
8	Bolivia	39.0	8	Coeur d'Alene Mines Corp.[2]	United States	19.1
9	United States	36.0	9	Cia. de Minas Buenaventura S.A.A.[4]	Peru	15.3
10	Argentina	22.6	10	Hochschild Mining plc.	Peru	15.0
11	Canada	19.1	11	Kazakhmys plc.	Kazakhstan	13.1
12	Kazakhstan	17.6	12	Southern Copper Corp.	United States	12.7
13	India	11.0	13	Sumitomo Corp.[3]	Bolivia	12.4
14	Turkey	9.4	14	Kinross Gold Corp.[5]	Canada	12.1
15	Sweden	9.1	15	Industrias Peñoles S.A.B de C.V.	Mexico	11.4
16	Guatemala	8.8	16	Xstrata Zinc[6]	Switzerland	11.1
17	Morocco	7.3	17	Teck Resources Ltd.[3]	Canada	10.1
18	Indonesia	6.0	18	Hecla Mining Company[2]	United States	9.5
19	Iran	3.5	19	Yamana Gold Inc.	Canada	9.3
20	Papua New Guinea	3.0	20	Eti Gümüş A.Ş.	Turkey	8.4

[1] Reported metallic silver production
[2] Primary producer
[3] Estimate
[4] Includes production from minority subsidiaries
[5] Reported silver sales
[6] Reported silver in concentrate and lead bullion

Figure 3.3 Top Countries and Companies That Produce Silver
SOURCE: The Silver Institute.

began accumulating the metal. The holdings of the U.S. Treasury surged a peak of 3.2 billion ounces by 1962, the largest single silver stash ever held by a country.[3] The U.S. Treasury began disposing of that silver in the 1960s and has virtually no silver remaining. Today, only Russia, China, and India are significant government suppliers of silver on the market. But their sales of the white metal fell sharply in 2011 in part because the countries' silver stocks have fallen significantly due to large disposals on the market in recent years that likely left them with little metal to supply the market with.

It is in relation with governments that silver and gold are so different in terms of supply: Central banks around the world hold 1.01 billion troy ounces of gold worth approximately $1.7 trillion. Governments, which a century ago held a substantial part of all silver on the market, today own almost nothing. If federal governments or central banks ever decided to try and manage the price of gold, their control over large gold holdings might allow them to try and do so. In fact, there is an organization that for years has claimed that governments are actively manipulating the price of gold. (This issue is discussed in Chapter 14.) But lacking any significant silver deposits—as, for instance, the U.S. Treasury once held—would make it difficult for any government to have more than a temporary influence on the price of silver. (See Figure 3.4.) In this sense, silver's price is perhaps a truer reflection of what the free market believes it should be, while gold can be affected by central bank activity, which can be significant from year to year. Consider that in 2011, central banks bought more gold than they had in any of the past 40 years, which had a positive effect on the metal's price. They could also be selling, which they did aggressively in the late 1990s, near the bottom of the gold bear market. No such activity has occurred in the silver market in recent years. (See Figure 3.4.)

After proceeds from the mining industry, scrap sales are the largest component of silver supply to the market. In 2011, scrap sales jumped

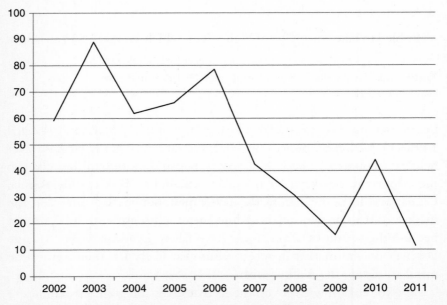

Figure 3.4 Government Sales of Silver (millions of ounces)
SOURCE: The Silver Institute.

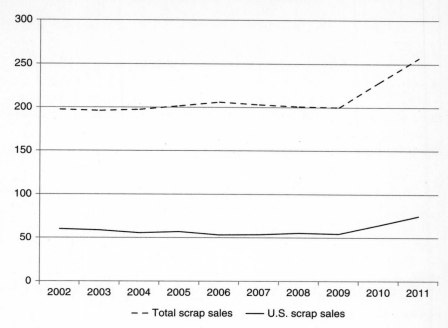

Figure 3.5   Silver Scrap Sales (millions of ounces)
SOURCE: The Silver Institute.

20 percent over the previous year to a record 257 million ounces as sellers scrambled to take advantage of high prices, which averaged $35 an ounce during the year. Scrap sales have averaged around 22 percent of total silver supply over the past decade, but over the past two years higher silver prices have caused a sharp increase in scrap supply (see Figure 3.5). In 2011 scrap silver supply rose to represent 25 percent of all silver sold on the market, the highest in many years. (See Figure 3.6.) Although China, India, and Japan are large scrap sellers each year, they are eclipsed by silver sales from the United States, which reached 75 million ounces in 2011, a big jump from the previous year. That amounted to more than double the scrap sales made in China, the next largest supplier to the market, and more than three times what was sold in India, also a very important player in the global silver market.

Scrap can come from anything from metal recycled from industrial processes, flatware, jewelry, medals, and old coins, which used to have a large silver content. In fact, silver coins used to circulate commonly in many countries until the 1960s and in virtually all countries before the 1930s. Dimes and quarters in the United States used to contain silver, but

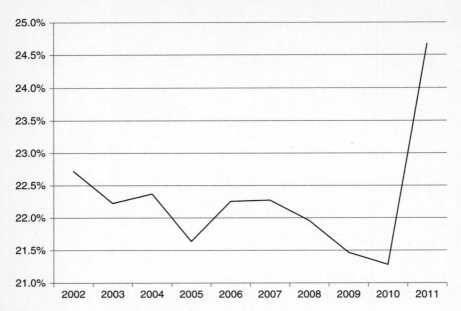

Figure 3.6   Silver Scrap as a Percentage of Total Supply
SOURCE: The Silver Institute.

the metal was removed from all coins after 1964. (This episode is discussed at greater length in Chapter 10.) The vast majority of coins from earlier times have been melted down, the silver consumed in industrial processes over the past 50 years. Much of scrap silver over the past two or three generations came from coins, but today most silver coins that remain are rare coins. Hence scrap today comes primarily from jewelry and industrial recycling.

Silver Demand

The sources of demand for silver have changed significantly in recent decades. Silver went through a period of demonetization that lasted over a hundred years ending in the 1960s, as monetary systems began adopting purely gold standards in the nineteenth century. They were following the lead of the Bank of England, which abandoned bimetallism in 1717, and China was the last country to be on a purely silver standard until 1934, when the country was forced off a metallic monetary standard and entered a severe inflationary crisis. The final chapter of silver's demonetization happened in the 1960s, when the last coins containing silver were either melted down or hoarded in collections to be replaced with coins made of less expensive metals.

Coin use today is completely different, as silver is no longer employed in commerce, and buyers are either collectors and/or investors. Silver coin demand has been climbing sharply in recent years rising from a paltry 3 percent of total demand a decade ago to 10 percent of total silver demand today. Roughly $3.5 billion in coins were minted in the world last year, which is a dramatic rise from the roughly $140 *million* in new coin sales a decade ago. The sharp rise reflects not only the increased volume demand (up threefold), but the sevenfold rise in average silver prices. But here is some perspective on the $3.5 billion in purchases: This total demand for newly minted silver coins (from all over the world) is the value of what trades in shares of Starbucks, a single security on the Nasdaq exchange in the United States, in two weeks. A recurring theme throughout this book is the tiny size of the silver market in comparison with the financial ocean of $200 trillion in investments.

Although coin demand is strong in countries like Canada, Austria, and China, the United States market is by far the largest, accounting for 40 percent of total global demand (see Figure 3.7). When coin demand is added

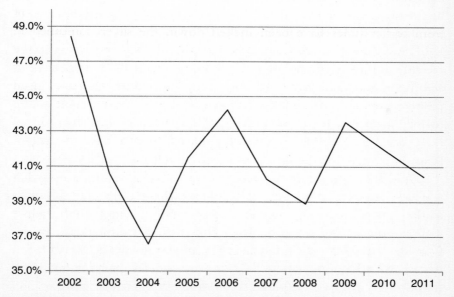

Figure 3.7 U.S. Silver Coin Sales as a Percentage of Total Global Coin Sales
SOURCE: Silver Institute.

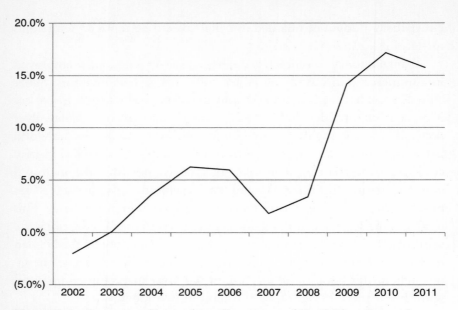

Figure 3.8   Investment Demand as a Percentage of Total Silver Demand
Source: Silver Institute.

to demand for other silver investment products—mainly in the form of silver bars—total investment demand for new physical silver entering the market accounts for 27 percent of total silver on the market, as shown in Figure 3.1.

Considering photography's importance to the silver industry until very recently, it is worth mentioning. Between 1977 and 1993, 34 percent of all silver industrial demand was from photography. With the rise of digital photography, silver use in film developing collapsed, a factor contributing to sluggish prices in the 1990s. In 2011, only 6 percent of all silver produced each year is used by the photography industry, which makes it a minor factor in considering the supply and demand dynamics of silver.

Despite the significant rise in demand for silver coins and bars—what is widely regarded as the physical market—what truly pushes the silver market up and down, often in dramatic price swings, is the paper market—silver futures and options. This market is substantially larger. Consider that while total investment demand for physical silver reached a record 282 million ounces in 2011, the average *daily* volume traded on the Comex, the world's largest commodities exchange, was of 389 million ounces (see Figure 3.8).

Chapter 4

Poor Man's Gold
Is Different from Other
Inflation-Protection
Assets

S peaking some time ago to a reporter at a major financial newspaper, I asked him—following a somewhat lengthy discussion about gold—if he owned any. His response was straight to the point: "I put money into my 401K, and whatever I have left over would never be enough to buy even an ounce of gold. I don't have the option to buy gold within my 401K. There might be a way to do so in my account, but I haven't figured it out." He seemed resigned to the fact that he probably would not be buying any gold soon.

Having written two books about gold and being manager of a gold fund, I have had a great many conversations with people about gold in relation with their other investments—mostly stocks, bonds, and real estate. Among the wealthy friends I have, the decision has been fairly simple: Most own gold—some a lot, some a small portion of their total wealth—and have owned it for several years. For many, their private wealth advisors have recommended this. (I remember seeing some time ago that Credit Suisse, which has one of the largest and most prestigious private wealth management operations in the world, had openly recommended that its clients—generally of the $10 million–plus net worth variety—hold at least 5 percent of assets in gold.) Some also have investments in silver, but these are in a minority.

But my chats about gold with *normal* people—that is, with those whose family income is nearer the American median level of $50,700, or at lot less—often hit a brick wall fairly quickly. Because—let's face it— most people can't put $1,750 on the table to purchase a single coin, the price of an ounce of gold. It is not an easy proposition for most people, regardless of their thoughts on the metal. Even those that can, and for whom that amount represents a lot of money, the prospect of investing almost $2,000 into a single coin makes many people nervous. Two thousand dollars represents a significant portion of an average American's take-home paycheck. Furthermore, a great number of people with 401Ks are, for a multitude of reasons—like the one in the first paragraph—unable to invest in gold directly using the investment accounts that monthly draw from their salaries. There are a number of investment vehicles in planning stages at this time that would allow investors to buy gold in their 401Ks, but a great many savers still do not have access to viable gold investment vehicles at this time. I think it's safe to say that the vast majority of American households do not own gold. And, as discussed at greater length in my previous book, pension funds barely hold any gold, either.

Silver has long been called *poor man's gold* simply because it is far less expensive per ounce than gold and hence more accessible to the majority of people in the world. And though the price difference between gold and silver is very high by historical standards (as discussed in Chapter 5), the disparity has always existed: Gold has long been a wealth preservation vehicle mostly for people of means. As an example, in the fourteenth century, an ounce of gold was worth the wages that a farmer earned in a week, which made the cheaper metal more widely used among the general public. But there is more to the description "poor man's gold" than price, as silver has long been a more volatile investment, regarded by many in my profession as a financial asset of poorer quality and for good reason.

If you read through the history section of this book, you will find that while silver has had some fantastic price rallies, the metal's story since the late nineteenth century has experienced a number of chapters of metallic disappointment that gold hasn't. Before then, gold and silver were monetary metals for thousands of years and their difference in value simply reflected the relative scarcity of each. Silver was roughly 14 times more abundant and consequently it was valued at one-fourteenth the price of gold: Aesthetic considerations aside, a gold ounce was equal in value to a stack of 14 silver one-ounce coins. But this changed completely in the 1870s.

Silver began falling sharply following the decision by a number of countries to abandon their bimetallic monetary systems, leaving silver behind and embracing an international (single metal) gold standard. Consequently, as it was being demonetized, silver entered a lengthy and volatile bear market that despite a brief surge during World War I's inflationary times would not end until 1933, when the price fell to a quarter, 25 cents. By then—just weeks before gold ownership was prohibited by the federal government—gold had become the premier monetary holding of central banks, commercial and investment banks, and the wealthiest individuals in society.

Silver also had a sharp decline in 1974, though it rebounded sharply during the rest of the inflationary 1970s. But at the end of that decade it suffered the worst fall of all: A 50 percent collapse in a single day, March 27, 1980. Shortly after it was revealed that two of the wealthiest families in the world had been trying to corner the silver market and had consequently been distorting silver's supply and demand dynamics. It was that singular event preceding a brutal bear market which, to this day, makes investors nervous about buying silver. Silver can be, no doubt, a volatile asset that should never represent a large enough part of your portfolio that it could cause you significant financial pain. It is an investment that should be considered very carefully.

All that being said, consider the possibility that silver is in the early stages of finally being reincorporated into the financial system as a mainstream investment asset, an imperfect alternative to gold. The market, that collection of global investors determining value based on supply and demand, has certainly been saying so over the past decade: Despite the volatility, silver has traded fairly closely with and has indeed outperformed gold, as well as all other major financial assets. Furthermore, few financial observers noticed that with the exception of gold and the highest quality bonds silver outperformed virtually all asset classes, including commodities and all stock markets during 2008. This during the worst financial crisis in four generations.

What Makes Silver a Singular Real Asset during Inflationary Times

As I write these lines, both the Federal Reserve and the European Central Bank are implementing policies that are widely regarded as inflationary: Hundreds of billions of dollars in new money will be printed by the two largest and most powerful central banks in the world in an effort to keep the world economy from stalling. Most likely they are soon to be joined by the Bank of Japan. Although we have pulled back from the economic cliff we faced in 2008 and 2009, with the Fed Funds rate locked at zero most monetary experts would regard this unprecedented level as an emergency rate, one called for in times of extreme economic distress. In fact, a J.P. Morgan strategist made this point:

> It's not an overstatement to say that we are living through the largest policy experiments of the last 300 years. In the U.S., Europe, Japan and the U.K., governments account for 75 percent of all borrowing that is taking place, and central banks account for 60 percent of all lending, both multiples higher than anything we have seen (or read about) before.[1]

Most asset managers today acknowledge the importance of assets that provide financial protection from the significant potential for a rise in inflation in the years ahead. If this notion, the idea that inflation is heading higher in the next few years continues to gain strength (as a great many economists believe), what are the options that most people have to protect their purchasing power? Silver has risen sharply in most

Growth needs to be reignited to push down unemployment, yet:	
Fiscal Policy Options Limited	**Monetary Policy Options Limited**
* Deficits at war-time (emergency) levels * Important U.S. states in fiscal distress (may require further federal assistance) * Structural deficits kicking in (demography) * U.S. unfunded liabilities massive (U.S. $202tr) and Fannie, Freddie still off govt. books (U.S.) * **Fear of 1937:** Fiscal restraint could cause double dip (Depression resumed in that year) . . . * . . . but without active (deep) deficit reduction, government debt/GDP continues rising rapidly	* Central bank rates at or near zero percent * Monetary policy today means: print money * Excess sovereign supply has already forced monetization (printing) to occur * Central banks must maintain independence to contain inflation expectations * **Risk:** hyperinflation emerges during *de*flationary periods and is always preceded by budget deficits. (Central banks need to be wary of supporting government spending.)

Figure 4.1 Keynesian Predicament Faced by the United States, European Nations, and Japan

inflationary episodes of history, often more rapidly than gold. Should silver be avoided entirely and gold be considered as the only viable precious metal inflation hedge in your investment portfolio?

Though the prospect of a recession is not being openly discussed among mainstream economists as I write, there are clear signs that the world economy is slowing down as global demand remains weak. The U.S. economy is growing at a stall speed annual rate; Europe is already in recession due to the ongoing credit crisis unfolding there; China is slowing, as is Japan. And virtually all developed nations have debt levels unprecedented in peacetime history. Unfortunately, the Catch-22 situation that our financial leaders find themselves in has not changed since I wrote *Hard Money* three years ago: Both fiscal and monetary tools available to our leaders are more limited than ever. (See Figure 4.1.) When we go into the next recession, whether it arrives sooner or later, the U.S. government will have fewer tax receipts with which to cover its climbing expenditures, roughly 30 percent of which are already being borrowed each year.

Even if the recession is not global (fortunately, a very rare event), a U.S. recession would likely prompt the Fed to increase the pace of monetary expansion even further than has been done already. There simply are no other powerful expansionary tools available to prevent the advent of deflation, a fall in prices that often leads to severe recession and at times depression, an economic catastrophe the Fed evidently wants to avoid. Consequently, financial professionals openly discuss the need to find investment vehicles that will provide adequate protection from the risk of rising inflation in the years ahead. Though stocks provide some degree of protection from rising prices, an investment term being used with increasing frequency in financial circles is *real assets*.

Real assets, to put it simply, are investment assets with a relatively fixed supply that cannot be reproduced easily or quickly, and that serve as historically proven stores of value during inflationary periods. Examples include precious metals (gold, silver, platinum, and palladium), commodities (like oil and copper), real estate, fine art, and some collectibles, like classic automobiles. One could also include such things as select rare wines from special years that produced spectacular flavors, though these are evidently assets that are difficult to store properly, not to mention sell at the right price.

The supply of real assets cannot change rapidly even if the pace of monetary expansion accelerates, as is occurring at present: As the amount of dollars in circulation rises more rapidly than the quantity of real assets in the market, real assets rise in price contributing to higher inflation. For example, there is a physical constraint on the amount of crude oil that is in the ground and what the global petrochemical industry can bring to market each year, at present roughly 88 million barrels per day. The same is true about copper, tin, and agricultural products like corn, wheat, and soybeans, a vital source of the world's food supply. Real estate, similarly, has a fixed supply over relatively short periods of time as it is difficult and complex to build new structures quickly. And real estate in prime locations—say the number of buildings surrounding Central Park in New York City—simply cannot be expanded much more.

Perhaps most importantly, real assets differ from *financial assets* (primarily stocks and bonds) in that the latter represent contractual claims on an underlying asset. Stocks and bonds differ substantially from a real asset like a home, which is a tangible asset over which one can have clear control and ownership. Derivatives, whose value is based entirely on other (generally financial) assets, are even further from being real assets since they also introduce *counterparty* risk into the equation—the possibility that the owing party in a transaction will not meet its obligations. There is also another factor that separates real assets from financial assets, particularly bonds: There is no limit—as we now know all too well—to the amount of bonds that the federal or any government can create and any company can easily expand its number of shares. Not that a company, like McDonald's, would want to simply increase the number of its shares in circulation, since this could impair its share price. The point is that there is no *physical constraint* on the supply of McDonald's shares.

Stocks are sometimes regarded as real assets because they can provide some degree of inflation protection: As inflation rises some companies benefit if they can pass along price increases to their customers. For example, if General Mills can increase cereal prices in line with inflation (and faster than its costs are rising), profits will rise and the company's stock would become a form of inflation hedge. However, during inflationary periods most companies are unable to keep up with rising prices (and can be affected by a number of different factors, like recession, or changes in fiscal policies), and stocks tend to underperform real assets. Furthermore, stocks can also be affected to some degree by public withdrawal from volatile equity markets during periods of rising inflation. Bonds, which pay a nominal rate of interest, are unable to keep pace with inflation and are widely regarded as providing poor protection against rising prices.

Though the financial future is always uncertain, the chart in Figure 4.2 can give you a sense of how real assets performed in the 1970s, a period of severe inflation. While the bond market was suffering during this turbulent decade and borrowers were forced to pay increasingly higher interest rates, stocks declined by roughly 50 percent in inflation-adjusted terms. Real estate did well although most people investing in real estate did so simply through the home they lived in as the large number of ways to invest in the industry available today—via bonds, stocks, derivatives, and other investment vehicles—had yet to be developed. Commodities fared far better in the 1970s, and as you can see precious metals outperformed most asset classes—and certainly stocks and bonds.

Forecasting which investments will fare better in the years ahead, considering the significant risk of higher inflation, is a difficult task. If real assets continue to perform well, it is most likely that silver will also rise as all real asset values tend to move in the same direction over history. But although silver has risen significantly in the last decade, there are three important reasons why I believe the white metal could continue to be one of the strongest performers in the real asset space.

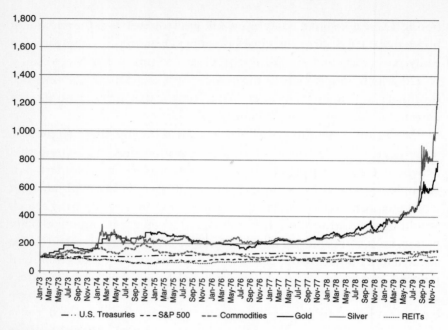

Figure 4.2   Performance of Various Asset Classes 1973–1980 (indexed at 100)
SOURCE: Bloomberg.

1. Silver is more correlated with gold than with anything else.

The first is simply that silver is more highly correlated with gold than anything else: For the past 40 years, silver—though more volatile—has moved in the same direction as gold, which I regard as the premier real asset for the financial environment we are living through. The correlation of silver with gold has increased in recent years: They have been moving in the same direction. In *Hard Money* I made two points about gold that I believe in strongly. One of them, which is related to inflation and thus to real assets in general, is that

> *Gold is the best vehicle for actually shorting government*; that is, betting on our leaders' failure to maintain our confidence in their ability to meet the ever-climbing liabilities they continue to incur (on our behalf) *with money the world believes in*. Expressed differently, gold is a good bet on a sudden rise in inflation. In the midst of surging government deficits across the world, readers of financial

history know that betting against government—that is, on a sudden sharp rise in inflation—has strong odds.[2]

There is no escaping the fact that the potential rise in inflation is directly tied to the severe fiscal distress afflicting governments across the world. Mohamed El-Erian, CEO of PIMCO, the largest bond fund manager in the world made this clear in 2010 when he wrote:

Today, we should all be paying attention to a new theme: the simultaneous and significant deterioration in the public finances of many advanced economies. At present this is being viewed primarily—and excessively—through the narrow prism of Greece. Down the road, it will be recognized for what it is: a significant regime shift in advanced economies with consequential and long-lasting effects.[3]

During times of rising inflation and fiscal distress, when the outlook for other real assets—like oil, copper, and real estate—is clouded by economic uncertainty, gold tends to perform better. This was the case during the 1970s, the 2008 crisis and the Great Depression, periods when gold performed far better than any real asset. If gold has historically been among the best performing real assets during periods of high inflation and crisis, it makes sense to consider a metal that is more correlated with gold than any other real asset.

2. Silver, like gold, is an easily storable real asset that can be entirely removed from the financial system.

A second, perhaps even more significant point I made about gold in my previous book is my belief that the metal is the only viable investment asset that allows a person to remove wealth from the financial system per se. The truest *real* asset, in my view, is that which has a finite supply and that you can hold in your hands, which is an attribute that silver shares with gold. Although oil, copper, and timber are real assets, the only practical way to invest in them is via a security or fund, both of which trade on financial markets. Hence, though they are real assets, for practical purposes these are *financial* assets in that they are held and managed through a third party and traded in markets that can be affected by such things as trading restrictions and illicit activity. Consider what happened

Figure 4.3   Price Performance of Sino Forest
SOURCE: Bloomberg.

to the company Sino Forest, a company engaged in forest plantation in Asia, when it was revealed that it likely did not have clear title to some of its assets. The stock collapsed, as shown in Figure 4.3.

Evidently, this was a mismanaged company and one could argue that there are far safer plays on timber. But the point is this: *when held physically, gold and silver do not require that anyone be trusted.* Even energy ETFs are *claims*, securities that require another entity to pay you. Gold and silver are not someone else's liability and can be held outside the financial system in a very physical sense: One ounce of gold is worth $1,650 and is a unit that is easily storable, as is an equivalent amount in silver. But $1,650 in barrels of crude oil would not fit in most homes. And where would you put the over 400 pounds of copper that you can buy with that amount of money?

3. Unlike gold, silver is affordable to the vast majority of families.

It is ironic that silver, widely regarded as more speculative and volatile, has outperformed gold as an investment since the beginning of this new century. Who would have thought that during a period in which the world experienced two stock market crashes and a severe real estate market meltdown that gold would have lost to a less noble metal? A trip to any coin shop or chat with any metals dealer will show you part of the reason—the most obvious one: Parting with $1,650 for a single coin is a tough proposition for most people. Buying a coin—a small real asset investment outside one's brokerage account, outside the financial system itself—for under $40 is an easier decision for most.

McBride's in Austin, Texas, is surely like most coin shops in the United States: Roughly 80 percent of what you see behind the glass display and most of what is sold is silver. In volume terms, the shop sells substantially more silver than gold. The same is true in India and China: Though many, if not most, would prefer to own gold, it is silver that the vast majority are forced to buy.

As discussed in other sections of this book, silver is far scarcer than one would think based on a price comparison with gold. Gold is not 50 times rarer than silver; it is not even 20 times rarer. If demand continues to rise for precious metals and more people are buying the metal they can afford, which is not as abundant as is widely believed, it follows that the price of silver could continue to rise.

But there is no escaping the reality that all investments present risks, and silver is vulnerable to a change in market conditions. Keep in mind that silver is unlike gold in two important respects: For one, gold has the advantage of being a central bank reserve asset, a metal whose market is far deeper (with far more buyers and sellers than silver's market), and one that has proven investment characteristics that are defensible before a professional investment panel. Silver is more of a hybrid metal, as roughly half of total demand is industrial, which can cause the metal to under-perform gold during a period of economic distress. The white metal was also affected by two major factors over the last forty years, which gave rise to significant volatility: the attempted market manipulation incident in 1979 and 1980, which crippled silver investment for over a decade, and the rise of digital photography. But both of these events have no effect on silver's present. Silver demand from the photography industry is now small relative to what it was in the 1980s and 1990s. And as investment demand for silver has surged in recent years, its correlation with gold has increased.

Chapter 5

The Gold-Silver Ratio, a 3,000-Year-Old Exchange Rate, Is Out of Historical Balance

The gold–silver ratio, simply the price of gold divided by that of silver, is the oldest continuously observed exchange rate in the world. As I write these lines, the ratio is 58, which means that today gold is 58 times more expensive than silver. One gold bullion coin is worth a tall stack of 58 silver ones.[1] At first glance, the number is not surprising as most know that gold is scarcer than silver, a fact that has been understood for thousands of years. But for most of history, the ratio was closer to the *actual* difference in the scarcity of each metal, which has been closer to 14 to 1—not four times that level, which is where the ratio stands now. Today, the price difference between gold and silver—the number 58—does not reflect the relative scarcity of each metal: Silver appears more plentiful than it really is.

It makes sense to think that, when averaged out over the thousands of years in which metal values have been recorded, the prices of gold and silver have been inversely proportional to their supply. Silver, being roughly 14 times more abundant than gold, over time has been worth about a one-fourteenth the price of the rarer metal. That is, if silver was selling for 1 unit of currency, gold was selling for 14. Since both silver and gold were regarded as money for thousands of years, a farmer receiving payment for some corn a few decades before Rome was founded—or 10 decades later—would be equally satisfied with an ounce of gold or 14 ounces of silver.[2] He might prefer the shine of gold or the fact that it was easier to buy and sell using silver (the more common money), but these considerations aside, the golden coin and the silver stack were worth the same. And he could turn around and use his gold coin or 14 silver ones as they each commanded exactly the same purchasing power.

But the gold–silver ratio, as the exchange rate has come to be known, has never actually stayed at 14, as shown in the average mentioned above. It has shifted significantly over time in part due to varying levels of production of each metal. Gold was likely used earlier than silver simply because it could be washed out of ores using crude methods, while silver could only be extracted by smelting, which made gold's sister metal relatively scarcer millennia ago.[3] The gold–silver ratio fluctuated in a fairly tight range between 9 and 16 for more than three thousand years from 1670 B.C. through the 1870s. And during the past 200 years of that period, the range was significantly narrower, as the gold traded in between 14 to 16 times the price of silver.[4]

But the ratio began to surge (gold became more expensive) in the late nineteenth century, when the world's leading central banks began to abandon their bimetallic monetary systems that had been based on both gold and silver. England had led the way when the Bank of England adopted the gold standard in 1717, and others would follow. The United States, then the world's dominant emerging market—what China has become today—formally adopted a pure gold standard in 1873 (before the Federal Reserve had begun operating). However the importance of silver to the American monetary system had already been in decline for

Figure 5.1 The Gold-Silver Ratio, 1800–Present

SOURCE: Roy Jastram, *Silver: The Restless Metal* (New York: John Wiley & Sons, 1981), Bloomberg, Thomson Reuters Datastream, World Gold Council.

some time thanks mostly to massive gold discoveries in the young country. As the world's economies began demonetizing silver—that is, using it less and less in their coinage—demand for gold's sister metal began to fall sharply while that of gold began to do the opposite. (Silver demonetization is discussed at greater length in Chapters 7 and 8.) This led to increased volatility in the gold-silver ratio and to its rise over time: The world's preference for gold climbed as silver was left behind (see Figure 5.1).

The consequent changes in the gold–silver ratio were dramatic. From a low well under 20 in the 1850s and 1860s, the ratio varied between 15 and 40 from the 1870s to 1929, the eve of the Great Depression. The U.S. government silver purchase program under President Franklin D. Roosevelt, which caused a temporary surge in silver prices in the mid- to late-1930s, was not able to prevent the ratio from climbing to 54 by 1935. Then the ratio surged to an all-time high of over 100 in 1940 and 1941—gold was 100 times more desirable than silver on world markets. It would not reach that triple-digit level again until 1991, but only briefly (see Figure 5.2).

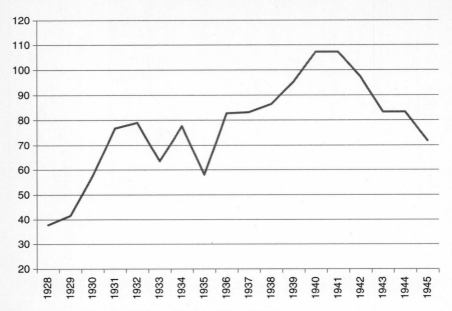

Figure 5.2   The Gold–Silver Ratio, 1928–1945

SOURCE: Roy Jastram, *Silver: The Restless Metal* (New York: John Wiley & Sons, 1981), Bloomberg,
Thomson Reuters Datastream, World Gold Council.

The inflationary boom in the 1960s and 1970s, which drove up
commodity prices, pushed silver prices higher while gold stayed at $35 an
ounce by government decree. Under the Bretton Woods agreement
signed when World War II ended, the U.S. government exchanged
dollars for gold at a fixed rate of $35 per ounce, which had effectively
frozen the price of gold. This ended in 1971, when President Nixon
devalued the dollar against gold and allowed the metal's price to trade
freely on global markets. But before that occurred, the gold–silver ratio
had fallen to a low of 18 in 1970, the lowest ratio recorded since the
nineteenth century (see Figure 5.3).

Since the end of Bretton Woods in 1972, the gold–silver ratio has
alternated dramatically as gold began trading freely for the first time in
decades. During the 1970s inflationary crisis, both metals climbed
significantly and gold surged an impressive 2,300 percent to its peak
in 1980, while silver rose 2,600 percent to its peak in the same year.
However, as can be seen in the chart in Figure 5.4, silver entered a deep
bear market and the gold–silver ratio climbed as gold outperformed its

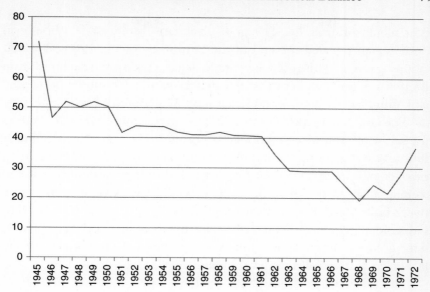

Figure 5.3   The Gold–Silver Ratio, 1945–1972

SOURCE: Roy Jastram, *Silver: The Restless Metal* (New York: John Wiley & Sons, 1981), Bloomberg, Thomson Reuters Datastream, World Gold Council.

Figure 5.4   The Gold–Silver Ratio, 1972–2000

SOURCE: Roy Jastram, *Silver: The Restless Metal* (New York: John Wiley & Sons, 1981), Bloomberg, Thomson Reuters Datastream, World Gold Council.

sister metal substantially. The gold–silver ratio broke to 100 briefly in 1991, which signaled the end of the ratio surge of the 1980s. Though choppy (as always), the gold–silver ratio began a protracted decline during the 1990s, as gold weakened sharply in large part due to substantial central bank dumping while silver traded around $5 per ounce (see Figure 5.4).

The gold bull market began in 2001 with the gold–silver ratio trading just below 60. But silver continued being affected by the sharp decline in film-developing demand. In 2001, photography demand still accounted for over one-quarter of total silver demand, but it was collapsing and keeping a lid on the price of silver. It would take several years before silver's bull market began in earnest, as it finally recovered its correlation with gold in *its* bull market in 2002. The impact of silver's rise can be seen in the gold–silver ratio at the time, which peaked at 80 and began a steady decline to almost half that level by late 2006.

The financial crisis of 2008, which caused a severe decline in commodities as the dollar surged, caused silver and gold to decouple in August of that year. The gold–silver ratio, which had been trading at just above 50 surged to 84 in two short months, an almost unprecedented

Figure 5.5   The Gold-Silver Ratio, 2000–2012

SOURCE: Bloomberg.

move caused by the severity of the financial crisis: When the chips are down in a financial disaster, for the past 140 years investors have picked gold over silver without question. But when signs of financial relief began appearing, silver began to recover very rapidly and to outperform gold on the way out of the crisis. In fact, driven by the surge in silver, the gold–silver ratio plummeted almost to 30 in April 2011. It has since rebounded to above 50, where it remains as of this writing (see Figure 5.5).

What Will Ultimately Drive the Gold–Silver Ratio Down?

The gold–silver ratio once mattered a great deal because governments had once established a set ratio between the two as both metals formed the foundation for monetary systems around the world. For example, when the newly formed United States set up its monetary system in 1792, it determined that gold and silver would trade at a ratio of 15 to 1. This, Treasury Secretary Alexander Hamilton had determined, made sense simply because 15 was the free market rate in the country at the time. And so it was in Europe in the late eighteenth century, where gold was 15 to 16 times more costly than silver.[5] Consequently, the ratio reflected the actual availability of silver supply on the market relative to what one could find in gold.

But today, the ratio has lost its significance because precious metals are not formally part of any country's monetary system: The 58 level does not matter if there is no legal ratio anywhere that contradicts it. (There is not a central bank somewhere that is willing to buy one ounce of gold and pay with a fixed amount of silver ounces or vice versa, as once was the case.) While many central banks hold gold as a financial asset—and numerous monetary authorities have been accumulating the metal in recent years—there has been no national currency linked to gold since 1972 nor to silver since the 1930s. And consequently, the present 58 gold–silver ratio is purely a reflection of market forces, the supply and demand dynamics of each metal, which today are being deeply influenced by investors. Gold is simply more desirable than silver on financial markets at present price levels. And if the gold–silver ratio, which once mattered greatly in the global financial system, went to 200 or 1.245, so what?

I believe there are two reasons why the gold–silver ratio will begin to matter once again. The first is that it should become a key reference point for investors to consider silver's value as the metal continues to gain importance relative to gold. If the bull market in precious metals persists and more funds continue to increase allocations to the so-called hard asset space, there will be an increasing need to value individual metals. But since hard assets do not provide cash flows (like stocks and bonds, which pay dividends and interest payments), there are few ways to assess whether silver is under- or overvalued.

For example, applying basic supply and demand analysis to precious metals does not work the way it does for other commodities for a simple reason. Precious metals are easily storable and transportable, traits that made people begin using them as money—portable wealth—thousands of years ago. Agricultural commodities are perishable and others, like oil and copper, are difficult to store as investments since they require large storage facilities. So their supply and demand are rarely far from balance: It is expensive and/or risky to store them for long. But consider gold supply for a minute: There are literally *trillions* of dollars in gold kept in central banks and private vaults—some of which have been there for centuries—and the expense of storing it is extremely low compared to doing so for, say, coal. And the difficulty of determining with any precision how demand will evolve in the years ahead makes supply-demand analysis for gold problematic. There is far less silver (roughly $800 billion), but considering climbing investment demand over the last decade, to think that a rising or falling supply will be useful in determining where the price is going is a tough call: Silver can be stored as an investment for generations, literally forever, just as can be done with gold. The gold–silver ratio could once again become a useful reference point for considering silver's potential over- or undervaluation since the metal has been so highly correlated with gold over time.

But the main reason investors may begin to focus on the gold–silver ratio is that it is far off balance from a historical perspective. The ratio, which has thousands of years of price data that can be used for reference, is extremely high relative to where it held for thousands of years, particularly considering present actual mining production, new supply of the metals, as well as aboveground total supply: Silver is far scarcer than the ratio would imply. Silver has important industrial uses, but if its use as a financial asset continues to increase as it has in the last decade, the gold–silver ratio will point to this imbalance and investors will likely focus on it, as well.

Consider the 58 gold–silver ratio in light of the quantities the mining industry produces each year. A typical gold mine contains 1 to 3 grams of the precious metal per *ton* of ore; for silver mines, a grade in the hundreds of grams is common and there are mines where silver has been found at grades of 800 grams per ton. Although this difference in grade confirms the fact that gold is far rarer than silver *underground*, what matters considering what is bought and sold in new production of each metal is the *total* that is brought *above*ground. The 762 million ounces of silver produced globally by the mining industry each year are only eight times more than gold production in volume. Furthermore, if one subtracts from silver and gold supply the ounces that are destined for noninvestment- and jewelry-related uses (industry, etc.), the scarcity of gold relative to silver is even lower: The silver available for investors is only four times higher than gold. But that is just in volume terms, the number of ounces of each metal. When compared in dollar terms, the total gold produced by the mining industry at $153bn is far above the $25bn produced in silver (see Figure 5.6).

If one considers the supply of gold and silver that are ready for delivery, the aboveground bullion that could be purchased today, there is actually far more gold than silver. That is to say, considering what is available for sale today silver is rarer than gold. Although some governments (like India, China, and Russia) hold silver, the amounts are relatively small, and while silver is more abundant underground, there is less available than gold aboveground.

It is demand alone that makes gold more valuable than silver, since one could argue that silver is becoming rarer more rapidly than gold. In addition to the fact that there is far less aboveground silver than gold, millions of ounces of silver are destroyed in industrial production each year. The quantities are stunning: Roughly 2 billion ounces were used up—permanently—by industry in the past 20 years alone. Despite recycling efforts, a small amount is recovered each year: Close to 900 million ounces of silver are used in fabrication processes and only 180 million ounces come back as scrap. In contrast, the vast majority of gold used in various ways is recycled (think of the "We buy gold" signs around the world), and hence most of what has been mined and refined in

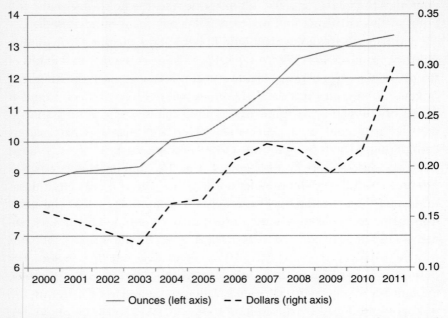

Figure 5.6 Ratio of Silver to Gold Mining Production (in millions of ounces and dollars)

SOURCE: The Silver Institute, World Gold Council.

human history is with us today. This is not the case for silver as much is lost each year.

Ultimately, I believe the key driver of the gold–silver ratio will be the continuing rise of silver as an investment asset as such. Silver's collapse in 1980, when it lost half its value on a single day, is not something the global investment community has forgotten. Regardless of the extraordinary nature of the event—the two wealthiest families in the world tried to corner the silver market—there is this lingering sense that silver remains a junk metal. A friend and commodity expert at one of the world's leading firms says that "Silver rushes up the stairs to jump out the window." And silver's often intense volatility and price swings remain, which makes long-term investors—particularly the large institutions that truly move markets—hesitant to make it a serious investment.

That being said, I believe silver has passed two important investment tests that have helped the metal to continue recovering credibility. The first was the financial crisis of 2008, the worst—by far—since the 1929 stock market crash. While the price of crude oil, the most important commodity, collapsed by 77 percent; while king copper plunged almost 70 percent; while the GSCI, the leading measure of commodity price movements in the world economy fell off a cliff by over 65 percent, silver declined a mere 23 percent. In doing so, silver—that volatile metal that few investors can trust—outperformed commodities and all major stock markets in the world by a wide margin during the worst financial crisis in four generations.

Secondly, I believe silver passed another important test in 2011. In that year, the metals' price began to gain steam as it did in 1980. There was widespread anticipation among precious metals investors during February, March, and April that silver would overcome its 1980 roughly $50 peak as it surged a whopping 80 percent in those early months of the year. But then, as if fate was forcing it back to junk status, it fell a sharp 30 percent over the next two weeks. (See Figure 5.7.) It then recovered

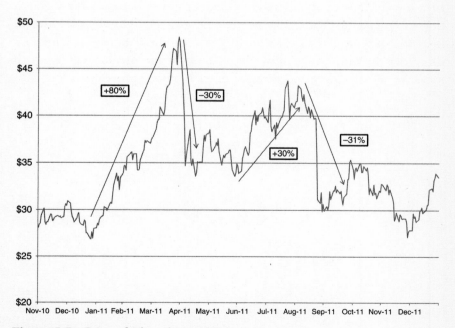

Figure 5.7   Price of Silver during 2011
Source: Bloomberg.

ground into the summer before plunging—along with gold, which declined far less, as usual—25 percent in the space of a few days.

The year 2011 was the most turbulent for silver since 1980, but how did the years compare? In 1980, silver began the year trading at $32.20 and ended the year at half that price, $15.50. In the beginning of a brutal bear market, which prompted the shutting down of multiple refineries and precious metals dealerships, silver would not recover that $15.50 level for 27 years. But in 2011, despite the extreme price swings, the price of silver fell a mere 10 percent for the full year to 27.84, and it started 2012 above that level. When viewed on a long-term chart, it looks like silver was simply letting off steam after a strong run (see Figure 5.7).

The market will eventually give its final verdict on the gold–silver ratio. Considering the broad swings of history through the millennia, the ratio's move above 20 followed by the significant movements it has had between 20 and 100 over the past century reflect a financial relationship over a tiny slice of history. For 3,000 years the gold–silver ratio held between 9 and 16, which was due to the actual relationship between the physical supply of each metal. And at present gold is 58 times more expensive simply due to financial demand. Now that silver is far scarcer following decades of industrial permanent destruction of the metal and the metal is trading more closely with gold's movements, perhaps the market will begin to focus on actual supply and demand of each metal again.

Chapter 6

Always Keep in Mind the Risks of Investing in Silver

Anyone who enters the silver market is surely put on guard by history's lessons.

—Roy Jastram[1]

During the present rally in silver prices, I have heard a number of serious investors say things like "I believe in silver." Some of the large precious metals owners I have come into contact with trust silver money more than the fiat currency of any nation, and they believe wealth is more secure invested in silver than in the stock market or kept within the banking system. Trusting that silver's value will shine through what for some is a sense of monetary and financial deception, they feel certain that many in the world are about to pile into the precious metal, leaving stocks, bonds, and other financial assets far behind. While there are important grounds to believe the metal will surge in the years ahead, as outlined in this book, it is important to understand the risks inherent in silver investment. Silver has broken many financial hearts.

History Has Been Unkind to Silver at Important Times

Consider a few facts. First, history has not always been on silver's side and its worst episode occurred during one of darkest chapters in American financial memory, the Great Depression (see Figure 6.1). In the early 1930s, the world had been transferring much of its wealth into gold, a proven refuge during times of financial adversity. In fact, to stop people from rushing into bullion, a move that was pushing the metal's price higher and rapidly depleting federal gold reserves, in 1933 the U.S. government decided to prohibit private ownership of the metal. But while gold demand was rising—*surging*—during the 1930–1932 period its sister metal was going in the opposite direction, as you can see in Figure 6.1.

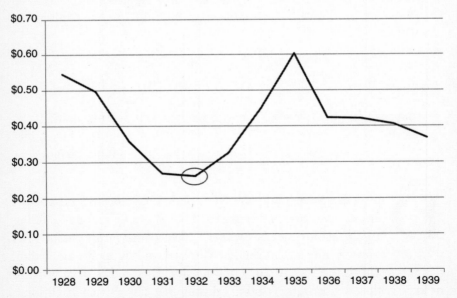

Figure 6.1   Price of Silver during Great Depression Years
SOURCE: Roy Jastram, *Silver: The Restless Metal* (New York: John Wiley & Sons, 1981).

Considering that silver has moved with gold for the past 40 years, it is surprising to think that the metal's price actually declined sharply during the Great Depression, when demand for gold was rising. But this was not a sudden event in the 1930s. For reasons discussed in Chapter 8, silver had been falling years before the 1929 stock market crash.

While the white metal had remained above $1.29 per ounce for much of the nineteenth century, by the early twentieth century the price was hovering well below 80 cents. And despite a surge in prices related to the advent of World War I, by the early 1920s silver prices began to sag once again. The financial turmoil and closing of banks in the early 1930s, which drove investors to the safety of gold, cash, and government bonds, pushed investors even further away from silver. The price per ounce plummeted along with stock prices to an all-time low of 24½ cents, which caused the ratio of gold to silver to surge to more than 80, nearly the highest level ever. (Figure 6.1 does not show this because it graphs only yearly closing prices, which do not show the price spike.) Silver's price actually fell in half during the Depression. (That silver then proceeded to triple in price after it bottomed—one of the most amazing rallies during the second half of the 1930s—is another story addressed in Chapter 9.)

If a serious regional war erupted—say a conflict in the Middle East escalated to involve numerous countries—one might expect demand for silver to rise sharply, which it tends to do (along with other commodities) in times of armed conflict. For instance, silver prices surged during World War I and II and during the Vietnam War era as industrial demand for the metal rose and speculative investor interest jumped along with it. Hence, if Israel were to attack Iran this year, as some have speculated might occur, and the world's military powers aligned with the countries on either side they supported, one would expect the price of silver to surge. And I would be surprised if it didn't.

But consider that during the years of the Civil War in the 1860s, the war that caused more economic dislocation than any other American conflict, the purchasing power of silver fell while the value of other commodities—wheat, rice, steel—soared. This was an extreme event, "one of the rare occasions in price history anytime, anywhere, when a precious metal did not respond to a national calamity," as the late silver historian Roy Jastram commented.[2] But bizarre as silver's fall during the Civil War was, the event *did* occur: Silver's purchasing power halved in three years.

There are a number of drivers that can continue pushing the price of silver higher in the years ahead. But the point of this chapter is that this is no sure thing. And history has shown that silver can fall when one would least expect it. Even the biggest silver bull would have to admit that the metal has a weaker investment track record than gold.

Silver Price Volatility Has Been High for over a Century, and Investors Should Not Expect That to Change

The dramatic rise and fall in silver prices that occurred in 1980, when the Hunt family tried and failed to corner the market provides a number of lessons about investing in silver. The first is that the metal's price volatility can make your head spin. As you examine the charts in Figures 6.2 and 6.3, consider the intense disappointment of investors in this bubble—and how can you not call it a bubble? As of this writing, the price of silver is *still* below the peak of 1980, which was reached 32 years ago, while gold has more

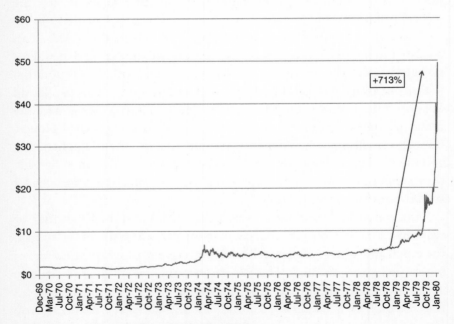

Figure 6.2 Price of Silver during the 1970s
SOURCE: Bloomberg.

Figure 6.3   Price of Silver during the 1980 Surge and Crash
SOURCE: Bloomberg.

than doubled in value since that year. And these have been 32 years of intense volatility caused by dramatic shifts in industrial demand and investor interest in silver.

One can be optimistic that silver will rise "over the long run"—a favorite saying of investors that have just lost a lot of money—but consider a recent silver entry point and its effect. If you bought silver as it was surging in early 2011 near its peak of $48, by the end of the year you were down over 40 percent. Even though silver declined a mere 10 percent during 2011 (after a 1,000 percent surge over the previous decade), there are surely a number of investors that lost a lot of money! And the price of silver, as of this writing, is still below that 2011 level (see Figure 6.4).

It is important to understand that silver is simply a volatile investment. It can surge more than 5 percent in a day or fall like a rock. Like stocks, bonds, and real estate, silver has its investment warts and volatility can be one of the ugliest ones. This is one of the reasons why silver has not made it onto the radar screen of a number of professional investors like pension funds and insurance companies: While a number of them have begun to

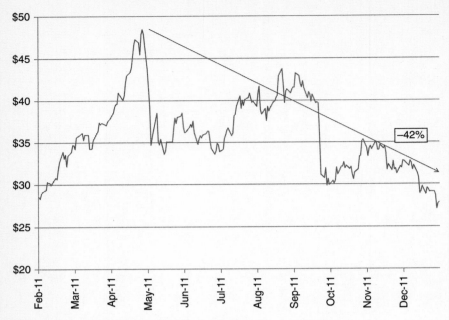

Figure 6.4   Silver's Price Performance since 2011 Peak
SOURCE: Bloomberg.

invest in gold, silver's intense volatility and the difficulty in predicting its price behavior have kept them away from the metal, at least for now. For volatility to diminish, there need to be a lot more investors in the silver market, a lot more bidders and sellers that can mitigate the intense ups and downs in the market. Unfortunately, there are few buyers when the white metal is on the downswing.

While Many Investors Jump on the Silver Wagon on the Way Up the Hill, the Metal Has Very Few Friends on the Way Down

A second lesson from the 1980s silver surge and collapse is that the metal often attracts few investors, the "bottom-fishers" seen in the equity and bond markets—and even in gold—when its price is falling. When gold prices have been declining in recent years, a number of investors have become more active. During 2011, central banks increased their purchases of gold

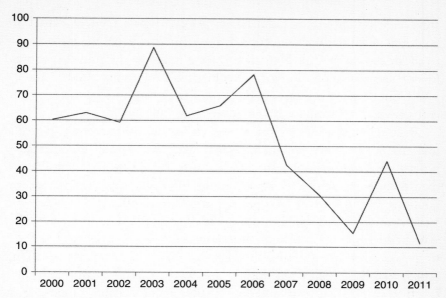

Figure 6.5   Government Sales of Silver (in millions of ounces)
SOURCE: The Silver Institute.

more than in any of the past 40 years. Monetary authorities from Mexico to Kazakhstan have been accumulating significant tonnage in gold markets, but there is no such interest in silver even though some governments make minor purchases. Actually, the opposite is true: For years governments collectively have been net *sellers* of silver, as the chart in Figure 6.5 shows.

Fortunately, there has been increased buying interest in silver on downswings in recent years, particularly from India and some investment funds. But there is no comparison to the demand for gold that has been seen in market sell-offs, where individual investors, banks, hedge funds, and central banks have often become more active.

Silver Has No Mainstream Financial Advocates, No Gurus or Recognized Investment Authorities Saying "It Is Time to Buy Silver," as Many Are Now Doing with Gold

In 2010, a senior colleague and I spoke with one of the world's investment authorities, a person quoted frequently in *Barron's*, the *Wall Street Journal*, and seen every month on financial news TV channels. He is an expert on gold, predicted the financial crisis of 2008, and has been making perceptively sharp market calls ever since. As we spoke about gold, he recommended a sizeable position for individual and institutional funds. When I asked him about silver, he sounded completely surprised by the question and answered, "I suppose it will go up, as well."

A large number of investment experts have come to recognize gold's investment attributes and believe the metal has earned a respectable position in mainstream investment discourse. Gold is seen as an asset class that despite its perceived shortcomings (it doesn't pay dividends or coupons and is difficult to forecast), provides significant diversification benefits and performs well in times like the present. The man we spoke with believes gold is one of the most logical investments to own in a time of negative real interest rates and central bankers' fight against inflation, which involves money printing.

But silver is not an investment any major financial figure feels comfortable speaking up for, and for good reason. The price of silver is even harder to forecast than that of gold, and its volatility makes it difficult for anyone to advocate as a serious investment consideration. Whether this makes sense, considering the drivers outlined in this book, is beside the main point I'm making: As of today, there are no widely respected financial authorities that are openly recommending that investors consider silver. Silver is simply not on mainstream radar screens, which makes this something important to consider. Financial experts are only willing to stick their necks out for gold, at least for now.

Final Thought on Silver's Risks

I believe the most significant risk to silver as an investment is that traditional investment assets, like stocks and bonds, become extremely attractive again. The silver bear market that began abruptly in 1980 was not only caused by an unprecedented market manipulation event (as discussed in Chapter 11); that year also marked the beginning of a financial markets boom, the most spectacular ever. As shown in Jeremy Siegel's classic *Stocks for the Long Run*, the roughly 20-year period that began in the early 1980s offered the best returns for stocks and bonds in the history of the country—or at least since 1802, when the first record of American financial market performance is available.[3]

In the precious metals research I have done over the years, I often find an effort to explain why silver and gold performed so poorly in the 1980s and 1990s—a fact that some have attributed to direct market manipulation by government. (See Chapter 14.) And there are grounds to believe this, as central banks dumped millions of ounces of gold during this period all the way up to 2008. But I believe the dumping of gold by monetary authorities—which indirectly affected silver investment prospects—was probably not due to attempts to "prop up the system," as some might say. It was the unbridled optimism of the time, the faith in the U.S. dollar and Treasury bonds of the U.S. government. There was a sense that the economic cycle had been permanently tamed. And with the collapse of Communism in Europe just a few years prior, optimistic books like *The End of History* were being written.[4]

For most who were investing in the 1990s precious metals were far, far from our minds simply because there were so many drivers for traditional asset classes. Amazing new companies were being formed, inflation was under control, the economy was steady and corporate earnings were strong. That a number of those companies would implode in time, that a bubble was in the making and that the problems we face today were created, in part, by the precautions not taken then is beside the point: Almost nobody cared about investing in precious metals in the late 1990s! There was simply no investment demand for gold and silver to think of at the time.

The surge of precious metals is driven in part by the decline in faith in traditional financial assets, which rely on a stable economy and government balance sheet for strength. The challenges of today—most notably, the mountain of debt and alarming deficits in major economies—will be overcome in time. And while I believe silver and gold both have investment drivers that have yet to be fully appreciated in financial markets today—even after the rally metals have enjoyed—I understand that the rally must end. Though precious metals should be part of a diversified portfolio, stocks and bonds are the asset classes of choice for long-term wealth accumulation. At present traditional finance is being undermined by out-of-control government leverage, as our leaders struggle to sustain economic growth without causing fiscal crises. But in time, there could be another 1980, a time when tremendous compensation for risk appears for stocks and bonds in the form of rock-bottom low valuations and high inflation-adjusted interest rates. This is the main risk for silver—that alternative investments become so compelling as to make owning the white metal less attractive. But fortunately for silver bulls, today's financial environment remains dramatically different from 1980.

Part Two

A BRIEF HISTORY OF SILVER IN THE UNITED STATES AND WHAT IT MEANS FOR THE METAL'S FUTURE

Chapter 7

1792: The American Monetary Foundation on a de Facto Silver Standard

/

The major monetary metal in history is silver, not gold.
—Nobel in Economics Laureate Milton Friedman, 1993[1]

G iven their deep financial connection throughout history, before considering silver's story it is important to understand the position of gold, the premier monetary metal. Odd as it sounds, gold is quite new to the world of modern financial asset management. Its history as an asset class that U.S. fund managers could actively invest in, with the potential for appreciation or the risk that its value could decline, dates merely to 1971. This was the year in which the Nixon administration stopped intervening in the gold market to keep the metal's price frozen at \$35 per ounce. Before then, the metal was effectively uninvestable and with an immovable price, trying to obtain a return on gold was impossible, anyway. Considering that gold started trading freely in 1971, from a fund manager's perspective gold is really a 40-year-old security.[2]

American citizens were actually prohibited from owning gold bullion legally between 1933 and 1974, which is why the U.S. Mint did not produce gold (or silver, though ownership was permitted) coins during that period and only resumed production in the mid-1980s. The only way for American gold investors to evade this restriction legally was to buy jewelry or transact in the tiny numismatic market, where gold and silver rare coins have always traded freely.[3] Prior to 1933, when private ownership of gold was legal (and common), the notion that it could be regarded as an "investment" was nonsensical as it was money itself under the Gold Standard, not the asset that rises and falls daily in global financial markets, as occurs today. That gold can be regarded as an *investment*, which implies taking financial risk, is an entirely modern concept.

Gold's very short history as a true investment asset, one trading on the international open market with significant price movements, is an important fact that separates it from silver, its sister metal. Silver has been trading freely since the rise of the international Gold Standard in the late nineteenth century, when most governments left their bimetallic gold-silver monetary systems for the simplicity of using the single, rarer metal, gold. While there were a few exceptions (like China, which remained on a pure silver standard until 1934), silver began to be demonetized, its price left to the whims of the market. By the 1960s, when silver was finally removed from the dimes and quarters where the metal was still to be found in American money, silver's demonetization was complete. The metal's formal withdrawal from the monetary system has had significant effects on the metal's history as an investment and I believe it will have a deep effect on its future.

While gold preserved its value due to rising monetary demand in the late nineteenth century, the abandonment of silver by the world's leading financial authorities caused a sharp price decline that lasted several decades. Despite moving in tandem with gold for thousands of years, for the first time ever, silver decoupled from its sister metal and, despite a brief surge during World War I, the white metal's price would not recover until the Great Depression. Then, beginning in 1934, silver would rapidly climb threefold in value during some of the worst years in U.S. economic history due to active government intervention in the silver market before declining again in the years leading up to the Second World War. The post–World War II economic expansion and rising inflation would drive silver prices higher into the 1960s, and despite decades of turbulent trading, since 1971 the price of silver once again began to move closely with gold, as it has done to this day.

Given its lengthy trading history, the opportunities for tremendous profit and deep investment disappointment in silver existed long before gold finally ceased being frozen at $35.00 an ounce. Since it began trading freely in 1971, gold has only had one bear market and two bull markets, including the present one. Silver has had numerous bear and bull markets for over a century, as shown in Figures 7.1 and 7.2. Considering its deep, sharp price movements over the years it has long been the restless metal.

This section of the book makes a brief trip through the history of silver in the United States, as it points to the significant political and economic events that have affected the metal's value. Perhaps the most

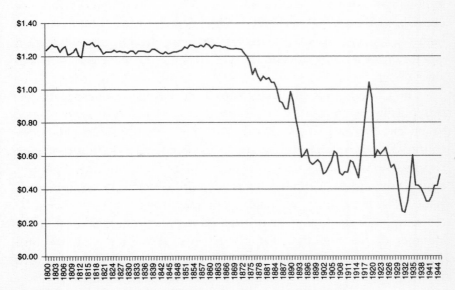

Figure 7.1   Price of Silver, 1800–1945 (Year-End Closing Prices)
SOURCE: Roy Jastram, *Silver: The Restless Metal* (New York: John Wiley & Sons, 1981) and Bloomberg.

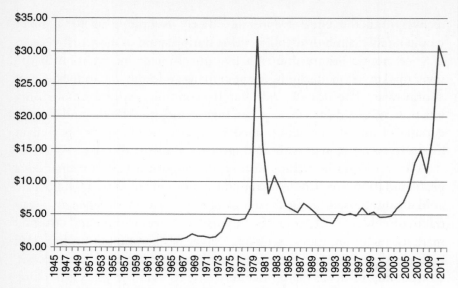

Figure 7.2   Price of Silver, 1945–2011 (Year-End Closing Prices)
SOURCE: Roy Jastram, *Silver: The Restless Metal* (New York: John Wiley & Sons, 1981) and Bloomberg.

important message is seeing that, after a great number of important financial events over the past 40 years silver has traded alongside gold. Despite its higher volatility, the metal has begun to act more like the monetary metal it was for thousands of years, and less like the industrial metal that it has also always been.

The United States' monetary foundation—American money itself—was initially based upon both gold and silver, although this system proved to be entirely theoretical. By the late eighteenth century, the new country's leaders were well versed in the historical experience of pure paper money and its negative consequences: there was nothing to prevent leaders from printing money as needed and eventually destroying its value. (The bankruptcy of France in the eighteenth century, caused by the temporary abandonment of hard money, had occurred within the lifetimes of the Founding Fathers' parents.) To avoid such financial disasters, the leaders of the new republic, as set forth in the Coinage Act of 1792, were prohibited from making "anything but gold and silver coin a tender in payment of debts." In his *Report on the Establishment of a Mint*, dated the year before, Alexander Hamilton set the formal gold-silver exchange rate to be maintained by the U.S. government at 15 to 1. That is, each ounce of gold would be worth 15 ounces of silver.

Although Hamilton gave signs of a preference for a pure gold standard, which England had adopted in 1717, the reality was that gold was very hard to obtain in the new country and was often hoarded by its wealthiest citizens. There was actually a scarcity of all universally acceptable money, which at the time was *specie*, gold or silver. These metals, credible stores of value in the eyes of potential depositors, were the reserves banks needed to back paper currency that the new nation's citizens would gradually gain the confidence to use as money.

Although the country's new monetary system was initially bimetallic, the "United States was effectively on a silver standard however read the law," wrote historian Roy Jastram.[4] At its inception, American banks had extremely low reserves and what reserves they had were almost entirely in silver. Gold had practically disappeared from circulation. Much of it had been exported to Europe, far from the new political experiment which was the United States, the first emerging market.

A rapidly growing nation needy of money with which to conduct transactions ended up using whatever was at hand, much of it highly suspect as a store of value. There was simply never enough gold or silver to meet the demand for money, the lifeblood of economic activity. This surging demand prompted a printed supply, but much of the new paper money (backed in writing by gold and silver) making its way into circulation in the early years of the new democracy was counterfeit, issued by banks that didn't even exist. By the 1850s, with so many entities commissioning bank notes of their own design (and in denominations, sizes, and colors of their own choosing), the money supply became a great confluence of more than 10,000 different kinds of paper that continually changed hands, baffled the uninitiated, and fluctuated in value according to the whims of the market. Furthermore, thousands of different kinds of gold, silver, and copper coins issued by foreign governments and domestic merchants complicated the mix.[5]

With so many forms of money being highly suspect and gold, if it could be found, too valuable for daily transactions—visualize shopping for groceries with a $500 bill—silver became the most acceptable and hence useful form of money for early American citizens. The Spanish silver dollars circulating throughout the world were in widespread use and legal tender in the United States until 1857.[6]

The extensive use of silver money made sense. Though industry was in early stages of development, the nascent United States was largely an agrarian country expanding westward into new territory. Commercial transactions were often conducted with persons never seen before, at times in different languages, in open fields far from law enforcement. Although barter was common, paper notes issues by, say, the Bank of Massachusetts, were seen by many west of the Mississippi as we would regard Monopoly money today: unacceptable. New businesses being established in growing communities across the country often had giant money reference books used to confirm the validity of a given currency note presented. A merchant selling a bag of corn, having consulted one of the 80 or so "counterfeit detectors" published during the pre–Civil War period, might give a stranger 20 cents on the dollar for his Merchants' Bank of Utica $10 bill—or less. Counterfeiting was a thriving business.[7]

In such a time, absent a universally accepted means of exchange backed by a credible and solvent national central government, silver and gold were unquestioned as a means of exchange. However, silver was preferred partly due to the difficulty of conducting minor transactions with gold, whose purchasing power was 16 times stronger than its sister metal. But the main problem with gold was that there simply was not enough of the metal on the market. By 1830, with so much gold continuing to be exported to Europe and virtually no domestic mining production, U.S. Mint gold production amounted to only 11 percent of the total silver coinage.[8]

What changed the course of monetary history in the United States was a dramatic increase in new discoveries of gold in the Americas, Russia, and Australia. A surge in gold found in California and other places was reaching the mint and gold coins began to circulate across the country very rapidly. With gold abundance came an increasing preference for the metal over silver. And by the 1850s, there was already some talk in Congress about adopting a pure gold standard, and for practical purposes the metal became the key medium of exchange for large transactions, silver being used for smaller ones.

Chapter 8

1873: The United States Joins the International Gold Standard and Leaves Silver Behind

1873 was not the year in which the United States decided to abandon silver and adopt gold as the sole foundation of its monetary system. The transition had been occurring decades before, and the change was largely fortuitous. Gold had been rising in importance since the 1850s, thanks primarily to the increasing abundance provided by unprecedented discoveries around the world. The scale of production was remarkable: From levels of close to $15 million per year in 1840, new gold supply rose 10-fold in the years following 1850. In fact, between 1851 and 1875, more gold was produced in the Americas than silver, in dollar terms. As much gold was produced in the third quarter of the nineteenth century as in all 350 years following the discovery of the Americas, a fact that would transform the global monetary system.[1]

At the time, silver coins in any denomination were becoming increasingly hard to find. The United States had been under a paper money standard since the 1860s, as the exigencies of financing the Civil War led the federal government to issue greenbacks, currency notes without gold or silver backing or any promise of redemption in these metals.[2] The country was using virtually no hard money at all in the 1870s for ordinary transactions and a significant part of gold production was making its way across the Atlantic into European central bank vaults, the formal backing for paper money issued by governments.[3] (The American Federal Reserve would not begin operations until 1914.) Also, substantial silver tonnage had been leaving the United States and was being sold in India and China, where demand was rising sharply due to the metal's extensive use in coinage. Meanwhile, in the United States banks were amassing gold as reserves to back their balance sheets upon which new loans could be made. Yet it was not until 1879 that the United States actually formally adopted a gold standard as the basis for its monetary system, thereby entering the international club of gold standard nations.

But the year 1873 is an important marker in the history of silver because in that year Congress passed the first act of monetary legislation that omitted mentioning silver, an action that would have important implications for silver decades later. The "right of free coinage" was an essential part of any metal-based monetary system, which was the case in the United States: The U.S. Mint at its inception would take any amount of refined gold or silver and mint the metals into new coins at no charge to the person presenting the raw minerals. But the Act of February 12, 1873, made no mention of free coinage of silver, which effectively put the United States on a gold standard.

At the time this had no significant consequence for the workings of the American financial system. And the persons who would later make the silver question a major political issue did not even notice what would be regarded as "The Crime of 1873," the demonetization of silver, when it was committed. An observer at the time commented: "So completely without observation was this measure passed, that it was not for a year or two that the fact of demonetization was popularly known."[4] In fact, one could argue that the United States had been on a de facto gold standard

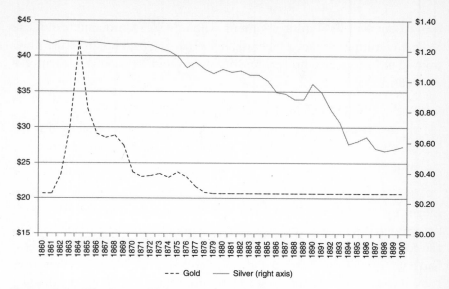

Figure 8.1   The Price of Silver and Gold, 1860–1900

SOURCE: Roy Jastram, *Silver: The Restless Metal* (New York: John Wiley & Sons, 1981), Bloomberg, World Gold Council.

since the 1850s, as gold rushed into the money supply thanks to discoveries in California. But in time, the 1873 decision on silver would gain political importance in the race for the White House and eventually as a major issue during the first Roosevelt administration during the 1930s (see Figure 8.1).

The so-called Crime of 1873 gained prominence, in the eyes of those with an ideological or economic interest in the metal, because it was in the early 1870s that the price of silver started to fall sharply. Gold and silver for the first time went their separate ways, as shown in Figure 8.1: gold was frozen at a set value while the price of silver was allowed to fall. Commodity prices, including silver, began a protracted decline toward the end of the Civil War and by the late 1870s they had fallen roughly 40 percent. This deflationary period hurt farmers the most since the products they brought to market were declining in value, while their liabilities—interest and mortgage payments—were payable in constant gold terms. Western agrarians found a voice in a new political platform that joined silver mining with other antideflationary interests into a larger constituency that became the "free-silver" political movement. The movement had its shining moment when 1896 Democratic candidate William Jennings Bryan, a Nebraskan with strong backing from the silver mining industry, gave his famous "Cross of Gold" speech at the national convention:

> We will answer their demand for a gold standard by saying to them: You shall not press down upon the brow of labor this crown of thorns, you shall not crucify mankind upon a cross of gold.

The American public never had to decipher precisely what Jennings meant by this because he did not win the election. Presumably, large-scale purchases of silver by the U.S. government would provide support for commodity prices, such as corn, wheat, and other commodities that had been moving in lockstep with silver as their prices declined. But there was no respected economic research to support the idea that a rise in silver prices would lead to increasing prices for other commodities. What was found in abundance was a growing number of congressmen that began tying the concept of "free silver" to the need for inflation in commodity prices. Decades would pass before this movement gained sufficient strength to prompt legislative action, but the opportunity finally arrived thanks to the Great Depression.

Chapter 9

1934: The Federal Government Speculates in Silver

The price of corn went negative in 1933 in South Dakota. The county elevator listed corn at *minus* three cents. Collapsing consumer demand driven by the economic devastation of the Great Depression became so extreme that growers had to pay silos bursting with corn to take their new production. Across the country, farmers were blockading highways to intercept livestock, butter, and eggs and prevent them from getting to market and contributing further to plunging prices.[1] Unemployment was surging across the country, and in time it would become clear that this depression was different. In contrast with nineteenth-century depressions, which though often harsh were usually brief, the depression which started in the late 1920s would last a number of years and take on a global dimension. Industrial production

109

collapsed, there was an unprecedented surge in national foreclosures as evictions skyrocketed, and the stock market would not recover its 1929 peak for 25 years.

Such was the environment under which President Franklin D. Roosevelt (FDR), fresh from taking the United States off the gold standard and setting in motion a wide range of new economic policies, decided to "do something for silver." While this is not the place for a lengthy discussion on FDR's economic and financial experimentation, which produced mixed results, the impact his policy had on silver is hard to understate. Though the metal's price would briefly surge during World War One years, as discussed in the previous chapter silver had been on a declining trend since its demonetization in the 1870s, when the price per ounce was well over one dollar. Silver reached an all-time low of 24½ cents per ounce in December 1932, a few months before FDR would take office the following year. It is ironic that during some of the worst years of the Depression, the president would offer silver speculators a tripling of the metal's price with consequences for the white metal's market that would last for decades (see Figure 9.1).

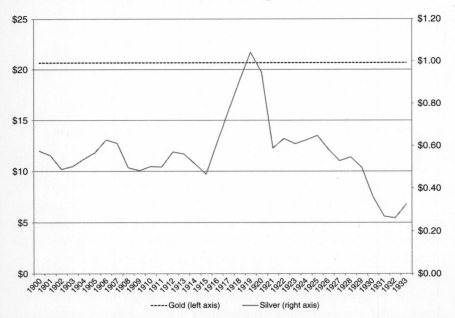

Figure 9.1   The Price of Gold and Silver, 1900–1933

Source: Roy Jastram, *Silver: The Restless Metal* (New York: John Wiley & Sons, 1981), Thomson Reuters Datastream, World Gold Council.

As mentioned throughout this book, after the rise of the international gold standard in the late nineteenth century and the end of bimetallism, silver became a speculative metal whose price began to vary with substantial volatility. After moving in lockstep for more than 3,000 years, silver and gold began to move in different directions, and these movements were most dramatic in the early twentieth century. While gold was fixed in price, during the pre-depression years there were three major breaks in the price of silver, each of which were separated by periods of a fairly level price.[2] Despite the metal's fall below $1.00 per ounce in the early 1900s, silver would surge to a peak of $1.37½ by November 1919, the first major break. But silver would collapse in the months following, losing half its price value by the end of that year. That was the second important shift. Between 1921 and 1926, silver remained fairly stable as supply and demand were fairly balanced, though supply had increased moderately due to sources of demonetized silver from European recoinages.[3] A final break came with the advent of the Great Depression, which caused silver to plunge to record lows. In England, the price of silver had fallen to the lowest level in six and a half centuries, one-third the price of silver at the time of Magna Carta.[4]

It was at this point that silver agitation in the United States, the political movement to remonetize silver (expecting that this would indirectly push crop prices higher to help American farmers), reached its highest intensity in Congress. Though today such a movement would seem bizarre—a free silver movement—at the time the United States was the world's largest silver producer and had a substantial agricultural population. The movement had immense political support in the West, but was opposed by conservatives in the East, a simplistic geographic division that carried weight in the popular mind at the time.[5] Its advocates were united by a simple idea, controversial as it was then—and is becoming today—that inflation was needed for the country's prosperity. Whether the United States would prosper via inflation remained to be seen, though clearly silver miners and farmers personally thought *they* would.

That the Silver Purchase Act of 1934 is one of the more malodorous political compromises in U.S. history is not only due to the nature of the deal cut between the president and Congress. By manipulating the global silver market, the United States produced devastating monetary effects on a number of nations, including China, which was on a silver standard at the time and would eventually go into an inflationary crisis. Feeling that it was being forced upon him—in part by silver speculators lining up to profit from a deal—the president had actually resisted the bill initially. In fact, the Treasury Department had prepared a 26-page list of speculators that included banks, corporations and businessmen, "two of whom had helped give a dinner for Congressmen interested in silver."[6] The list would serve as ammunition for the president to evade the silver bullet by showing that the bill was being pushed by profit-hungry speculators and not by those with the country's best interests in mind. But political circumstances forced his hand into voting in favor of the silver interests.

For one, Roosevelt needed to keep congressmen in session to pass controversial labor and housing legislation. And several key senators were threatening to filibuster all presidential efforts in Congress unless a silver deal was struck. Furthermore, he and others were disappointed by the inflationary results of his radical decision on gold: Although the dollar had been devalued by over 40 percent, inflation based on the wholesale price commodity index at the time had merely risen 21.5 percent over the preceding 13 months. The Roosevelt administration was seeking a much sharper increase in commodity prices, particularly agricultural ones, and the doubtful economic science predicting that rising silver would lead to an increase in other prices was appealing to many at the time.

Ultimately, the political forces pushing for government purchases of silver won with the signing of the Silver Purchase Act on June 19, 1934, "one of the finest achievements of any political lobby in Washington" in the twentieth century, as one observer put it.[7] Among its main features was the order to increase monetary stocks of silver until they reached one quarter of the total value in relation with gold. At the time this implied a massive purchase of 1.2 billion ounces of silver. But since the Treasury Department has also been purchasing gold, an additional 125 million would ultimately have to be purchased.[8] These were paid for primarily with silver certificates, which added to the money supply as these instruments were legal tender.[9]

Although the agreement was clearly bullish for the price of silver simply by virtue of the massive volume of purchases the U.S. government would embark on, there was an additional point that would provide ample support to the price level: The U.S. Treasury would only be able

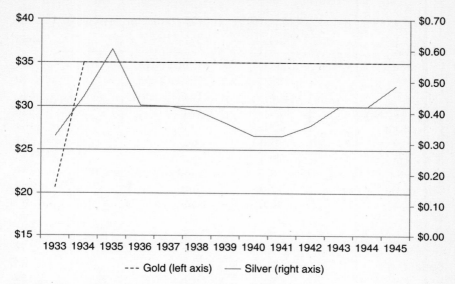

Figure 9.2   The Price of Gold and Silver, 1933–1945

SOURCE: Roy Jastram, *Silver: The Restless Metal* (New York: John Wiley & Sons, 1981), Thomson Reuters Datastream, World Gold Council.

to sell silver when government stocks exceeded 25 percent of total—or when the price of silver was above $1.29, the silver price during much of the previous century. But considering that silver was trading at below 50 cents per ounce at the time, it was quite clear that the Treasury department would not be selling any time soon (see Figure 9.2).

In 1933, as shown in Table 9.1, the United States had the largest holdings of gold of any country in the world. But with the silver purchase, its holdings would almost triple and the nation would become the largest silver owner, as well. Through its domestic and global market activity, by 1938, the United States had purchased 1.7 billion ounces— over 400 million ounces in 1938 alone—and had amassed the largest silver deposit ever accumulated.[10] Thanks in part to government intervention, 1933 proved to be one of the best buying opportunities for silver ever. Few could have known at the time that the bull run in silver that started in 1933 would last 45 years, despite temporary downswings, and by 1979 it would have outperformed commodities and gold as an investment by a wide margin. In inflation-adjusted terms, silver rose 241 percent between 1933 and 1979.[11]

Table 9.1 The World's Gold and Silver in 1933 (in millions of ounces)

	Gold		Silver
United States	196.0	China	1,700
France	157.0	British India	1,050
Others	263.0	United States	640
United Kingdom	28.0	Others	1,550
Switzerland	23.0	Hong Kong	162
Spain	21.0	Spain	144
Netherlands	20.0	Germany	135
USSR	18.0	Netherlands Indies	111
Belgium	17.0	Japan	107
Italy	15.0	United Kingdom	89
Argentina	12.0	Mexico	78
Japan	10.0	USSR	78
Germany	9.0	Iran	73
British India	8.0	France	66
Canada	4.0	Italy	48
Netherlands Indies	2.0	Netherlands	35
Australia	2.0	Ethiopia	34
Siam	1.5	Egypt	23
Egypt	1.5	Switzerland	21
Austria	1.0	Philippine Islands	19
Mexico	0.0	Siam	19
Philippine Islands	0.0	Canada	17
China	0.0	Australia	15
Hong Kong	0.0	Austria	10
Ethiopia	0.0	Argentina	0
Iran	0.0	Belgium	0

SOURCE: Dickson H. Leavens, *Silver Money* (copyright 1939).

There is no major economist or historian, to my knowledge, that would argue this silver purchase episode provided any economic advantage to the United States. In retrospect, many would agree that the government's silver policy in the 1930s was driven by the "narrow short-term self-interest of a small but politically potent group," as economist Milton Friedman said.[12] And yet, the effect outside of the United States was detrimental to a few important economies, most notably that of China, the only populous country remaining on a silver standard in 1933. As its economy had been evading the foreign effects of the depression with a weak currency (driven by falling silver prices), the United States' new policy provoked a massive outflow of silver from the country and caused its currency to appreciate. Consequently, Chinese exports plummeted and the agricultural economy went into an even deeper crisis than what it had been living through.

The severity of Chinese deflation, which came as a direct consequence of silver being exported to the attractive U.S. market, caused the country to go off the silver standard on October 14, 1934.[13] Freed from the shackles of a currency linked to a fixed commodity, the Chinese Nationalist government in time would print money at an unprecedented scale leading to inflation rates of more than 150 percent per year in the 1940s. This would pave the way for the Communist Revolution that came shortly after. The effects of U.S. silver policy on China became, as Jastram put it, "a profoundly disturbing example of how one country, for purely domestic reasons, can devastate the economy of another country."[14]

Perhaps the most significant effect of FDR's silver purchase order was that it contributed to the complete demonetization of silver and its removal from virtually all monetary instruments. Despite gold's triumph over silver in the 1870s as the world's leading economies adopted the gold standard, as late as 1933 more than 30 percent of all silver produced from 1493 to 1932 was in monetary use. By 1979, partly as a result of the instability created by the FDR administration in the 1930s, coinage represented a mere 5 percent of total silver consumption, a level roughly in line with where it is today.[15] But while silver miners had lost one of their most important markets, the monetary one, the industrial market was about to surge.

Chapter 10

1960s: As the Last Silver Dime Is Minted, Silver Demand Surges in the Electronic Revolution

T hough a distant memory to most in the years following the end of World War II, the Silver Purchase Act of 1934 remained in force and continued having a remarkable impact on the international silver market. U.S. Treasury Department stocks had risen from a breathtaking level of 1.7 billion ounces in 1938 to 3.2 billion ounces by 1962, a silver trove amounting to more than 10 percent of all the silver ever mined and refined in world history. The driver of this acquisition policy—which had driven up the government's silver holdings sixfold in a quarter century—was the stipulation that (1) silver would be purchased until it became a quarter of monetary stocks and (2) the price of silver had

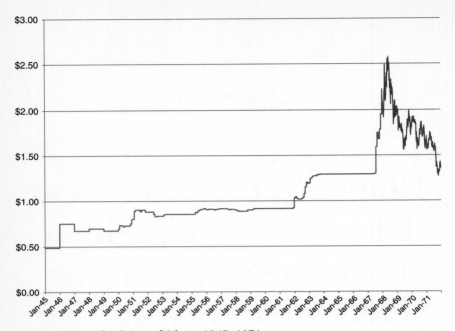

Figure 10.1   The Price of Silver, 1945–1971
SOURCE: Roy Jastram, *Silver: The Restless Metal* (New York: John Wiley & Sons, 1981), Bloomberg.

passed the level of $1.29 per ounce. Since neither of these legislative requirements had been met and the law had not changed, purchases continued, and silver mining companies must have been as happy as early Apple shareholders. (See Figure 10.1.)[1]

However, this artificial demand, which had been created by what effectively was a massive government subsidy, was no longer required. In the 1950s silver consumption began to rise at a 4 percent annual rate, which exceeded the 1.5 percent growth in global mining production.[2] Domestic production actually declined slightly between 1958 and 1963 while domestic consumption for coinage and industrial use rose sharply. Though in 1942 net silver industrial consumption in the United States exceeded 100 million ounces for the first time due to military demand, a true surge well beyond that level would come in the 1960s. (See Figure 10.2.) The annual deficits, the silver demand that exceeded supply, of 100 million ounces in the 1950s jumped to 187 million in 1963 and then to 289 million ounces the next year.[3]

Silver's high electrical and heat conductivity, resistance to corrosion and light sensitivity made the metal a vital input in a number of industrial

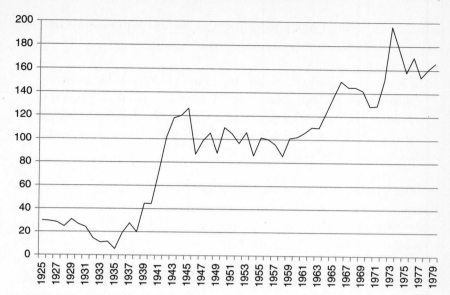

Figure 10.2   Net Industrial Consumption of Silver, 1925–1979 (millions of troy ounces, fine)

SOURCE: Roy Jastram, *Silver: The Restless Metal* (New York: John Wiley & Sons, 1981).

processes during the rise of the electronic era. Not only was demand surging in the United States, the recovering West Germany and Japan began importing large amounts of silver from the American mining industry. Between 1950 and 1958 foreign industrial demand doubled and by 1964 it had risen by another 50 percent.[4]

   While the U.S. Treasury held in excess of 3 billion ounces of silver in late 1961, there were only 22 million ounces of "free silver"—less than 1 percent of government holdings—due to the restrictions imposed by the Silver Purchase Act. With pressure building on the domestic silver supply, then-president John Kennedy caused a stir when his statement became public knowledge: "I have reached the decision that silver metal should gradually be withdrawn from our monetary reserves."[5] The president's words caused such a stir in the silver markets that within 24 hours, according to Jastram, the white metal had surged 10 percent in price and would continue on its upward path in the months ahead. In time, the president would be forced to repeal the Roosevelt-era legislation so that his administration would be able to begin supplying the market with silver in larger quantities. But this did not prevent a building silver mania from erupting in full force.

> It was as emotional as a chain-letter craze. Children were collecting coins in emulation of their elders. Wild tales of fabulous prices that could be got for a simple dime (if it had just the right combination or markings) were the centerpiece of conversations over bridge tables and corner bars.[6]

The public's hoarding of dimes, quarters, and nickels due to their silver content contributed to the chronic shortage of coins already being created by the technological marvel of the time: the coin-operated vending machine. By the mid-1960s, there were around 12 million automatic coin-operated vending machines—parking meters, phone booths, and dispensers of hot and cold beverages, sandwiches, candy, cigarettes, as well as laundry machines.[7] And their numbers were rising faster than the population. Machines were consuming the nation's coins along with hoarding hands putting the metallic disks into cookie jars in expectation of higher prices for silver.

An additional factor putting pressure on supply, which is given little weight by Jastram or a key Federal Reserve study from the time, was the rise of clandestine smelters. These illicit operations sought to take advantage of the reality that American coins' silver content was becoming more valuable than the face value of each individual coin. U.S. War nickels (minted between 1942 and 1945), silver dollars (up to 1935), as well as dimes, quarters, and half dollars (which would be minted through 1964) all contained relatively high amounts of silver. "As the price of silver climbed, so did the number of would-be and actual illegal smelters," wrote coin specialist Henry Merton in the 1980s.[8] Though it is difficult to quantify how many coins were withdrawn from circulation permanently, there is no way to calculate with precision how many actually went to the melting pot.

By 1964, the coin shortage had become extreme and banks actually started rationing dimes and nickels. Whether it was hoarders, smelters or simply the increased use of coins in commerce, clearly a lot of coins were disappearing. It was a truly bizarre situation: In mid-1964 there were an average of 240 coins for every woman, man, and child in the entire country, and yet there was a coin shortage.[9] The government responded with even more supply—a "crash program"—as the nation's two operating mints worked almost continuously with tremendous results: 5.5 billion coins were minted in 1964 versus 3.4 billion the year before.[10] The idea was that a flood of coins would satiate demand and cause coin prices to fall and indirectly prevent silver from rising above the critical $1.2929 level. At a silver price above $1.3824, many coins would be worth more than face value due to their silver content, which is what hoarders were betting on.

By early 1965, the U.S. Mint reported that the coin situation had come under control after the unprecedented experience: Between 1959 and 1964, coinage had tripled while the population had only increased by 8 percent, the economy by 28 percent, and vending machine sales by 47 percent.[11] But the cost of the coinage surge and booming industrial demand was a dramatic decline in Treasury silver stocks. By June of 1965, supplies had fallen sharply to a mere 1 billion ounces. In the space of less than four years, the Treasury Department's holdings had fallen by more than two-thirds and the government faced the prospect of a complete depletion of silver holdings in a short period of time.

The unsustainable situation ultimately led the Lyndon Johnson administration to remove silver from American coins completely. In the Coinage Act of 1965, silver was formally removed from U.S. dimes, nickels, and quarters and the element was replaced by cupronickel, the most widely used coinage material in the world at the time, which would cover a copper core in silver-colored American coins. Though similar to silver—new coins would be virtually indistinguishable from the ones being replaced—cupronickel differed in one important regard: In 1965, it cost 45 cents a pound—about 2 percent the cost of a pound of silver, which was almost $19. The new legislation also aimed to prevent further hoarding of the existing coins that contained silver by, among other measures, prohibiting the melting, alteration, or export of any U.S. coins. By 1966, thanks to the construction of new minting facilities and the reactivation of a production facility in San Francisco, production surged, and in time the silver excitement seemed like it would begin to wane.

But Treasury silver holdings told a different story. Although the government used only 54 million ounces of silver for coins in 1966—a steep decline from the 320 million level of the previous year—domestic and foreign industrial demand continued to surge. So Treasury stocks continued their rapid decline from 1.2 billion ounces in December 1964 to 804 million a year later and to 594 the following year. And now authorities faced a significant dilemma: There were a large number of silver certificates issued in the 1930s and '40s that could be redeemed for silver, and most remaining supplies were earmarked for redemption: Paper silver might become physical silver.

Once again, the government was forced to legally impede a silver surge as the public—most notably silver speculators, which even school children were becoming at the time—was aware of the predicament, which made them even more bullish on the price of silver. To guarantee continued availability of silver, the government restricted supply to those presenting silver certificates and to sales for "legitimate domestic concerns." While the government tried to control the price of silver at $1.30, the international price rose much higher, which effectively created a dual market: In London, silver rose to $1.70 an ounce. Eventually, the Treasury Department halted all sales of silver at the old price and announced that it would only sell 2 million ounces a week. This control of supply led indirectly to an even more intense rally in silver prices on global markets. By June of 1968, silver had almost doubled to $2.56 an ounce.

Chapter 11

The 1970s Silver Boom, the 1980 Crash, and the 20-Year Bear Market

By 1970, silver had become one of the most popular speculative investments in the United States. Within a few years, a book entitled *Silver Profits in the Seventies* offered an enticing proposition for the get-rich-quick crowd: "Within our lifetime, and perhaps within this decade, silver could become more valuable than gold."[1] This implied that silver could surge more than tenfold in value (which it eventually did) and a lot more if gold took off, as well. But despite the excitement this notion presented, by 1970 and 1971 silver's slowing ascent was beginning to disappoint investors, who began reducing their speculative positions. Industrial consumption also slackened as many companies had accumulated stocks in prior years and, combined with supplies from investors, the market finally had a surplus, which led to a sharp decline. By the spring of 1971, the price of silver had lost almost half its value from the peak and was trading near $1.70 per ounce. But few knew at the time that the silver bull market that had begun in 1963 was merely taking a break.

Moving into 1972 and 1973 currency markets faced a number of significant dollar devaluations driven by climbing U.S. deficits. Though extremely low by today's standards, the growing federal deficit, which forced demand to rise faster than the economy's supply, began to cause inflation, inflation that we exported to other countries via the dollar.[2] Given the United States' weight in the international economy and the resulting synchronization of countries' business cycles, other central banks were forced to follow the Fed's lead. But U.S. dominance combined with the government's continuing Vietnam War–driven expansionary policy began to cause concern among world financial leaders.

France led the charge in criticizing the United States for requiring the world to fund its deficit spending, and in the 1960s, the European nation had begun converting its dollar holdings into gold, effectively forcing the American government to begin selling down its massive gold holdings. Gold, the French finance minister at the time explained, is "the only monetary element outside the scope of government action," implying that the dollar was rapidly losing credibility as a store of value for political reasons that pertained to the United States, not the global monetary system. Despite President Lyndon Johnson's assurances that he would defend the value of the dollar (that is ensure that gold stayed at $35 an ounce by dumping the precious metal on global markets), a gold rush was gaining force—moving in lockstep with the silver rush. Though American citizens were prohibited from owning gold bullion until 1974 (they were limited to buying jewelry and rare coins, which were already climbing rapidly in value), foreign central banks and individuals began amassing large amounts. The fever, much like the silver fever, was fed by a flurry of articles in the world media and by books on gold.

Economists monitoring the U.S. money supply reported a troublesome trend—more and more dollars in circulation and a declining amount of gold in U.S. vaults with which to back the American currency's value. Although the world was no longer on a gold standard, the Bretton Woods international monetary system had been founded at the end of World War II based on the dollar. And central banks from other countries were allowed to exchange their dollars for gold from the U.S. government upon demand. This was not a concern in 1948, when the United States held two-thirds of all monetary reserves and much of the world's gold and silver bars. But by the late 1960s, gold stocks—much like silver stocks—had been falling sharply. The precious metals-based monetary foundation of the United States was weakening.

By 1971, the flood of dollars into gold and other currencies, like the German mark (predecessor to today's troubled euro), had become unsustainable. And in that year President Richard Nixon, facing the prospect of a complete depletion of gold from federal vaults, ordered the closing of the "gold window": foreign central banks—much as had happened to American citizens with silver a few years before—could no longer convert their U.S. currency into gold. The dollar was suddenly no longer as good as gold and the Bretton Woods system collapsed. All currencies began to trade freely in what would become a decade of surging inflation.

In a world seeking alternatives to the dollar, silver resumed its climb rising to $3.28 by December of 1973. But silver reacted even more strongly to a supply shock in the oil industry that began with the Arab oil embargo, which provoked a very sudden surge in global energy prices. Silver, an asset that traditionally reacts very positively to inflation, became explosive and doubled in value in two months, rising to $6.70 in late February as speculators stormed the market.[3] Gold, which had begun trading freely just a few years before, jumped along with silver. The correlation of the two metals, which had broken down in the late nineteenth century due to the end of bimetallism and rise of the gold standard, resumed: From the early 1970s to this day, gold and silver have continued to trade in the same direction.

Notwithstanding the surge in gold and inflation due to climbing oil prices, the rise in silver was also driven by supply and demand factors in the metal's market itself. Industrial demand driven by new uses of silver—mainly photography and electric processes—rose from 129 million to 190 million ounces in the 1972–1973 period, which more than compensated for the decline during the previous two years. Also, since gold prices had been surging and causing jewelry demand to fall, silver jewelry buying rose sharply as customers sought the cheaper alternative.

Meanwhile, supply was disrupted by the nine-month closing of Idaho's Sunshine mine in 1972 due to a fire and eventually a strike the following year. At the time, one-half of U.S. silver production came from the Coeur d'Alene mining district, a 20-by-30-mile strip in northern Idaho. The Sunshine mine, which reached large-scale production in the 1920s, had become the major driver of Idaho silver production.

Despite sharp price swings throughout the mid-1970s, silver continued trading near $5 an ounce until 1978, when prices began to move sharply higher. Few knew that two of the richest families in the world at the time, the Hunts of Texas and the Saudi royal family, were about to embark on one of the most audacious attempts to corner a market in financial history. It would cause the biggest, fastest surge ever in the price of silver and prompt the metal to reach an all-time-high of $48.70 that has yet to be surpassed. Silver rose over 700 percent during 1979. But it also led to a spectacular crash, the temporary shutting down of silver trading on the American silver futures market and to a bear market in silver that would last years.

Ironically, the strategy for manipulating the silver market was already known to anyone paying attention, as it had been explained—just weeks before it actually happened—in the magazine *Euromoney* in early 1979:

> If 150 million ounces of silver were owned by parties who intended to hold it for a 30–40 percent appreciation after interest cost, those parties would have a major impact on supply and might well succeed in achieving the price they ask. Someone who wanted to buy that much silver could do so with a billion dollars, which sounds like a lot, but since he could borrow 80–90 percent of the funds to do it with, a silver squeeze could be financed for $100 million. Whether it will really happen is hard to predict; most people with $100 million to spare have better things to do.[4]

But, as journalist Stephen Fay wrote at the time, billionaires Bunker and Herbert Hunt as well as the princes of the Saudi royal family were not "most people."[5] The story of the trade's initial success and its catastrophic failure are chronicled in Fay's classic book on the episode, *Beyond Greed*.[6] Though the speculative conspirators took the right steps to corner the silver market, they ultimately underestimated how authorities would react: "A common characteristic shared by the architects of market corners is the conviction that they have thought of everything."[7] The Hunts and Saudi royals were caught off guard when Comex authorities ultimately decided to cancel silver trading and forced holders to suffer as the price began to plummet. While the average prices between 1978 and 1980 showed a dramatic increase and then collapse, the violent monthly moves provide a deeper illustration of just how volatile the market had become (see Figure 11.1).

Although the metal traded in the $5 to $6 range throughout 1978, in 1979 silver rapidly broke into $7 and by September the white metal's price had gone double-digit. Silver skyrocketed, which was intensely destabilizing for the persons working away from financial markets in the physical world, refiners and silver dealers. While physical silver in the form of jewelry, flatware, and anything people could sell was flooding the market, refineries and dealers were unable to deliver on orders. "Quoted turnaround times stretched out to three months, six months, a year, or more," a silver dealer writing about that time explained.[8]

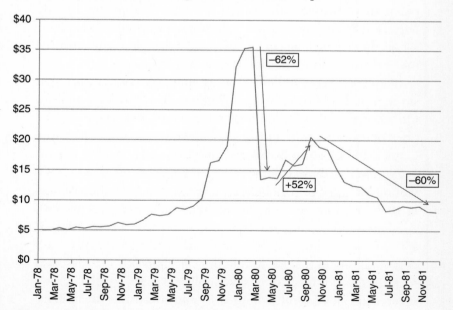

Figure 11.1   Price of Silver, 1978–1981
SOURCE: Bloomberg.

Overloading the refining system wasn't the only problem, he explained; it was how this was affecting the futures market. Refiners and dealers need to "hedge" or "lay off" their silver purchases by selling futures contracts as they buy physical silver, and vice versa. Acting as middlemen, they are not trying to profit by speculating on market direction, but rather to simply profit from a spread on volume of activity: "Selling doesn't hurt them, buying doesn't hurt them, but a market going nowhere *kills* them." In a simple trade, they can buy 5,000 ounces of physical silver (bars, jewelry, flatware, or scrap in some other form) and sell a futures contract for the same amount so as to lock in profit in a "fully hedged" position. But as speculative positions of unprecedented size began to be placed by the Hunts in 1979, the situation became unsustainable for the metals market, as metals expert James Blanchard explained:

> In 1979–80 . . . exchange brokers kept shorting (selling) silver all the way up, and their pain increased to the breaking point. Even though their actual position, balancing futures against physicals, might have been flat (neither long nor short), they still had to meet phenomenal margin calls against their short futures contracts. By January 1980 they were actually threatened with *losing* (a once-in-a-millennium experience), so they did what powerful financial interests always do when a loss threatens: *They changed the rules*.
>
> On January 21, 1980, the Comex effectively closed trading in silver. You could only buy or sell to liquidate existing positions. Off-exchange physicals dealers and investors were trapped. The price of silver began to break. Trading volume statistics from the Comex and Chicago Board of Trade eloquently tell the tale. In 1979, total trading volume was 34 billion ounces. In 1980, volume dropped to 6.99 billion ounces. From 1.1 billion ounces in 1979, open interest dropped to 309.3 million ounces in 1980.
>
> Silver on the commodity exchanges may have been trading at $50 an ounce, but unless investors already had the silver on deposit in an exchange warehouse, *they couldn't get more than 65 percent of its value*. Coins, silver dollars, wafers, ingots, sterling silver, and bars all went to huge discounts because of the refinery overload. Dealers and refiners discounted everything. Some refused to buy at any price.[9]

Few at the time could know that the silver trading suspension on the Comex would initiate a two-decade grizzly bear market that would take the metal from its peak of $48.70 to a bottom below $4 an ounce in the early 1990s, a value collapse of over 90 percent from which the metal has yet to recover fully. In 1980 alone, silver lost almost over 30 dollars in value from its peak. The pain trade continued into 1981 and 1982, when it touched $5 an ounce—a return back to 1978 levels, before the Hunts had set up their market corner. And despite a recovery above $10 an ounce in 1983 with signs of economic recovery, silver was unable to sustain a rally and would not break the $10 mark for more than 20 years. But the Comex move was not the real cause of the silver bear market, nor that of the gold bear market that began in the early 1980s.

Rather, it was the Federal Reserve's fight against inflation. As the Fed, under new Chairman Paul Volker, drove the cost of borrowing higher and higher into the early 1980s, the move caused a sharp economic deceleration and consequent decline in inflationary pressures. During the late 1960s and into the 1970s, many investors had moved money into real assets like gold, silver, other commodities and real estate and away from traditional financial assets, like bonds and stocks, which performed very poorly in the inflationary environment of the time. But higher interest rates began making bonds increasingly attractive, especially as it became clearer that the Fed would be successful in containing the runaway inflation of the 1970s. Real interest rates—that is, interest rates adjusted for inflation—were reaching some of the highest levels ever, which would become an irresistible magnet for foreign investment into dollar-denominated assets. This pushed the dollar higher and a strong dollar is generally negative for gold, silver, and commodities. And as interest rates finally began falling in the 1980s, stocks—which were trading at some of the most attractive valuation levels ever seen—began to rise sharply as the economy recovered. It was the beginning of one of the most fantastic performance periods of financial assets in history, one that would leave gold and silver behind.

The sharp decline in silver investment that began in 1980 with the Comex-driven crash coincided with a sudden surplus in production that had arrived in 1979. After years of silver mining and scrap production being insufficient to meet industrial demand from new processes, supply had finally risen to meet demand, a phenomenon that was occurring across the commodity complex: There was plenty of supply, a glut in a number of commodity markets that caused severe economic difficulties for a number of countries, like oil-rich Mexico, whose currency collapsed leading it into a devastating recession.

The silver market had grown accustomed to deficits (a bullish market condition since it tends to push the market toward higher prices), which averaged 55 million ounces per year between 1971 and 1978 (see Figure 11.2). But in 1979, there was a small surplus: And with the market-distorting silver conspiracy fiasco, tons of silver flooded the market resulting in a 200-million ounce surplus in 1980. From then on, the silver market went into surplus for 11 years and would not move back into deficit until 1990, just in time for digital photography to take off.

In 1983, 38 percent of all silver fabrication demand came from film photography, making the print developing industry of vital importance to the metal's market. The growing threat of digital photography, which does not require significant amounts of silver, was well known as far back as the 1970s. The technology leading to what would become digital photography was invented in 1969 and shortly after Sony began

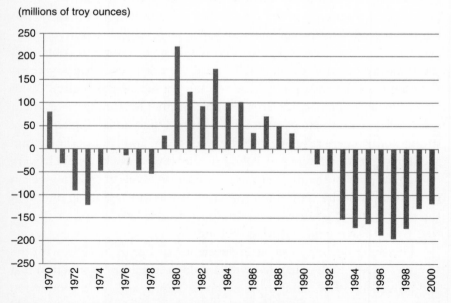

(millions of troy ounces)

Figure 11.2   Silver Deficits and Surpluses, 1970–2000
SOURCE: The Silver Institute.

developing the first cameras that would appear on store shelves in the early 1980s. But it was not until 1994 that the first cameras for the mass market became available. Few could have visualized that within a decade, traditional photography would become a small part of global picture-taking. Needless to say, the effect on silver prices would in time be significant, as the rise of the digital camera caused silver consumption for film developing to decline sharply (see Figure 11.3).

The collapse of traditional photography gathered strength in the 2000s, driven by falling camera prices. In late 2002, when 2-megapixel cameras could be found for under $100 and 1-megapixel cameras for $60, a milestone was reached: digital cameras outsold film cameras for the first time. The next year, disposable digital cameras were available, like the Ritz Dakota Digital, a 1.2-megapixel camera for only $11. Kodak, whose name had become synonymous with traditional photography, stopped producing Kodak-branded cameras in 2004 and would eventually be driven to the

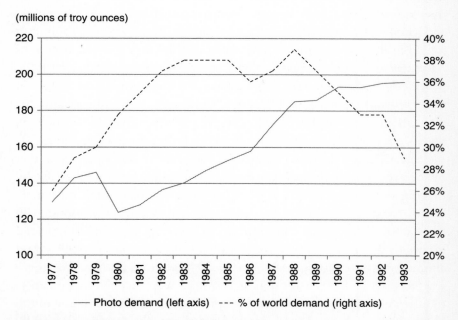

Figure 11.3 Photography Industry Use of Silver (in ounces and as a percentage of total silver demand), 1977–1993

SOURCE: James Blanchard, *Silver Bonanza* (New York: Simon & Schuster, 1993).

brink of bankruptcy. Nikon stopped producing most film cameras and Konica Minolta decided to pull out of the camera business completely.

In 2002, despite the amazing rise of the digital camera, the photography industry was still absorbing almost a quarter of total silver supply as traditional film cameras were still in widespread use. But from that year forward, silver demand for photographic use began to plummet. Silver consumption halved in six years and by 2011 a mere 66 million ounces were used in the photography industry, an amount representing a third of demand from a decade earlier. As a result, photography has become far less important to the silver industry, as it represents only 6 percent of total supply at present. Film photography's replacement by digital technology was one of the factors that prevented the price of silver from rebounding from its bear market as quickly as gold did: gold bottomed near $250 in mid-1999 and silver would not trough until it nearly fell to $4 in late 2001. Hence, silver's bear market lasted two years longer than gold's.

Toward the end of the 1990s, silver remained in a malaise as an investment, as the metal continued to trade near $5 an ounce. When silver moved into deficit (with industrial demand outpacing supply from mines and scrap) in the early 1990s, ending a decade of bearish surpluses, optimism surged in the precious metals investment community. The publication of *Silver Bonanza: How to Profit from the Coming Bull Market in Silver,* in 1993, provided grounds for this optimism, though it underestimated the impact on silver demand of digital photography: "Contrary to conventional assumptions about "revolutionary" technologies replacing silver in technology, silver's place in photography is quite secure for the foreseeable future."[10]

Silver bulls were also excited by the surprise announcement that billionaire Warren Buffett had joined their ranks, however briefly, by making a major purchase in 1997. With silver trading at $4.50 an ounce, it was revealed that the sage of Omaha had bought a whopping 20 percent of global silver consumption that year, a move that appeared bizarre to the tech stock-crazed investment world of the late 1990s. And although silver briefly surged above $7.50 in reaction to the move, there was very weak follow-through as investors were deeply concerned— rightly, as it turned out—about the rapid decline of silver demand in the photography industry. Few followed Buffett into silver and by mid-1998, silver was back down to below $5. Silver would have to wait another three years for the end of the bear market.

Chapter 12

2001 to the Present: The Bull Market Begins as Silver Reenters the Financial System

The effects of the 1990s digital photography revolution on silver were severe, and it took a number of years for other sources of silver demand to compensate for the decline in photographic demand for the metal. Silver, though highly correlated with (its price generally moves in the same direction as) gold, would really not enter the bull market that gold had already begun for another two years (see Figure 12.1). The rise of both gold and silver in the early 2000s coincided with a commodity market boom. The rising affluence within emerging economies provoked a surge in demand for agricultural and mining products as well as energy. Meanwhile, the lack of investment in energy

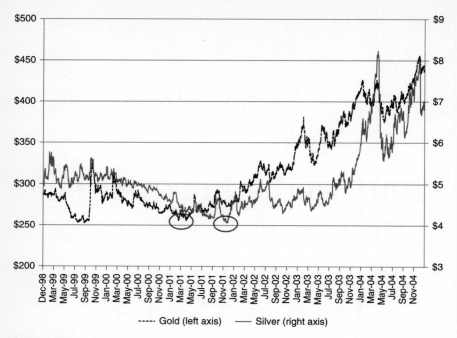

Figure 12.1   Price of Silver, 1999–2004
Source: Bloomberg.

and mining over the preceding commodities bear market made for a weak reaction in supply to meet the growing demand, which intensified the price increases for crude oil and natural gas as well as for copper, iron, lead, tin, and the various food commodities.

But beyond the drivers related to commodities, in general, precious metals—and gold, in particular—were gaining importance as financial assets that were being considered alongside stocks and bonds as investment vehicles for global portfolios. The movement began very gradually, as memories of the grizzly bear market of the 1980s and 1990s had made gold a pariah among institutional fund managers. But with the dramatic decline in interest rates that began with the 2001 recession, when the Federal Reserve began pushing the Fed Funds rate down to unprecedented levels, commodities and precious metals—which do not offer dividends or pay interest—were becoming increasingly attractive as investment alternatives.

In the professional asset management industry, commodities are widely regarded as a *tactical* investment, something to invest in temporarily to take advantage of short-term dynamics that tend to dissipate over time. *Strategic* investments are for the long run and the unquestioned ones are stocks and bonds, which have a long-term history of providing attractive risk-adjusted returns. Although the percentage of stocks and bonds that large, professionally-managed portfolios hold vary significantly over time, they have a permanent position in portfolios— never a zero weighting.

Until very recently, gold was widely regarded as a commodity, an investment that did not deserve a strategic allocation, a long-term position in a well-diversified portfolio. Gold positions in large portfolios had traditionally been at zero or near zero. But in recent years, views about gold have changed primarily considering the diversification bene-fits that the metal provides to a portfolio. Over extended investment periods gold does not move in the same direction as stocks, and consequently, holding the metal can mitigate the negative impact on portfolios that equities have when these are performing poorly. Gold, an inert element that does not pay dividends or interest, might not outperform stocks or bonds over the long run, but it helps reduce the volatility of equity-dominant diversified portfolios and enhances long-term returns. This realization led to gradually increasing allocations to gold in the 2000s. Some professional investors have come to believe, as I do, that gold merits a relatively small, but significant and permanent position in well-diversified portfolios (see Figure 12.2).

Silver, though a metal that is more correlated with gold than with anything else, has not received the same attention as gold primarily because the metal's price movements can be volatile and extreme. Consider the sharp, sudden downswing silver suffered in May and September of 2011, as shown in the chart in Figure 12.3. Such violent downswings—the key investment differentiator from gold, which almost never experiences movements of this intensity—make silver a metal to which few fund managers want to make significant allocations.

Though it is not as rare as gold in nature, ironically, there is less silver available for investment in the world today. This makes silver an asset that is harder to invest in, as the metal is less liquid (easy to buy and sell in large quantities) than gold. Most professionals in the investment industry would regard silver as a commodity, notwithstanding its close relation-ship to gold, and hence as a tactical (short-term) investment at best and

Figure 12.2   Relative Performance of Gold, Silver, and Commodities, 2000 through the Present (Indexed to Start at 100)
SOURCE: Bloomberg.

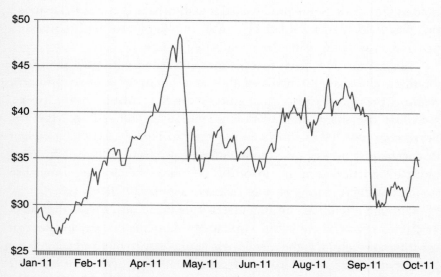

Figure 12.3   Price of Silver from January through October 2011
SOURCE: Bloomberg.

as a speculative uninvestable asset at worst. But notwithstanding the growing number of research reports focusing on gold's positive invest-ment attributes—and none about silver—investment in gold's sister metal began climbing sharply in the 2000s, as well. More and more investors began to realize that, despite being more volatile, during gold bull markets silver tended to appreciate faster than gold. And despite its higher volatility, silver has outperformed gold over the past decade as an investment.

The increased investment in gold and silver was facilitated by the rise of new precious metals investment vehicles. Though barely perceptible to those without a direct interest in the precious metals world, silver and gold investing has been transformed in recent years by the rise of the exchange-traded fund. John Hathaway, portfolio manager of the Tocqueville Gold Fund, believes the launch of the first gold exchange-traded fund (ETF) in 2003 was "the single most important development in the gold market since Nixon closed the gold window in 1971."[1] (See Figure 12.4.) SLV, the first silver ETF, was launched three years later, in April of 2006 and the impact is hard to underestimate. When Barclays Global Investors first filed the paperwork for the initial public offering of SLV, silver was trading at just over $7 an ounce, not far from the average of the previous 30 years. Within a year, silver would surge above $10 an ounce (see Figure 12.5).

By giving them tickers, ETFs allowed gold and silver to trade along-side stocks like Google, China Telecom, and Petrobras in the global arena, a significant investment to be considered in portfolios.[2] Gold, long seen as an asset that helps protect a portfolio from inflation, can now be used in a simple way by portfolio managers who are considering it alongside other inflation protection vehicles, like Treasury Inflation-Protected Securities (TIPS). Silver, which is highly correlated with gold (though significantly more volatile), can be used in the same way. ETFs can also finally be used with simplicity as a basic portfolio diversification vehicle, something that was extremely difficult to do just a decade ago. Though ETFs have been trading for several years now, some of the most significant investors in these vehicles have only begun doing so in recent years. (See Figure 12.5.) The China Investment Corporation, one of the largest investment funds of any kind in the world, made its first invest-ment in a gold ETF in early 2010, just a few years ago.

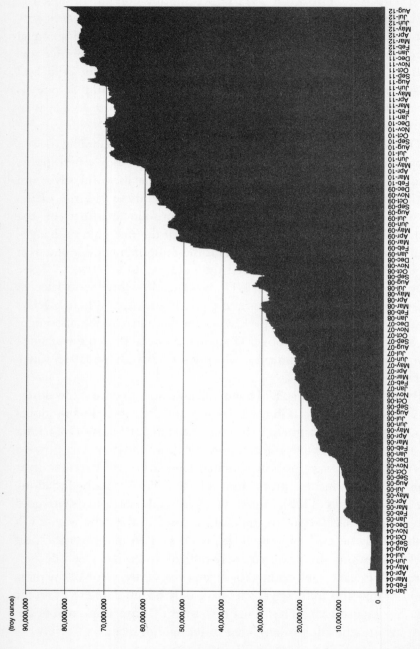

Figure 12.4 Global Gold ETF Holdings since Inception

Source: Bloomberg.

(troy ounce)

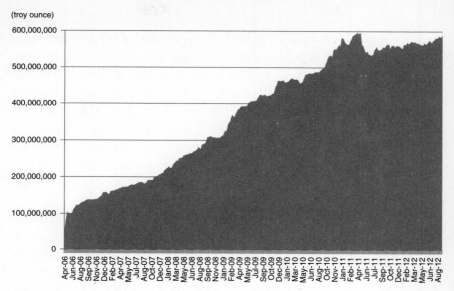

Figure 12.5   Global Silver ETF Holdings since Inception
SOURCE: Bloomberg.

Prior to the existence of ETFs, precious metals investment required more cost and effort: Investors were forced to own precious metals physically (typically via coins or bars) and had to pay significantly higher prices—as much as 5 percent for a retail transaction—than could be obtained by, say, central banks buying gold. Alternative strategies using the futures market, which implies using leverage and frequent trading, were not accessible to or practical for most fund managers, especially for the thousands who manage long-only equity funds. Today, aside from a recurring management fee of around 0.40 percent for gold (for GLD, the most liquid and widely held gold ETF, and slightly less for some others) and 0.50 percent for SLV (the most liquid silver fund), ETF investors pay essentially the same price as any central bank does when buying gold and substantially less for silver than when buying physical. And new ETFs that offer the possibility of exchanging them for physical gold or silver, like the ones offered by Sprott (PSLV for silver and PHYS for gold) have been listed in recent years.

Another inconvenience was the need to store the metals, either at home (a potential safety risk) or by paying a storage fee to secure the asset in a safety deposit box at the bank. Perhaps most importantly, considering the effect the launching of ETFs has had on gold and silver demand, ETFs have made gold and silver investable to a great many funds that could not have legally owned it before. The pension fund I work for, Teacher Retirement System (TRS) of Texas, is not allowed to physically own any assets directly as all need to be held by way of a custodian. The creation of the GBI Gold Fund, which we launched in 2009 and which holds gold and silver ETFs, would not have been possible in its present structure without the existence of these vehicles. As such, gold and other precious metals are truly new as investment assets to a great many of the world's largest funds.

Since the launch of gold and silver ETFs, both precious metals—as well as commodities, in general—remained in bull markets until the 2008 financial crisis. Although financial conditions were turning intensely volatile as the U.S. housing market began showing signs of significant distress, commodities continued to rise sharply in early 2008, many climbing to new record highs. Silver broke $20—a level not seen in almost three decades—in March of that year, and gold reached $1,000 an ounce for the first time. Crude oil rose to $145 per barrel, a new record. However, during the summer energy and food commodities and metals began a deep nosedive that made 2008 end as one of the worst years in the history of commodities investing. But even though the financial outlook had become extremely uncertain, one thing was becoming clear: Gold would emerge once again as a proven investment vehicle for financial protection, as the following table shows. When the dust settled after the financial devastation, gold was the only asset that had risen in value during 2008 that was not a fixed income instrument. Unless you were lending money to an unquestioned government entity regarded as safe—that is, you owned a sovereign bond—gold was the only place to hide in that terrible year (see Figure 12.6).

Silver was dragged down along with other commodities during 2008, as investors began speculating that industrial demand for the metal would fall sharply as multiple economies around the world went into recession. 2008 was a dark year for the metal, as its value fell by more than half from its peak for the year at over $20 to below $10 an ounce in October of 2008. And while it would recover some ground later in the year, it would still close the year down 23 percent. But considering the deep decline

Name	2008 Performance
Stocks:	
S&P 500	(37.0%)
Russell 1000	(37.6%)
Russell 2000	(33.8%)
MSCI US REIT	(38.0%)
MSCI AC World	(42.2%)
EM Asia	(53.0%)
EM Latin America	(51.4%)
EAFE & Canada	(43.6%)
Fixed Income:	
U.S. Treasury Bonds	13.7%
Japan Government Bonds	3.7%
US TIPS	(2.4%)
EM Government Bonds	(6.9%)
US Investment Grade Credit	(3.1%)
Commercial MBS	(20.5%)
US High Yield	(26.2%)
Money Market	1.8%
Commodities/Real Return:	
Global Hedge Fund Index	(23.3%)
Crude Oil	(53.5%)
Copper	(54.2%)
Agriculture	(28.9%)
Silver	**(23.0%)**
Gold	**5.8%**

Figure 12.6 Performance of Major Asset Classes during 2008
SOURCE: Bloomberg.

suffered by other commodities and the stock market, silver, the speculative metal so often criticized by professional investors for its volatility,
actually emerged better than most investment alternatives, as Figure 12.6
shows. Silver dramatically outperformed all commodities and stock
market indices around the world. And since the price bottom
in 2008, silver has outperformed gold and commodities, as shown in
Figure 12.7.

The price performance of silver during the 2008 bear market, the
worst financial market crash since the Great Depression, shows that it

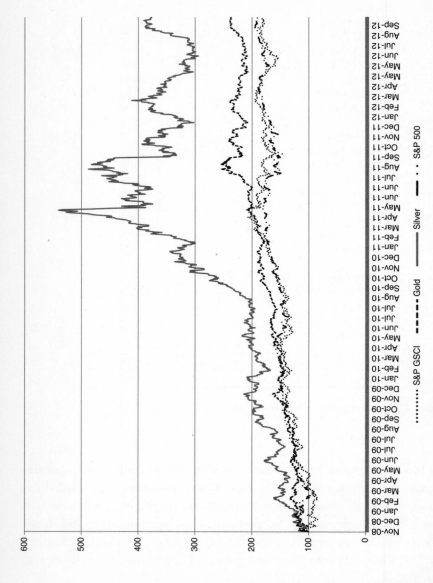

Figure 12.7 Relative Performance of Gold, Silver, Commodities, and U.S. Equities since November 2008 (Indexed to Start at 100)

SOURCE: Bloomberg.

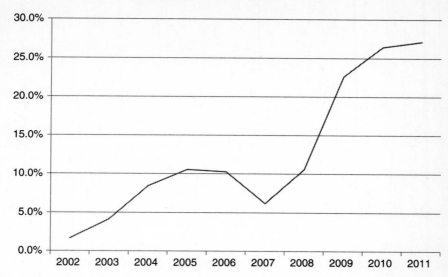

Figure 12.8   Investment Demand for Silver as a Percentage of Total Demand
Source: Silver Institute.

continues to recouple with gold despite having higher volatility. Notwithstanding its history as an unstable metal, one that has caused
numerous investment disappointments in the past, silver is behaving
more and more like gold and less and less like a commodity, such as
copper or oil. Consider the climbing percentage of silver supply that is
going into investment, which basically rose fivefold over the past decade
(see Figure 12.8).

Demand for silver coins, which is virtually all for physical investment
purposes, has tripled over the last decade to 118 million ounces in 2011
and demand for bars has also soared. If one includes jewelry, which in
many Asian countries is regarded as both body adornment and investment, the percentage of silver demand that accounts for investment
climbs to over 40 percent, as Figure 12.9 shows. This is the percentage of
silver demand derived from investment and jewelry, which is to say,
nonindustrial demand for silver.

Meanwhile, the drag that the collapse in photography silver usage
was causing on demand for the metal over the past two decades is gone:
At present, photography accounts for a mere 6 percent of total demand
compared with a quarter of total a decade ago. In that sense, all the

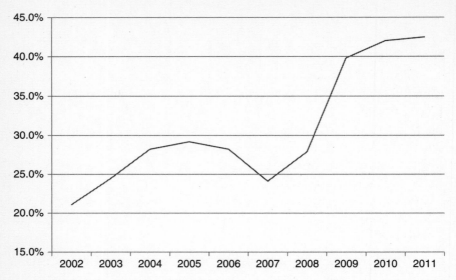

Figure 12.9   Combined Investment and Jewelry Demand for Silver as a Percentage of Total Demand
SOURCE: Silver Institute.

demand that was lost as a result of digital photography has been made up by investors in the metal.

As we enter 2013, the professional investment community continues to struggle with silver as an investment for a number of important reasons. For one, the silver bull market has been stronger than gold's. Silver bottomed near $4 an ounce in 2001 and surged to a peak of just over $48 on April 28, 2011, a fantastic rise of 1,000 percent. This compared with the gold's bull market, which took it from a low near $250 in 1999 to a high of $1,900 in September 2011, a surge of 660 percent. This gives investors pause as to how much more the metal could rise in the years ahead.

Secondly, there is lingering concern regarding the volatility of silver and the sharp downswings the metal suffers every so often. As silver approached its all-time high near $50 an ounce in April of 2011, a sell-off ensued that ultimately pushed the metal's price down to a low of $27 before it recovered ground. But as of this writing, silver is still down over 30 percent from that time, a reminder that silver can disappoint investors—and disappoint them very suddenly. Another factor that has caused concern for some is the rising silver surpluses that have been seen in the market in recent years, which gives rise to the concern that silver could be sold by investors in the future.

Regarding the first concern, the risk of buying after the sharp rise that silver has seen in recent years, it is important to keep in mind that the metal remains below its all-time high of $49.45 reached in 1980. Consider that the price of gold as of this writing is at a level *double* what it was at the peak of 1980, a mark it passed in 2009. In this sense, silver is still catching up with gold after struggling with the effects of the decline of film photography in the 1990s (see Figure 12.10).

Unfortunately, the volatility of silver is simply one of the characteristics of investing in the metal, a reminder that it should never hold a dominant position in any diversified portfolio. As seen repeatedly in the history of silver, something discussed in a number of chapters of this book, silver can have a way of falling sharply after strong upswings. That being said, the sell-off seen in May of 2011 was significantly different from important downswings seen in the past. This is shown in Figures 12.11 through 12.14.

Consider that after the collapse of 1980, a large number of metals traders, coin shops, and refiners were wiped out in the ensuing silver bear market that lasted decades. But the sharp sell-off of 2011 barely caused a dent in the market, as silver declined a mere 10 percent following its 1,000 percent climb over the previous decade. Furthermore, in average terms the price of silver was 50 percent higher than the price average of 2010. This reflects, in part, the fact that silver is now traded broadly by market participants of many types around the world. In 1980, the market was dominated by silver speculators in the U.S. and U.K. futures market, and the two wealthy families trying to corner it. The volatility in today's silver market pales in comparison to what has been seen in the past. During the deep sell-off in May of 2011, holdings in silver ETFs—where a significant amount of the world's silver bars are held—showed minimal withdrawals, a reflection of the increasing comfort numerous investors have with holding silver in the present financial environment.

Rising silver surpluses is something that several analysts have pointed to as a cause for potential concern. A surplus in the silver market is defined as demand from traditional sources, primarily industrial, minus supply from mining activity and scrap. When a surplus is generated, it is assumed

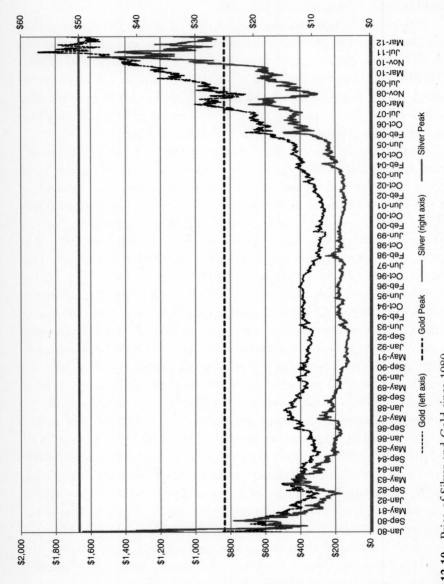

Figure 12.10 Price of Silver and Gold since 1980

Source: Bloomberg.

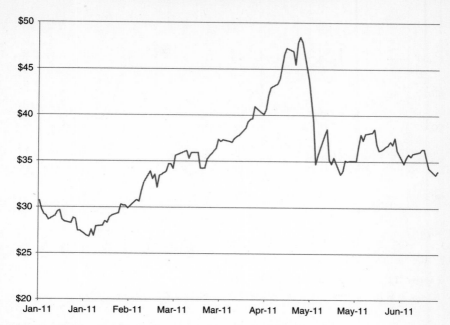

Figure 12.11   Price of Silver from January through June 2011
SOURCE: Bloomberg.

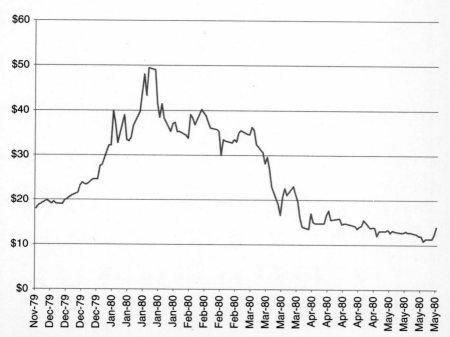

Figure 12.12   Price of Silver during 1980
SOURCE: Bloomberg.

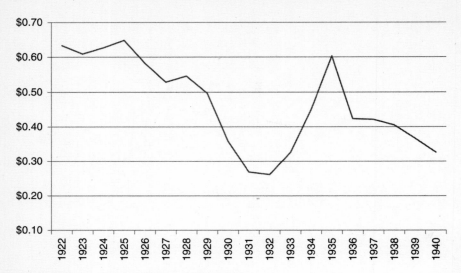

Figure 12.13   Price of Silver, 1922–1940

SOURCE: Roy Jastram, *Silver: The Restless Metal* (New York: John Wiley & Sons, 1981).

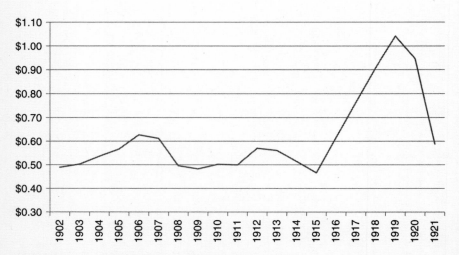

Figure 12.14   Price of Silver, 1902–1921

SOURCE: Roy Jastram, *Silver: The Restless Metal* (New York: John Wiley & Sons, 1981).

that—since it is not being sold—investors are comfortable holding it at the present price level. The new silver joins the existing aboveground silver that is held in the form of coins, bars, industrial inventories, and jewelry by individuals, governments, and companies around the world. Why are surpluses a concern for some analysts? Because in the 1980s, when surpluses began to rise after the Hunt Brothers' fiasco, silver was in a brutal bear market: There was plenty of silver for anyone who wanted to own the metal and eventually mining production had to adjust to the new reality. Now that we have surpluses again, as shown in Figure 12.15, there is a worry that silver holders could begin selling.

While it is certainly true that owners of silver coins, bars, and ETFs could begin dumping their holdings at any time, consider the situation that gold is in. There are tens of thousands of tons of gold that are held by central banks, investment firms, ETFs, and individuals around the world worth trillions of dollars. This is all a gold "surplus" and yet those holding these millions of ounces are comfortable preserving them in their possession at the present price level. Indeed, the vast majority of gold

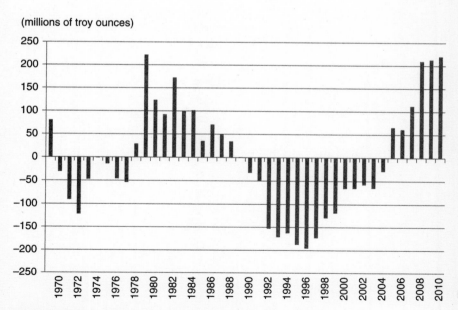

Figure 12.15   Silver Surpluses and Deficits
SOURCE: The Silver Institute.

does not change hands each year as, like the wedding ring on my finger, it is held with comfort. This has been the case throughout history.

But clearly silver is not gold, notwithstanding the many characteristics the white metal shares with its more valuable sister metal. Gold, for one, is a store of value that central banks purchase and hold, an open and clear judgment by the world's economic authorities that the metal is a store of value. But silver is a metal that governments of only a few countries—mainly Russia, China, and India—openly hold. It was only recently, thanks, in my opinion, to the rise of ETFs and more sophisticated ways of storing silver (which requires substantially larger storage space than gold) that more and more individuals and institutional investors have become comfortable owning silver. It is simply easier to own silver in large quantities than it ever has been.

In the history of silver, it has only been in recent times that the metal has come to be seen as a speculative way to ride the commodity cycle. And yet, considering the large number of coins being sold in the United States and the world, clearly there are a growing number of people who want to own silver as a method of wealth preservation.

Part Three

HOW TO INVEST IN SILVER

Chapter 13

Deciding on the Best
Way to Invest in Silver[*]

When thinking about silver as an investment, there is no question more important than what the right amount for you to own should be. More precisely, *you need to carefully consider what percentage of your total wealth should be in silver*, perhaps with the help of a financial advisor. Most likely, an advisor would recommend that you only invest an amount that you can *truly* put at risk—that is to say, an amount of money that would not hurt your financial situation significantly if your investment in silver took a substantial hit. As pointed out in Chapter 6, you should always consider the significant risks involved in silver investment and that, though the metals tend to move in the same direction, *silver is not gold*. And even gold—like stocks, bonds, and all other asset classes—presents its own specific investment risks.

[*]Parts of this chapter were taken from my book *Hard Money: Taking Gold to a Higher Investment Level*. Reprinted with permission by John Wiley & Sons.

Beyond the vital question of quantity, the most basic consideration is whether you want to own physical silver or hold the metal indirectly via a security, the way you would invest in a stock or bond. This is widely regarded as "paper silver," and the most common vehicles for owning it are exchange-traded funds (ETFs) that provide a representative interest in physical silver held by a custodian in a secure vault. SLV is by far the largest and most liquid (easy to buy and sell) ETF and it essentially provides the same investment return (minus a 0.50 percent management fee) as silver without the complications related with possessing the physical metal. It generally trades at below 0.30 percent of net asset value and its custodian is J.P. Morgan. One disadvantage of owning SLV is that should you ever want to convert the shares to silver, this would not be possible, much as it is impossible to convert a Tech stock ETF into the individual stocks underlying it: The security, a liquid, low-cost method for owning silver, was simply not structured nor designed for this. One ETF manager (though not of SLV) told me some time ago, simply: "Those who want to own their own bars should just go out and buy them"—and he has a point: Investors can pay more and store precious metals at home or in a bank vault, if they prefer to do so.

For those who like the convenience of ETFs but not the inability to convert into physical silver on demand, in 2010 Sprott Asset Management launched Sprott Physical Silver Trust (PSLV), the first North American ETF that is redeemable for physical silver. (Similar ones have been trading in Europe for a few years.) The metal purchased by Sprott to become the assets of the trust is deposited in Canada with the Royal Canadian Mint. PSLV trades at a premium to its net asset value (NAV) in part because the vehicle is taxed at the (lower) capital gains rate, while SLV is taxed at the collectible rate, like physical precious metals. However, PSLV's premium to NAV has displayed tremendous volatility in its range since the fund's inception as a closed-end fund, climbing as high as 33 percent early in 2012 and sinking to as low as 2.36 percent in July 2012. The premium to NAV was nearly 5 percent as I was writing this, reflecting some investors' willingness to pay a significant amount over the price of silver for the advantages offered by this investment vehicle.

Table 13.1 shows a number of silver and other precious metals ETFs listed on the market around the world today.

Table 13.1 Silver and Other Precious Metals Exchange–Traded Funds

Ticker	Company Name	Exchange	Market Cap (Local)	Purpose	Inception Date
Silver					
DBS	PowerShares DB Silver Fund	NYSE Arca	67,826,263	Single Long Silver	1/5/2007
SLV	iShares Silver Trust	NYSE Arca	10,404,050,781	Single Long Silver	4/28/2006
PHAG LN	ETFS Physical Silver	London	851,923,706	Single Long Silver	4/24/2007
PHAG IM	ETFS Physical Silver	BrsaItaliana	658,769,287	Single Long Silver	6/20/2007
PHAG NA	ETFS Physical Silver	EN Amsterdam	666,385,864	Single Long Silver	5/18/2007
SLVR LN	ETFS Silver	London	67,712,135	Single Long Silver	9/27/2006
USV	E-TRACS UBS Bloomberg CMCI Silver ETN	NYSE Arca	7,430,700	Single Long Silver	4/1/2008
SIVR	ETFS Physical Silver Shares	NYSE Arca	606,270,813	Single Long Silver	7/24/2009
HUZ CN	Horizons COMEX Silver ETF	Toronto	20,016,500	Single Long Silver	6/25/2009
1542 JP	Mitsubishi UFJ Japan Physical Silver ETF	Tokyo	4,948,218,262	Single Long Silver	7/2/2010
PSLV	Sprott Physical Silver Trust	NYSE Arca	1,388,743,652	Single Long Silver	10/29/2010
PHS/U CN	Sprott Physical Silver Trust	Toronto	1,384,591,797	Single Long Silver	10/29/2010
Leveraged Silver					
AGQ	ProShares Ultra Silver	NYSE Arca	846,411,011	Double the performance of Silver	12/3/2008
LSIL LN	ETFS Leveraged Silver	London	139,344,589	Double the performance of Silver	3/11/2008

(continued)

Table 13.1 (*Continued*)

Ticker	Company Name	Exchange	Market Cap (Local)	Purpose	Inception Date
ZSL	ProShares UltraShort Silver	NYSE Arca	144,410,355	Twice the inverse performance of Silver	12/3/2008
SSIL LN	ETFS Short Silver	London	25,115,776	Single short on Silver	2/22/2008
HZU CN	Horizons BetaPro COMEX Silver Bull Plus ETF	Toronto	105,375,999	Double the performance of Silver	6/30/2009
Gold					
GLD	SPDR Gold Trust	NYSE Arca	74,728,367,188	Single Long Gold	11/18/2004
2840 HK	SPDR Gold Trust	Hong Kong	56,117,621,094	Single Long Gold	7/31/2008
GG9B GR	Gold Bullion Securities Ltd	Frankfurt	6,148,402,344	Single Long Gold	4/15/2007
GBS LN	Gold Bullion Securities Ltd	London	7,950,273,438	Single Long Gold	3/31/2004
GBS IM	Gold Bullion Securities Ltd	Brsaltaliana	6,153,626,465	Single Long Gold	4/20/2007
GBS FP	Gold Bullion Securities Ltd	EN Paris	6,146,501,953	Single Long Gold	11/7/2005
GOLD AU	ETFS Physical Gold/Australia	ASX	653,868,347	Single Long Gold	9/17/2002
GLD SJ	NewGold Issuer Ltd	Johannesburg	21,011,429,688	Single Long Gold	11/2/2004
DBP	PowerShares DB Precious Metals Fund	NYSE Arca	394,814,392	Single Long Gold	1/5/2007
DGL	PowerShares DB Gold Fund	NYSE Arca	453,646,362	Single Long Gold	1/5/2007
IAU	iShares COMEX Gold Trust	NYSE Arca	11,428,649,414	Single Long Gold	1/28/2005
CEF	Central Fund of Canada Ltd	NYSE Amex	5,767,973,633	Single Long Gold	9/14/1983
CEF/A CN	Central Fund of Canada Ltd	Toronto	5,653,494,629	Single Long Gold	11/15/1961
GTU	Central GoldTrust	NYSE Amex	1,275,277,954	Single Long Gold	8/26/2003
GTU-U	Central GoldTrust	Toronto	1,246,522,461	Single Long Gold	7/7/2003

Ticker	Name	Exchange	Value	Category	Date
PHYS	Sprott Physical Gold Trust	NYSE Arca	2,909,040,771	Single Long Gold	2/26/2010
PHY/U CN	Sprott Physical Gold Trust	Toronto	2,897,326,172	Single Long Gold	2/26/2010
1540 JP	Mitsubishi UFJ Japan Physical Gold ETF	Tokyo	27,057,867,188	Single Long Gold	7/2/2010
3081 HK	Value Gold ETF	Hong Kong	1,183,949,951	Single Long Gold	11/3/2010
SGOL	ETFS Gold Trust	NYSE Arca	1,952,363,892	Single Long Gold	9/9/2009
BULL LN	ETFS Gold	London	233,557,510	Single Long Gold	9/27/2006
HUG CN	Horizons COMEX Gold ETF	Toronto	14,264,251	Single Long Gold	6/25/2009

Other Precious Metals

Ticker	Name	Exchange	Value	Category	Date
PTM	E-TRACS UBS Long Platinum ETN	NYSE Arca	39,060,001	Single Long Platinum	5/9/2008
PGM	iPath Dow Jones-UBS Platinum Subindex Total Return ETN	NYSE Arca	32,521,511	Single Long Platinum	6/24/2008
PHPT LN	ETFS Physical Platinum	London	786,531,128	Single Long Platinum	4/24/2007
PHPT IM	ETFS Physical Platinum	BrsaItaliana	608,758,667	Single Long Platinum	6/20/2007
PHPT NA	ETFS Physical Platinum	EN Amsterdam	608,161,072	Single Long Platinum	5/10/2007
PHPD LN	ETFS Physical Palladium	London	297,694,305	Single Long Palladium	4/24/2007
PHPD IM	ETFS Physical Palladium	BrsaItaliana	229,584,000	Single Long Palladium	6/20/2007
PHPD NA	ETFS Physical Palladium	EN Amsterdam	232,376,389	Single Long Palladium	5/10/2007
PPLT	ETFS Platinum Trust	NYSE Arca	825,132,996	Single Long Platinum	1/8/2010
PALL	ETFS Palladium Trust	NYSE Arca	478,794,983	Single Long Palladium	1/8/2010

Equity Longs (ETFs)

Ticker	Name	Exchange	Value	Category	Date
GDX	Market Vectors—Gold Miners ETF	NYSE Arca	9,587,328,125	Equities—Senior and Intermediate Producers	5/22/2006

(continued)

Table 13.1 (*Continued*)

Ticker	Company Name	Exchange	Market Cap (Local)	Purpose	Inception Date
GDXJ	Market Vectors Junior Gold Miners ETF	NYSE Arca	3,017,549,072	Equities—Junior and Emerging Producers	11/11/2009
PSAU	PowerShares Global Gold and Precious Metals Portfolio	NASDAQ GM	37,667,503	Equities—Global Precious Metals	9/18/2008
PLTM	First Trust ISE Global Platinum Index Fund	NASDAQ GM	8,063,307	Equities—Platinum and Palladium	3/12/2010
SIL	Global X Silver Miners ETF	NYSE Arca	376,384,064	Silver Miners Equities	4/20/2010
GLDX	Global X Gold Explorers ETF	NYSE Arca	38,145,397	Gold Miners Equities	11/4/2010
Leveraged (ETFs)					
DGP	PowerShares DB Gold Double Long ETN	NYSE Arca	525,947,449	Double the performance of Gold	2/28/2008
UGL	ProShares Ultra Gold	NYSE Arca	369,881,287	Double the performance of Gold	12/3/2008
HBU CN	Horizons BetaPro COMEX Gold Bullion Bull Plus ETF	Toronto	54,292,000	Double the performance of Global Gold Equities	1/23/2008
LPLA LN	ETFS Leveraged Platinum	London	8,372,214	Double the performance of Platinum	3/11/2008
DZZ	PowerShares DB Gold Double Short ETN	NYSE Arca	58,505,100	Twice the inverse performance of Gold	2/28/2008

Ticker	Name	Exchange		Description	Date
GLL	ProShares UltraShort Gold	NYSE Arca	97,168,091	Twice the inverse performance of Gold	12/3/2008
HBD CN	Horizons BetaPro COMEX Gold Bullion Bear Plus ETF	Toronto	4,708,000	Twice the inverse performance of Gold	1/23/2008
PTD	E-TRACS UBS Short Platinum ETN	NYSE Arca	3,300,000	Single short on Platinum	5/9/2008
SPLA LN	ETFS Short Platinum	London	1,595,945	Single short on Platinum	3/11/2008
Swiss Offerings	Zürcher Kantonalbank (ZKB) is wholly owned by the canton of Zurich				
ZGLD SW	ZKB Gold ETF	SIX Swiss Ex	5,268,506,836	Single Long Gold	3/15/2006
ZSIL SW	ZKB Silver ETF	SIX Swiss Ex	1,563,210,083	Single Long Silver	5/10/2007
ZGLDUS SW	ZKB Gold ETF–A USD	SIX Swiss Ex	3,060,424,072	Single Long Gold	1/15/2009
ZGLDEU SW	ZKB Gold ETF–A EUR	SIX Swiss Ex	1,215,605,469	Single Long Gold	12/9/2008
ZPLA SW	ZKB Platinum ETF	SIX Swiss Ex	537,983,643	Single Long Platinum	5/10/2007
ZPAL SW	ZKB Palladium ETF	SIX Swiss Ex	208,089,294	Single Long Palladium	5/10/2007
ZSILEU SW	ZKB Silver ETF EUR	SIX Swiss Ex	347,808,167	Single Long Silver	12/9/2008
ZSILUS SW	ZKB Silver ETF USD	SIX Swiss Ex	643,950,500	Single Long Gold	12/9/2008

This chapter points to the pros and cons of various ways of owning silver, via paper markets, physical ownership, or somewhere in between. If you would like to consider investment methods for adding *leverage*—that is, seeking ways to magnify your returns on investment—by way of commodity options and futures, this is not the book for you. There are a number of great books covering options and futures, which are a different animal and require some degree of preparation. Another way of leveraging your precious metals investments is to buy one of the growing number of ETFs that provide leverage to silver or other precious metals investment. For example, AGQ (also shown in Table 13.1) aims to provide double the performance of silver.

But there are some important considerations for these investments. First, to obtain the return magnification, portfolio managers of these funds need to resort to the derivatives and futures market to gain the leverage needed. And since managers are forced to face the reality of contract expiration, things can move in unexpected directions and harm the fund managers' portfolios, a fact that is likely clearly indicated in the prospectuses that virtually no investor reads. Despite the potential risks that come with the use of derivatives, some precious metals investors are buying these investment vehicles to move away from financial markets, to some extent. And yet precious metals magnification investments like these can do the opposite. There is nothing wrong with using derivatives properly, and these instruments offer a dynamic way to leverage precious metals' performance without the time limitations presented by other vehicles, like futures and options.

However, investors in these instruments need to understand that they are not actually buying precious metals, themselves, which sets these vehicles apart from ETFs like SLV that represent ownership positions in actual silver held in a vault. Another important consideration is that the liquidity of these investment vehicles is not particularly high, something that might not be a consideration for some individual investors, but it might be for others. Finally, these new investment vehicles have yet to be tested under several periods of severe market stress.

Owning physical silver provides the comfort of knowing that your investment in the metal is completely outside the financial system, something that may not have been worthy of consideration for most before 2008, when the largest bank in terms of total assets (Royal Bank of

Scotland) and largest insurance company (AIG) in the world both collapsed. This is an important issue for many precious metals investors and some will only hold physical silver and gold. But holding silver in a physical form presents some difficulties.

For one, silver is bulkier than gold: Five ounces of gold, which you could hold in your pocket, is worth the same as 16 *pounds* of silver. And it needs to be stored somewhere secure, like a safety deposit box at a bank. And obviously, bigger safety deposit boxes cost more to rent.[1] Storing it at home in a safe or some other place presents the risk of theft or some a natural disaster affecting the deposit. In early 2012, I remember reading that a London man's home was invaded and virtually all of his wealth, which was invested in silver held in a safe, was stolen from him at gunpoint. Evidently, these are risks to take seriously and stupidity (apparently the man was bragging about his silver throughout the neighborhood) is not recommended. Despite these considerations, many silver investors find the best way to store the metal themselves as a way of keeping the metal (and any other precious metals holdings) isolated from other investments, like stocks and bonds held in a brokerage account. If you are interested in buying physical silver, read the last section of this chapter, "How to Invest in Coins and Bars."

Table 13.2 is a list of the major ways in which you can own silver (and gold) today. I presented this table in my books about gold, but have updated it based on silver, changes in financial conditions, and the addition of new investment vehicles that have become available since then. I scored each of the ways to own silver or gold based on four factors that I discuss; however, this is not scientific. *I would not suggest buying silver or gold (or other precious metals) based on the best score, but rather on what fits a reader's individual needs.* And it is important to point out that I cannot recommend any specific investment vehicle nor vouch for its reliability. Before briefly explaining the way I scored the investment vehicles, I'll describe two you might not be familiar with.

GoldMoney

GoldMoney was launched in early 2001 as an innovation allowing investors to buy and sell physical precious metals online 24/7. Their

Table 13.2 Ways to Own Silver and Gold

				Pros	Cons	Investment Safety	Investment Potential	Liquidity	Government Risk	Score
Paper Gold	In between	Physical Gold								
1	Mining stocks/ gold funds			• Can rise faster than gold or silver • Very easy to buy and sell • Ability to leverage	• No silver/gold under your physical control • Many of same risks attached to other stocks • Will decline faster than metals in down market	2	5	5	3	15
2	Commodity options and futures			• Very easy to buy and sell • Futures can take physical delivery • Ability to leverage	• Risk of regulatory change affecting use • Delivery of metals not guaranteed (could be in cash if silver/gold unavailable)	4	5	5	1	15
3	ETFs			• Very easy to buy and sell • Represents silver/gold ownership • Highly liquid	• No gold under your physical control • Risk of government interference • Cannot be redeemed for gold	4	3	5	1	13
4		Redeemable ETFs (recently launched)		• Easy to buy and sell • Represents silver/gold ownership • Can be redeemed for silver/gold	• No silver/gold under your physical control • Risk of government interference • No track record of management reputation	4	3	4	1	12
5		GoldMoney.com		• Very easy to buy and sell • Silver/Gold is actually owned • Highly liquid	• No silver/gold under your physical control • Though metals are not lent, requires trust in mgmt. • Risk of government interference	4	3	4	2	13
6			Allocated bullion bank account	• Silver/Gold is actually owned • Individual bars assigned specifically to you • Stored safely	• No silver/gold under your physical control • You are allowing a bank to owe you something • Risk of government interference	4	3	4	2	13

No.	Category	Description	Investment Safety	Investment Potential	Liquidity	Government Risk	Score
7	Unallocated bullion bank account	• Silver/Gold is actually owned • Silver/Gold is pooled • Stored safely	• No silver/gold under your physical control • You are allowing a bank to owe you something • Risk of government interference	4	3	4	2	13
8	Gold bullion coins/bars	• Relatively easy to buy and sell • Transaction costs higher • Metals are owned/in physical possession	• Need to personally store • Risk of theft	5	3	4	5	17
9	"Common date" coins	• Can rise faster than gold or silver • Metals are owned/in physical possession	• Not easy to sell quickly • Down market periods can be deep, lengthy • Need to personally store	5	4	2	5	16
10	Rare coins	• Can rise faster than gold or silver • Historically has outperformed stocks • Gold is owned/in physical possession	• Not easy to sell quickly • Down market periods can be deep, lengthy • Need to personally store	5	4	1	5	15
11	Jewelry	• Gold is owned/in physical possession • Fashionable/aesthetically pleasing	• Likely to redeem only fraction of gold value • Not easy to sell quickly	4	1	1	5	11

Scale: 1–5, 5 is best

These numbers are based on the judgment of the author. I would not suggest buying silver/gold based on the best score, but rather based on what fits a reader's individual needs. For example, if you do not believe "government risk" is a concern, then bullion, commodity futures, and bullion bank accounts would be more attractive than the score above implies.

Investment Safety refers to ultimate safety, meaning which is safest in conditions of extreme financial stress. Hence, this is not an issue in normal conditions. Safety is low for mining stocks because of equity market and operational risks.

It is high for physical silver/gold, being outside of paper financial markets, yet it suffers from low liquidity.

Investment Potential: A score of 3 means the asset will rise or fall in line with the market price of silver/gold; 4 or 5 indicates the probability that the asset would rise more than silver or gold (or fall more in a precious metals bear market). Jewelry was rated 2 because it will typically be bought at or below melt (the price of silver/gold in the market).

Liquidity refers to the ease of buying and selling the asset. Rare and "common date" coins score poorly because they are difficult to sell in a hurry. Jewelry might be easy to sell quickly, but at a very low price.

Government Risk means risk that government could change the rules of the game in silver/gold ownership. A score of 5 means virtually no risk and 1 means high risk if the government decided (once again) to interfere with the private ownership of gold. Mining stocks receive a 4 because, in periods of financial stress, their corporate tax rate could be raised, especially if gold prices are rising rapidly. GoldMoney is based away from the United States to prevent the possibility of government intervention in its management. Rare coins, silver and gold coins with numismatic value, have never been confiscated.

Score is based on a simple addition of the four factors.

digital silver currency (gold, platinum, and palladium are also options) is then stored in specialized bullion vaults of their choice located in Zurich, London, and Hong Kong, thereby providing a degree of geographical diversification.

Customers have access to their metal similar to the way online banking gives you access to your dollars. So you can use the metal as currency by clicking a weight of it to another account, while the metal remains safely stored in the vault. The ownership of the metal changes, not its location. A unique benefit of GoldMoney is that your precious metals are very liquid and can be quickly turned into any national currency that can be wired to your bank account anywhere in the world. Customer assets in GoldMoney have risen tenfold to $2.2 billion since I wrote about them in my first book six years ago. Visualize an online bank that holds your money in the precious metal of your choice but does not lend out your money as a bank would.

Skeptical potential account holders might be concerned that they cannot actually see the gold being held on their behalf, which is a legitimate fear that extends to other forms of paper gold, as well. This is something to consider very seriously. In the early 1980s, International Gold Bullion Exchange, once the largest gold bullion dealers in the United States, shocked thousands of customers when it was discovered that gold bars in the company's vault were actually made of wood. Tens of millions of dollars were lost. To provide its customers with assurances of integrity, GoldMoney states that it has a well-defined governance procedure. This includes using a private storage company (Via Mat International Ltd., a highly regarded Swiss company) so that GoldMoney employees never actually handle any metal.

As with all investment alternatives mentioned in this chapter, you should consider each one carefully, perhaps with the help of a financial advisor before making an investment.

Rare Coins

Given that gold and silver coins once circulated as money in the United States, there are a large number of rare coins that have survived. Some are worth solely the metal they contain, such as low-quality Morgan and

Peace silver dollars from the decades before and after the turn of the twentieth century (1878–1935), and others that are worth millions, like a 1794 silver dollar that sold for $7.8 million in 2010.[2] Although rare coins are scarcer than modern bullion coins and can consequently appreciate faster than gold and silver, buying them at the right price and under the proper conditions can be challenging. I listed them in Table 13.2 because I think they are important, but learning the intricacies of rare coin investment requires time and study, so it is not for everybody. Considering the wide range of spreads that, say, a silver Morgan dollar can have over the spot price of silver, this is a market in which it is easy to be ripped off. *If you are simply interested in investing in precious metals, this is probably an investment arena you should stay away from.*[3]

In addition to listing the major pros and cons of the various ways of owning silver and gold as listed in Table 13.2, I scored each vehicle *based on my personal views* regarding investment safety, investment potential, liquidity, and what I call government risk. The scale is 1 to 5, with 5 being the best score. A higher score is positive, as it reflects combinations of ultimate investment safety, the potential to outperform the price of gold, the ease of buying and selling an asset, and low risk of government interference. I'll briefly define these terms as they apply to precious metals, which is not the same as they would be when used with other investment assets.

Here are the four investment factors to consider before buying silver or gold:

1. *Investment safety* refers to ultimate safety, meaning which vehicle is safest in conditions of extreme financial stress. Hence, this is not a consideration for normal conditions, but rather that of a situation of severe financial dislocation. While this may appear to be an extreme consideration, precious metals are assets that are often owned to deal with extreme situations. Considering this definition, safety is low for mining stocks because of equity market and operational risks, but high for physical bullion coins (which are outside financial markets).
2. *Investment potential* refers to the ability to rise faster than the price of silver, hence the emphasis is on *potential* and not on the higher volatility that such an instrument may present. A score of 4 or 5 gives a higher probability that the asset would rise more than silver or gold

(or fall more in a precious metals bear market), which is why mining stocks score high. Jewelry scores very poorly because it will typically be bought at or below *melt* (the price of gold or silver in the market). This means that jewelry will *always underperform precious metals* unless the transaction is carried out in parts of Asia, where jewelry items are often bought and sold based on weight (no retail mark-up).

3. *Liquidity* is simply the ease of buying and selling the asset, which is an important consideration for silver as several key investment vehicles can have low liquidity. Rare and *common date* coins score poorly because they are difficult to sell in a hurry. Jewelry *might* be easy to sell quickly, but it would fetch a very low price.

4. *Government risk* is the risk that the government could change the rules of the game in precious metals ownership, though this would most likely apply specifically to gold. (See Chapter 14.) A score of 5 means virtually no risk and 1 means high risk if the government decided (once again) to prohibit private ownership of precious metals. Mining stocks receive a 4 because, in periods of financial stress, their corporate tax rate or required royalty payments could be raised, especially if gold prices are rising rapidly. GoldMoney.com is based away from the United States to prevent the possibility of government intervention in its management (although this does not make it completely risk-free, since governments can monitor transfers). Rare coins, gold and silver coins with numismatic value, have never been confiscated, which is why they receive a high score on this metric.

The score I gave each of these silver and gold ownership vehicles is based entirely on my judgment. I would not suggest buying gold based on the best score, but rather based *entirely* on what fits your individual needs and what makes sense to you. For example, if you do not believe government risk is a concern, then commodity futures would be more attractive than the score in the table implies.

How to Invest in Coins and Bars (without Getting Ripped Off)

There has probably never been an easier time to buy silver and other precious metals than today, thanks to reliable physical delivery systems and the Internet. Much of the purchasing of physical silver and gold in the United States today is done in cyberspace, where a great many precious metals businesses, small and large, compete. Much like purchasing a book on Amazon.com, *once you have found a trustworthy precious metals dealer,* you can buy hundreds of thousands, if not millions, of dollars in silver and gold online and have the precious acquisition insured and mailed to you with confidence that the investment will arrive safely. Crazy as it sounds to *mail* gold, consider the win-win coin toss implied in over-insuring: If you mail $10,000 in metals but insure it for $12,000, heads you get your $10,000 in gold, tails you get $12,000 in cash. A great many millions of dollars in gold are mailed across the United States every year, though these precious packages are generally insured and labeled in a way that do not give away the contents.

Any business that involves money attracts sleazy people who will try to rip you off, and the gold business is no exception. There are several shops—some well known in the precious metals dealer community—that take advantage of novices who are perhaps nervously buying gold for the first time, and these firms prey on their clients' vulnerability. Here's an example: During the summer of 2006, the U.S. Mint released an eagerly-awaited new gold coin, the American Buffalo, the first U.S. coin minted in 24-karat gold (the previous ones had been 22-karat). A lot of excitement was generated by the release, and many new buyers, fearing the newly issued coins could get away from them forever, forgot the simple truth that the coin was still just an ounce of gold and that tens of thousands of them would be minted. With these coins being worth less than $750 each, there was a particular shop that was offering them openly, on the Internet, at $2,000 each. But as I wrote about that in the summer of 2007, the coin was available for under $1,000. And today, even after gold has risen significantly, you can find the coin easily over the Internet, day or night, in certified flawless condition still for well under $2,000 . . . or cheaper by the dozen! Buying a precious metal coin is often like buying a car: Even brilliant men and women with PhDs can be turned into gullible children. Remember that there is always a place for you to get ripped off legally, and the gold business is no exception.

Use the Internet to your advantage in two ways. First, choose a gold dealer with whom you can establish a relationship of trust and try to find an individual who has been at a firm for at least a few years. If you don't feel comfortable talking with him or her for any reason, speak to someone else! A solid metals dealer can steer you away from bad deals and direct you toward potentially profitable ones. They want you to profit because your disappointment will make them lose your business. A good place to start looking is to find a dealer with the Professional Coin Grading Service (www.pcgs.com) or the Numismatic Guaranty Corporation (ngccoin.com) listed on their websites. See if the dealer's website reveals the number of years the company has been operating, with less than 10 years possibly being a concern. A firm's website should also reveal whether it belongs to the local Better Business Bureau, which I think is an indispensable requirement. Personally, I prefer to deal with local dealers so that I can meet an individual face to face and see the firm's installations, although this is not possible for everyone.

Second, once you have determined what you are going to buy, get a price from your dealer and check it on the Internet. By Googling the precise product you are buying, like a 2009 American Eagle one-ounce gold coin, you can quickly find out what price you could pay by shopping elsewhere. If you find that you could buy the coin for a few dollars less at another, perhaps less trustworthy shop, it might not be worth the trouble, but if substantially more were involved, then you might ask your dealer if he can match the lower price. He might not be able to beat the price, but then you will need to consider the confidence you have in the other dealer you've found on the web. As with any purchase, be wary of prices that are too low, which might be a sign of trouble. Once you've decided to go ahead with your first acquisition with a new shop, you might want to start with a small purchase, perhaps using the company's website for an electronic transaction, and see how smoothly the process goes.

The physical gold and silver market really is a market: You can haggle! If you don't like a price, say so and you might get a better price. You can save money on your precious metals purchases by talking with a person instead of buying online. Quite often the 24-hour prices you see on websites for Internet orders are not the lowest you will be able to find. To protect themselves against an overnight rise in the price of precious metals dealers often list prices that are slightly higher than they would offer over the phone. Call a gold shop and try to get a better price, which most of the time you will. Like most other businesses, a coin dealer will not want to disappoint you, knowing you have many other places to buy silver or gold, thanks to the Internet. This might expose you to an undesirable conversation with a person who would like to sell you more, but with a "Thanks, I'm not interested in anything else," you could save yourself a lot of money.

Other than choosing the wrong dealer or not verifying that you are getting a fair price, perhaps the biggest mistake you can make is to fall into the urgency trap. Like autos at the car lot, precious metals products often seem to be running out, or their prices about to rise like crazy, and the coin you are interested in might be getting away from you. But, alas, they are still there tomorrow and next week . . . unless the precious metals market is heating up. When gold broke $500 and kept going past $600 in early 2006, dealer inventories were being depleted, prices were rising very rapidly and coins were getting away from buyers. But if, at the time you are buying, the market is relatively stable, be patient. Hang up the phone or step away from your computer and think about it before buying anything.

Chapter 14

Two Investment Considerations: Market Manipulation and Potential Confiscation*

T here are two issues regarding silver and gold investment that some readers might find important to consider. The first is the possibility that precious metals markets are being manipulated to some degree by government agencies and/or financial institutions. The second is that the federal government could someday once again prohibit private ownership of at least gold, which was the case between 1933 and 1974. I wrote about these issues at length in my second book about gold,

---

*This chapter includes updated sections of *Hard Money: Taking Gold to a Higher Investment Level* (Hoboken, NJ: John Wiley & Sons, 2010).

Hard Money, as topics in two separate chapters. But considering that the importance of at least one of them has been raised by results of a formal legal investigation into alleged silver market manipulation, in this book I am giving the issues greater weight by presenting them in a separate chapter, as they are relevant to silver, as well. Although many readers might not see this as vital to consider before investing in silver—if at all—some hard money investors regard these issues with the utmost seriousness and I would like to present my views on them. Each reader should weigh the issues to reach his or her own conclusion as to whether they are important considerations.

In 2008 the Commodity Futures Trading Commission announced that it was investigating "complaints of misconduct in the silver market" following a large number of allegations of illicit activity from numerous precious metals investors. And in 2010 CFTC Commissioner Bart Chilton said he believed there had been "fraudulent efforts" to "deviously control" the silver price. I believe there were grounds to believe in possible manipulation, considering silver market events in 2008, a grizzly bear year for commodities. At the time, the spreads between the cost of physical silver on the market and spot prices quoted on financial markets soared like never before, reflecting a surge in demand for physical silver. Deliveries for physical buyers were often delayed for months. And yet the price of silver plummeted along with other commodities, even though the decline was far smaller than that of all other major commodities, as shown in Figure 14.1.

2008 was a bizarre year for silver as well as just about everything else in the financial world. Institutions that had survived the Great Depression collapsed, along with the largest bank and largest insurance company in the world at the time, Royal Bank of Scotland and AIG. Although precious metals markets were behaving erratically, does this necessarily mean that they were being manipulated in 2008? The *Financial Times* reported in 2012 that the four-year investigation into alleged silver manipulation was likely going to be dropped because regulators had failed to find enough evidence to support a legal case.

In a great many conversations on the subject of market manipulation, I have found two sharply divided groups. Those who are firm believers that the market is rigged tend to work in the physical precious metals world, the metals dealers of the world (wholesale and retail), and some at

Figure 14.1   The Price of Silver during 2008
SOURCE: Bloomberg.

mining companies. The skeptics ("I don't believe in UFOs, either," someone once told me) tend to work in financial markets, be it for brokerage houses (commodities departments or mining research) or other institutions. I must admit that I fall in the skeptic camp.

Are the Prices of Gold and Silver Being Manipulated?

For many years the question of whether the prices of gold and silver are being regulated or actively controlled by government entities has been controversial. A movement in the precious metals investment world led by the Gold Anti-Trust Action Committee (GATA) is trying to expose what it sees as a concerted effort by financial authorities to suppress gold and silver prices. The organization believes precious metals prices would be substantially higher absent this alleged intervention in the market,

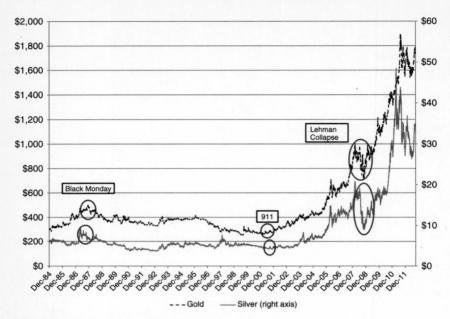

Figure 14.2   Gold and Silver Prices since 1985
SOURCE: Bloomberg.

done mainly via the commodities futures markets—mostly in the case of silver—and central bank gold lending.

Although a number of gold observers have wondered why the precious metal didn't spike during instances of severe financial distress (see Figure 14.2)—like the day in 1987 when stocks plunged more than 20 percent (see Figure 14.3) or during the 9/11 disaster—most conspiracy theories fail in the absence of a convincing motive. And in this case one should ask why the government would have any interest in suppressing the price of gold and/or silver, which have so little influence on the financial system today. Although ancient gold seems to have lost its relevance in our modern financial world run on flashing computer screens, I think there is a significant motive that makes GATA's conspiracy theory something to think about.[1]

The Treasury Department and the Federal Reserve certainly have an interest in seeing that the price of gold, the only major financial asset with no counterparty risk, does not increase substantially. Many would regard silver—which also has no counterparty risk—as being less relevant

Figure 14.3 Gold and Silver Price Movements at Time of 1987 Stock Market Crash

SOURCE: Bloomberg.

considering gold's dominant position as the premier metal in central bank vaults. But, at least in my opinion, the similar nature and elevated correlation of both metals makes silver highly relevant, as well: A spike or sharp fall in either metal most likely would impact the other, as has been occurring for decades. Hence a potential market manipulator could affect the price of gold or silver by moving the price of one or the other.

Think about this scenario: If gold and silver began to rise sharply in a crisis of financial trust and people found reason to begin dumping traditional investment assets—stocks, bonds, even cash—and buying precious metals, this could lead to even deeper trouble than a significant drop in financial markets would imply. (Keep in mind that the gold and silver investment markets are very small relative to others and that a relatively minor rise in investment would cause a surge in prices.) If the broad investing public saw rising gold and silver as compelling investments, in an extreme situation money could eventually be pulled out of anything from the financing of hot dog carts to major infrastructure maintenance and construction—and, most notably, government bonds—leading to a spike in interest rates, and ultimately deflation and another banking system crisis.

There is a precedent for this. In 1933, amidst a wave of bank failures during the worst deflationary crisis in U.S. history, the government was ultimately forced to confiscate gold to prevent individuals and institutions from continuing to dump financial assets in one of the deepest crises of financial trust ever. Remember "We have nothing to fear but fear itself!"? The words were uttered by President Franklin D. Roosevelt precisely at this time: Americans were running to gold. (But not silver at the time, as discussed in Chapter 9.) Our leaders evidently want to prevent something like this from ever happening again, and they—particularly Federal Reserve Chairman Ben Bernanke, a Great Depression expert—know that a rise in gold is something to be watched closely.

Gold offers ultimate financial insurance for individual investors and institutions, but since a gold and silver investment wave can suck resources out of the broader economy—most notably in that this can pull money out of bonds, the lending of money that requires some degree of trust in the issuer (like the U.S. Treasury)—it carries systemic risk that authorities may be forced to consider again in the future. Hence there is, and always has been, a motive for financial authorities to want to prevent a dramatic rise in the number of people wanting to convert their paper money into hard money, a situation that governments have faced many times over hundreds of years: People put their money in what they believe in, and precious metals investment surges reflect a severe distrust of government and the financial system it supervises.

I think there is a reason—one that goes beyond the ubiquitous logic that "gold only makes sense if you think the world is ending," and other such comments—why financial authorities almost never mention gold in public discourse. Why did monetary authorities buy more gold in 2011 than in each of the last forty years? Why do central banks hold hundreds of billions of dollars in gold? "Tradition," Fed Chairman Ben Bernanke answered evasively in July 2011.[2] It would certainly be relevant for, say, the U.S. Treasury secretary to discuss the precious metal considering that the country is the largest owner of gold in the world, by far. Gold is the largest reserve asset on the U.S. government's balance sheet, or so we're told. GATA would argue: The U.S. government has not allowed an independent audit of the nation's gold in decades.

Gold and silver compete with other financial assets based on perceptions of risk and potential return, and investors choose what they regard as the most promising ones. In recent years attention has partially moved away from trying to increase returns on investment to protection of principal, an environment in which gold (and often silver) investment tends to rise. The federal government and Federal Reserve would not like precious metals to be perceived as the most attractive asset class, as this could interfere with their authority over financial markets and the economy, which is exercised via government spending and taxation, as well as control over interest rates and the monetary base. The purchase of physical gold and silver moves investors and savers away from government and the financial system itself. This financial decision interferes with and impedes the government's control over the financial destiny of the individual, who is rejecting government-issued cash in opting for such a wealth transfer.

Although gold and silver investment has been rising in recent years, the increasing flows have been a trickle, relatively speaking, up to now—far more U.S. investment dollars have moved into the bond market since the 2008 financial markets' crisis. And, though I read GATA's reports, I have yet to see *convincing* evidence that the Federal Reserve, the Treasury Department, or major financial institutions have actually participated in the active suppression of gold or silver prices, merely suggestions that this may be occurring.

Consider this thought regarding JPMorgan Chase, which is widely regarded as an active silver market manipulator among a number of precious metals investors: the financial conglomerate has $2.2 trillion in total assets making it, by far, one of the largest financial institutions in the world and one that emerged stronger from the 2008 financial crisis. Now that the U.S. financial system is even more concentrated, to say the bank is "too big to fail" is an understatement, as its collapse would likely make 2008 look like a walk in the park. Would the bank jeopardize its reputation and standing in the United States and global financial system in an effort to make an illicit profit representing—at best—one one-hundreth of 1 percent of total profits? The silver market is tiny, virtually insignificant in comparison with almost any other that J.P. Morgan (JPM) deals in. The recent lawsuit was high profile as its result was published on the front page of the *Financial Times*,[3] which put tiny silver on the bank upper management's radar screen. Continued silver market manipulation—if it ever took place—would require that JPM CEO Jamie Dimon would permit this to occur, which would imply that he (and other bank conspirators) is in contact with Fed and Treasury Department officials who are allowing and encouraging it. To me, the idea is simply implausible.

But getting back to the possibility of direct government price manipulation, perhaps most importantly, the people I know who actually deal with central banks and the buying and selling of gold—not by the ounce, but by the tonne—see no evidence of government efforts to control gold prices, which directly affect those of silver. I believe the potential for government authorities to try to control the gold and silver markets could become a factor to consider at some time in the future for the reasons discussed above. And this is important to keep in mind as it would not be the first time this has happened. Considering the long history of currency crises and gold, one leading global investors to run toward the other, financial authorities certainly could have reason to do so in time. It certainly would not be the first time governments have manipulated gold and silver markets, as discussed in the history section of this book.

Would the U.S. Government Ever Confiscate Gold Again (and Would This Matter for Silver)?

In 1933, President Franklin D. Roosevelt ordered the confiscation of private citizens' gold to prevent a deflationary catastrophe. As people withdrew deposits from banks—and sold dollars, per se—to buy gold, money was being pulled out of productive activities in the economy. There was a need to *create* inflation and encourage people to spend so that economic activity could be reactivated—by force. Confiscation meant that individuals were forced to sell their gold at a depressed price, just before the government increased the dollar value of gold in an effort to raise the price level in the economy. The policy was aimed primarily at helping the depressed farming sector, which was suffering from a collapse in crop prices. Consider that at one point during the Depression in certain parts of the country the price of corn went *negative*: A farmer had to *pay* a silo to take corn off his hands. It was unfortunate that few investors considered silver at the time, which could be freely owned and which tripled in price in just over two years in part due to government intervention to reflate the economy. (This is discussed at length in Chapter 9.)

The aim of confiscation is clear and rational from the point of view of financial authorities, and the risk should not be dismissed outright: If a widespread gold rush were to begin, as it did in the early 1930s, money would be pulled out of productive activities and—most critically—the funding of government deficits via the bond market, which would perhaps lead to deflation. In bad times, governments often *force* people to spend in many ways, and there is a long history of government confiscation of gold that extends back for many centuries, even to the days of the Roman Empire. But there are five reasons why I think the risk of government confiscation of gold today is much lower than it was when FDR and his cabinet were considering the move in the 1930s.

1. **Financial markets today are international, capital flows can be virtually instantaneous, and most gold is held outside the United States.** GLD, the largest gold ETF in the world, holds its gold in London. In 1933, American citizens owned physical gold and typically held it in a safety deposit box at the local bank. Today, gold can be held in an electronic account on the other side of the planet. I could sell shares owned in a gold ETF listed on the Singapore stock exchange at 3 A.M. Austin, Texas time, and the funds could be transferred immediately to an account in Zurich, Switzerland, where I could order that funds be converted into gold bars—or something rarer, like Swiss Helvetia gold coins from the 1920s—all before I had breakfast. Any hint of gold confiscation in the United States could cause financial mayhem, the ultimate result of which would be completely unpredictable and likely bad.

2. **Any change in gold policy could cause a dollar crisis.** In 1933, despite the terrible economic environment, the dollar was very strong and FDR's efforts to make it fall—even when he ordered gold confiscation—were unsuccessful. The dollar remained strong because many other countries were in worse shape and American gold holdings were massive, a vital consideration in times when gold was used to back the value of money. Today, any hint that the U.S.

government was changing its policy on gold would lead foreigners—which today own most of the U.S. Treasury bonds in circulation—to question American motivations and wonder about the government's solvency. If gold was being confiscated, what next? In the 1930s, the United States had a positive net international asset position: We owned more of the world's assets than global investors held in American assets. But since 1985, our net international asset balance has moved to a net liability position largely due to our surging debts. A move to confiscate gold or restrict ownership in some way could lead to a fire sale of American assets, a serious risk that U.S. authorities are well aware of.

3. **Nobody owns much gold (or silver) today, anyway.** Gold confiscation is only a realistic risk in the possible future, when and if more institutions, governments and people own gold. It would not make much sense today. Even though precious metals investment has been growing rapidly, it has been doing so from a very low base. An extremely low percentage of Americans own gold as an investment, a diminutive fraction of our holdings in stocks and bonds, which run in the tens of trillions of dollars. Gold represents less than 1 percent of global financial assets under management and silver less than one-tenth of 1 percent. And the country owns in excess of $1 trillion in U.S. securities.

4. **A confiscation of gold, which might negatively affect global prices, could provoke a confrontation with China.** Even though Chinese authorities may not discuss it openly, gold has become a strategic asset for the nation. China is the world's dominant producer of gold and in recent years its leaders have given clear evidence that they are beginning to replace part of the nation's dollar-dominated reserves with gold. A confiscation move would rattle global gold markets, and China might react strongly if the United States carried out such a move. And the country owns in excess of $1 trillion in U.S. securities.

5. **Confiscation today would have to be a globally coordinated policy decision, a daunting objective.** Since markets are globally liquid and trillions of dollars move around the globe every single day, gold confiscation (in whatever form such a policy were implemented) would have to be carried out by all major economies.

Otherwise, an American announcement of capital controls—which is what gold confiscation would imply, by extension—would lead to money flowing out of the jurisdiction where the change in financial regulation had been announced. The United States has long been the financial market to which money has fled to in times of financial adversity, such as occurred in 2008 when the dollar soared. A unilateral announcement by the United States of capital controls might have the opposite effect on the dollar.

President Roosevelt ordered the confiscation of gold in 1933 because he wanted people to stop investing in an asset that was deflationary, one that pulled money out of productive activity and was leading the nation into a downward economic spiral. He was adamantly opposed to the (then) radical step of printing additional dollars, and forcing citizens out of gold seemed to be the next best option.[4] But in the 1930s, private capital mobility was extremely low and was conducted at a glacial speed by present standards, so there was not much worry about money being moved out of the country. Capital moved physically and there was a growing hesitance to invest abroad as economic turmoil took on an international dimension. The rest of the world was in a depression, as well, and new trade restrictions were also having an effect on capital mobility. Europe, still recovering from the devastation of World War I and a prostrate Germany, was not a place where dollars were likely to flow. Gold confiscation did not lead to any notable capital flight from the United States.

However, today there is a much deeper concern about the economic situation of the United States relative to the rest of the world and, considering both the size of American liabilities relative to GDP, as well as the need for foreign capital to finance our deficit spending, gold confiscation today could have dire consequences. Europe is experiencing serious financial difficulties at present, but there are a great many jurisdictions that have a history of respect for financial privacy and gold ownership, like Canada and Switzerland, to which money could be moved extremely rapidly. If limits were imposed on gold transactions and ownership, the stunned reaction in the investment community could lead to unpredictable movements in the foreign exchange markets. Consider that trillions of dollars are transferred every day in currency markets: The equivalent of U.S. GDP changes hands every week.

A change in gold rules could lead to speculation regarding further moves that would affect ownership of other U.S. assets, like U.S. Treasury bonds, the vehicles needed for funding government. Considering the probable tumultuous reaction that such a decision might provoke—as well as the simple fact that gold is an asset that very few individuals and institutions own today—I believe it is unlikely that U.S. authorities would attempt to confiscate gold. The financial world is far too complex for a 1930s strategy to work again.

What about silver? Silver's situation during the 1930s was completely different from that of gold, as discussed in Chapters 8 and 9. Silver had been demonetized in the late 1800s as the largest economies of the time followed England's lead to adopt a gold standard, leaving behind the centuries-old gold-silver bimetallic standard in place for many countries, including the United States. Global central banks and governments amassed gold to back their nations' monetary bases while tons of silver were sold, pushing down the metal's price. During the deflationary crisis of the Great Depression, silver prices had been falling sharply and reached a record low of 25 cents per ounce. China was the only major country that remained on a gold standard, and few Americans were buying silver as a financial refuge. Notwithstanding the interests of several well-connected political groups tied to silver at the time, the metal simply lacked any financial significance in the United States of the 1930s. Consequently, there was no need to even consider confiscating silver or limiting its trade in any way. That is something that would eventually occur, but many years later, in the 1960s (as discussed in Chapter 10).

Silver's situation today is completely different. The massive surpluses flooding the market in the 1930s went into federal vaults as the FDR administration launched a silver purchase program in 1934. The program, which remained in place into the early 1960s before President John F. Kennedy finally ordered its end, led to a federal stockpile that reached an astonishing 3.2 billion ounces in 1962. But coinage needs (dimes, quarters, and nickels still used silver at the time) as well as new uses of silver in industrial production led the government to begin rapidly selling down federal silver stocks to prevent the price from soaring. Yet the price of silver surged anyway, and it was not long before all government silver had been used, and in time, the market went into balance with no large stockpiles anywhere.

Notwithstanding the market surpluses of the 1980s as well as the rise of digital photography in the 1990s, which depressed silver prices substantially, the situation today is far more balanced as the mining supplies not absorbed by industry are being purchased by investors. But the market remains tiny in contrast with the 1930s: A mere $10 billion in physical silver was purchased in the global investment market during 2011, about what trades in Apple shares in a single day.

In the present financial environment, where deep concerns about surging federal debt and financial market instability remain important concerns, gold is becoming an important asset class once again. It would not be surprising to see governments begin to take steps to control the gold trade in the years ahead. But considering the relative insignificance of the silver market, at least at this time, I find it unlikely that its ownership would be prohibited any time soon.

Chapter 15

The Most Widely Respected Silver Investment Coins*

T his chapter presents the basic high-quality silver bullion coins that are generally accepted by coin dealers around the world without question. It also offers information on a few coins—like Morgan and Peace silver dollars—that are popular and easy to buy and sell primarily in the United States, but which might not be as liquid in other countries. There are a great many physical options for investing in precious metals that one finds at the coin shop or when shopping online.

---

*Some parts of this chapter are from my book *Hard Money: Taking Gold to a Higher Investment Level,* which was published in 2010, with permission from John Wiley & Sons. I would like to thank the staff of Austin Rare Coins & Bullion for their help in gathering information used in this chapter.

Some of them, like silver and gold *rounds*—which are not government-minted, as coins are—are best avoided if your objective is no-nonsense physical precious metals investment. I think this is best explained by a paragraph I wrote in my first book about precious metals investing. It was in reference mostly to gold coins (and I updated the prices), but the same applies to silver and all other precious metals coin investing:

> If a gold salesperson or website tells you of some uniquely valuable gold coin or medal, such as a coin commemorating the sixtieth anniversary of the end of World War II or Mickey Mouse's birthday, which is priced more than 10 percent above its gold content, I hope you truly love it. Because if you don't and decide to sell it in a few years you are likely to hear a dreaded word from a potential buyer at a coin shop: *melt*. Coins, medals, or bars that are not uniquely desirable in the marketplace—the large physical marketplace where hundreds of different coins and items made of gold are exchanged—will be bought at melt, meaning based solely on their gold content. If gold were trading at $1,700 an ounce and you bought a one-ounce coin for $1,955 (at a 15 percent premium for the once-in-a-lifetime opportunity) and decided to turn around and sell it, you would probably get $1,700 for it—less a charge for taking the coin to the gold scrap shop, where all the other unforgettable events are forgotten. I think this approach makes sense if you are buying gold as an investment: Unless you are Bill Gates, buy gold thinking you (or a relative or an heir) will probably want to sell it someday. You should try to buy gold in a form that will be relatively easy to sell (like a bullion gold American Eagle) because it is very well known and popular.[1]

The bullion coins—that is, coins that are not yet rare and hence lack numismatic value—presented in this chapter are a great way to invest in silver. By owning coins, you are segregating part of your wealth and keeping it outside the financial system. A 2012 or 1992 American Silver Eagle minted by the U.S. government will be widely accepted for decades, if not always due to its silver content and high quality. Millions of Eagles have been minted, millions are owned, and at least hundreds of thousands trade hands each year, making it the most liquid silver bullion coin in the world. And there are multiple advantages to investing in high-quality coins rather than bars, several of which many new investors in hard money might not know about:

- *High-quality gold or silver coins are widely accepted among precious metals coin dealers around the world.* While a bar can be looked at with suspicion—and large ones are hard to sell—high-quality coins are easy for dealers to work with and are often preferred.
- *Coins are the most liquid form of physical hard money.* Since they are minted in small denominations (generally an ounce per coin), values are relatively low, which allows a larger number of potential investors to be interested in the market. One hundred–ounce silver bars might be easier to store and handle for large holdings, but they will not be as easy to sell.
- *Coins command a (growing) premium over the price of silver.* While one always pays a premium over the spot price of gold or silver to acquire any coin, the premium can also rise for the seller, as has been happening in recent years as coin scarcity has grown. (One could have paid a premium over spot of 7 percent for an American Eagle in 2009 and sold the same coin at a premium of 10 percent—or a lot more—over spot in 2012.)
- *High-quality bullion coins are acquiring scarcity value.* There have been a number of times in recent years when the U.S. Mint has not had any coins for sale on its website, which implies that high-quality coins can be scarce at times. The mint has simply run out of coins several times and new issues have been selling rapidly in recent years. (Silver coins are unavailable on the U.S. Mint website as I write this, on October 10, 2012.)
- *High-quality bullion coins gain numismatic value over time.* Obvious as it sounds, the coins minted in 2012 will never be minted again. There can be no IPOs of 2012 coins, and hence their scarcity will grow. Hence, bullion silver American Eagles from certain years in the 1980s and 1990s are worth triple the value of their silver content. Think about that for a minute. If you bought a bullion silver coin when silver was trading at under $5 in 1998, you not only more than quintupled your money because of the rising price of silver—you also made money on the growing scarcity value of the 1998 coin. This is why it is important to protect the coin from scratches.

Although there are a great many gold and silver coins, you will notice that most of the bullion coins that circulate widely in the world have only been around since the 1980s, the exceptions being the gold South African Krugerrand and the Canadian Maple Leaf. There was a lengthy period during which silver and gold coins were not being minted, at least in any significant quantity, between 1933 and the mid-1960s. During this time, owning gold bullion was prohibited by law in the United States, a fact that influenced other world mints and this indirectly affected demand for silver coins (which the U.S. Mint was not minting, either). But in 1974, the U.S. government ended the ban on private ownership, which eventually gave way to mintage of most of the coins described in this chapter.

In terms of pricing, silver coins differ from gold ones in that dealers will quote gold in terms of percent over spot. For example, a gold American Eagle coin could be sold for 2 percent over the spot price of $1,750 per ounce, for $1,785. But silver coins are generally quoted in terms of dollars over spot, so with spot silver selling at $32 per ounce a buyer might be given a quote of $2 over spot resulting for a coin sold at $34. This is for simplicity and is done out of custom, but it also hides the fact that the spreads on silver coins are much higher than those on gold in the market: $2 is 6.25 percent of $32. Although it may be disappointing to investors wanting the best price, the spread over spot prices when buying is also seen when selling: due to market conditions, dealers generally pay a higher percentage premium over spot for silver coins than for gold coins.

American Silver Eagle

Silver American Eagles are struck in 0.999 fine silver and have been produced every year by the U.S. Mint since 1986. The obverse was modeled after the Walking Liberty Half Dollars minted from 1916 to 1947. These are sold only in 1-ounce sizes and have a face value of $1. Silver American Eagles come from the mint in tubes of 20 or in sealed green cases of 500 called "monster boxes."* They are the most popular

---

*If you opt for a red-colored monster box, you will need to write a high six-figure check, as these boxes contain 500 gold coins.

silver bullion coin for investors in the United States. Mintages have increased dramatically in recent years due to overwhelming investor demand. Premiums typically run $2 to $4 over spot depending upon quantity acquired. They are very popular with collectors and investors due to low premium and privacy when bought and sold (see Figure 15.1). Price (Oct. 23, 2012): $34.50

Figure 15.1   Silver American Eagle
SOURCE: Austin Rare Coins & Bullion.

Canadian Silver Maple Leaf

Canadian Silver Maple Leafs are struck in 0.9999 fine silver (the finest silver coin for normal production) and have been struck each year since 1988. They are sold only in 1-ounce sizes and have a face value of $5 Canadian. Today they come from the mint in tubes of 25 or sealed cases of 500 coins. They used to be packaged in mylar sheets of 10 per sheet, but they switched to rolls, due to demand. Like most silver bullion products, mintages have increased in recent years. Premiums typically run $2.75 to $4.75 over spot depending upon quantity. As shown in Figures 15.2, the obverse depicts Queen Elizabeth II, reverse has a Maple Leaf, but sometimes special issues are created with different reverses or privy marks. They are very popular with collectors and investors due to low premium and privacy when bought and sold.

Price (Oct. 23, 2012): $34.10

Figure 15.2   Silver Canadian Maple Leaf
SOURCE: Austin Rare Coins & Bullion.

Canadian Silver Cougar

This is just one of six coins from the popular wildlife series from the Royal Canadian Mint (RCM). There was a strict mintage limit of 1 million coins. They are produced in 0.9999 fine silver and come in rolls of 25 or sealed cases of 500. The Silver cougar coins cost between 0.50 to $1 more than normal Canadian maple leafs (see Figure 15.3).

Price (Oct. 23, 2012): $34.85

Figure 15.3   Silver Canadian Cougar
SOURCE: Austin Rare Coins & Bullion.

Australian Kookaburra

Produced by the Perth Mint in Australia every year since 1990, the reverse of the coin changes each year to show different pictures of the

Kookaburra. Each coin comes in an individual capsule. Australian Silver is considered by many as the finest produced silver bullion product in the world today. The coin is struck in various sizes: 1 ounce, 2 ounce, 10 ounce, and the impressive Kilo (32.15 ounces). Demand for this product has increased in recent years and these can be acquired for similar premiums as the Silver Eagle. Also, the larger the coin, the lower the premium. The obverse is Queen Elizabeth II (see Figure 15.4).

Price (Oct. 23, 2012): $34.50

Figure 15.4   Silver Australian Kookaburra
SOURCE: Austin Rare Coins & Bullion.

Silver Austrian Philharmonic

The front of this coin showcases the same musical instruments design as seen on the Vienna Philharmonic gold coin. The back depicts the great organ of the Vienna Musikverein Golden Hall in Austria. Produced each year since 2008, they come in rolls of 20 or in sealed mint boxes of 500 coins. They are very popular with collectors and investors due to their low premium and privacy when bought and sold. They are different from many silver bullion coins because they have slick, mirrored sides, whereas most coins have reeded edges. The design has not changed since 2008 (see Figure 15.5).

Price (Oct. 23, 2012): $34.40

Figure 15.5   Silver Austrian Philharmonic
Source: Austin Rare Coins & Bullion.

Australian 2012 Year of the Dragon
(1 kilo/32.15 troy ounces)

From the very popular Perth, Australia mint's Lunar Series, showcasing different animals from the Chinese Lunar Calendar–coin shown is a kilo size, $30 face value coin and struck in 0.999 fine silver. The popularity of this product has taken off in recent years due to the impressive designs and quality of production. The obverse features Queen Elizabeth II (see Figure 15.6). The Lunar Dragon design for 2012 has been by far the most popular in many years, although there are numerous other designs. Lunar silver comes in a variety of sizes: ½-ounce, 1-ounce, 2-ounce, 5-ounce, 10-ounce, half kilo, and kilo. Mintages are typically lower on Lunar Silver than most bullion issues. Each coin comes in an individual capsule. Mint packaging varies depending upon size of product. These can be acquired for similar premiums as the Silver Eagle. The larger the coin, the lower the premium.

Price (Oct. 23, 2012): $1,095

Figure 15.6   2012 Silver Australian Year of the Dragon
SOURCE: Austin Rare Coins & Bullion.

Chinese Silver Panda

The Chinese Silver Panda is highly popular and comes from the Shanghai China mint. Each coin contains 0.999 fine silver and comes in a hard plastic capsule sealed in a soft plastic sheet, which protects the capsule from scratching. Coins are sealed in sheets of 30, and cases contain 600 coins. The face value is 10 Yuan. The obverse design changes each year to show a different depiction of pandas in their natural habitats. The reverse shows the Temple of Heaven (see Figure 15.7). This is one of the most expensive silver bullion coins in terms of premiums over spot—routinely this coin will cost at least $10 over spot.

Price (Oct. 23, 2012): $43.25

Figure 15.7   Silver Chinese Panda
SOURCE: Austin Rare Coins & Bullion.

Johnson Matthey Bar

The Silver Bar, the Johnson Matthey Bar, is struck in various sizes ranging from 1 ounce to 100 ounces and produced in 0.999 fine silver (see Figure 15.8). The larger the bar, the lower the premium per ounce. One hundred ounce bars can typically be acquired for $1.50–$2.50 over spot. It should be noted that bars can be acquired privately; however, when sold in increments of 1,000 ounces or more in a 12- month period, they are required to be reported by the dealer buying from the investor. For this reason, these bars are not as popular as many of the items listed in this section.

Price (Oct. 23, 2012): $351 (10-ounce bar)

Figure 15.8   Silver Johnson Matthey Bar
SOURCE: Austin Rare Coins & Bullion.

Morgan Silver Dollar (Antique Coin, Minted 1878–1921)

Morgan dollars were minted in high quantities over a number of decades, which make them common to this day. For example, in 1889, 22 million Morgan silver coins were minted. They contain less silver (only 90 percent, the rest being copper) than modern pure silver bullion coins, which often makes them trade at a discount to the price of an ounce of silver. However, these coins are extremely popular and are generally the most abundant numismatic silver coins at coin shows. (See Chapter 16.) Though Morgan dollars in poor quantity are never far in price from spot silver, high-quality coins in high grades can be worth thousands of dollars. For example, certain Morgan dollars minted in 1886 were valued at $185,000 each in 2011 (see Figure 15.9).

Price (Oct. 23, 2012): $32 (for lowest quality Morgan, though collectibles are higher and vary in price substantially)

Figure 15.9   Morgan Silver Dollar
SOURCE: Austin Rare Coins & Bullion.

Peace Silver Dollar (Antique Coin, Minted 1921–1935)

Peace silver dollars were minted to commemorate the end of the Great War. Produced by the U.S. Mint from 1921–1935, Peace dollars replaced Morgan dollars and also contain 0.77345 ounces of pure silver. As with

Morgans, Peace dollars can be acquired in various states of preservation ranging from heavily worn to perfect (see Figure 15.10). The higher the state of preservation, the more expensive the coin. They are normally repackaged by dealers in tubes of 20.

Price (Oct. 23, 2012): $32 (similar to Morgans, this is for lowest quality Peace dollars, though collectibles are higher and vary in price substantially)

Figure 15.10   Peace Silver Dollar
SOURCE: Austin Rare Coins & Bullion.

Another Investment Option: Circulated U.S. Silver Coins

Dimes, quarters, half dollars, and silver dollars minted in 1964 and prior years are 90 percent silver. Today, these coins are bought and sold as "junk silver," due to the low quality of the coins, which circulated for years. These coins oftentimes trade very close to the melt value of their silver content. Normally, these coins can be purchased between one to two dollars per ounce over the melt value. Larger quantities can be acquired for lower premiums. The standard for "junk bags" is $1,000 face value, or roughly 712 to 715 ounces of pure silver. This material is oftentimes viewed as "barter silver" because the coins are fractional in size and would come in handy in a barter scenario. For example, each silver dollar has 0.77344 ounces of silver, half dollars contain 0.36169 ounces, each quarter contains 0.18084 ounces, and each dime has 0.07234 ounces.

Gold American Eagle

The Gold American Eagle, the most popular bullion coin in the United States, is minted in 22-karat gold and has been struck each year since 1986 (see Figure 15.11). The coin's obverse is similar to the $20 St. Gaudens gold coin commissioned by President Theodore Roosevelt, which was struck between 1907 and 1933, when gold was confiscated by the U.S. government. (Note of historical interest: surviving 1933 St. Gaudens coins, of which only a handful exist, are worth tens of millions of dollars each.)

Price (Oct. 23, 2012): $1,800

Figure 15.11   Gold American Eagle
SOURCE: Austin Rare Coins & Bullion.

Gold American Buffalo

The Gold American Buffalo is the first and only 24-karat gold coin ever minted in the United States. The first issue was struck in 2006, and has remained in production ever since. However, its supply at the U.S. Mint has been interrupted repeatedly due to continuing unexpectedly high demand for coins. The coin's beautiful design was modeled after Buffalo nickels that were produced during the early 1900s (see Figure 15.12).

Price (Oct. 23, 2012): $1,850

Figure 15.12   Gold American Buffalo
SOURCE: Austin Rare Coins & Bullion.

Platinum American Eagle

The Platinum American Eagle is the official platinum bullion coin issued by the United States and is the most popular platinum coin in the world (see Figure 15.13). The coin's obverse depicts the head of the Statue of Liberty and has been minted since 1997.

Price (Oct. 23, 2012): $1,547

Figure 15.13   Platinum American Eagle
SOURCE: Austin Rare Coins & Bullion.

Chapter 16

Your Local Coin Show, the Past Decade's Best-Performing Stock Market

U nlike the world's frantic stock exchanges, there's a lot of slow walking at this financial market, which likely looked almost exactly the same 50 years ago. Many of the same securities—literally the same ones—are still changing hands, though at substantially higher prices. The market is makeshift, set up in a large room, often a small town convention center hall or perhaps a high school gym, as not much space is required for the small number of people that will arrive. The cost of entering the trading floor is generally $2, though I've seen $2.50. Fortunately, the ticket is usually also a raffle ticket for a prize, generally of the hard money variety. The average age among the dealers on the floor before customers walk through the door is probably 55, and septuagenarians and their seniors are quite common. By noon, with customers including children on the floor, the average age has dropped to around 50.

The exchange is as low tech as can be: nobody is seen using laptop computers or iPads to look up prices and many transaction records are kept on ledgers. Though products are labeled, prices are generally negotiable and freebies often thrown in a bag after a good deal. When dealers are uncertain, references are made to thick books like the *Standard Catalog of World Coins* and specialty periodicals, like the *2012 Red Book* or *The Coin Dealer Newsletter*, a weekly that provides the freshest price information for innumerable collectible coins. The format for the publication—an indispensible font of price information with issues seen all around the room—is plain black type on recycled dark grey paper, and its cover has barely changed since its first edition 50 years ago. Collectible currency is also bought and sold, some of which are U.S. Federal notes that a century or two ago one could exchange at a federal agency for physical precious metals, a reminder that the United States was conceived on a foundation of gold and silver.

I'm describing the Cowtown Coin Show that I visited recently in northern Texas, one of the handful that take place every weekend in towns and cities across the United States. Despite the tremendous wealth the gold and silver coin market has generated for the small number of market participants—a market performance that has eclipsed the world's stock, bond and real estate markets for over a decade—it is rather unsophisticated. Unlike the commodities conference I spoke at in 2011[1] at the New York Stock Exchange, where most of the men and women were each wearing sharp business attire valued in the high hundreds, wardrobe frugality prevailed at the coin show I attended on September 16, 2012. Held at a recreation center in Fort Worth, Texas, sandals and shorts were de rigeur. The fine cocktails I shared with financial professionals last year as I chatted after hours amidst hundreds of blinking computer screens on the floor of the New York Stock Exchange offered little competition to the ice cold Big Red soda I sipped after pacing the Cowtown floor. As for food, I had to go elsewhere: "Bad news, folks: because of the rain the hot dog guy won't be able to set up his stand. Sorry!"

There can be no insider trading on this market—all products are in plain sight and can be examined manually, unlike the values blinking on a screen identifying stocks, bonds, and other securities that will never be physically touched. And while Wall Street is ever watchful of the next government regulation or interest rate decision from the Fed, the country's leaders have been extremely friendly to the coin market: a great number of policies the government and the Federal Reserve have implemented over the last decade seem to have benefitted the coin market in one way or another. The rise of government mistrust has done wonders for hard money markets. A dealer told me jokingly, "I don't care what anybody says. God bless the Fed!"

Although I have attended much larger events, such as the Houston Coin Show and the American Numismatic Association Coin Show held in a different city each year, most have attendance of less than 500 people a day. At the Cowtown show I counted around 40 dealers and assistants (many if not most of whom were family members), and their stations consisted of portable tables with six-by-three-foot surfaces. The tables support the dozens of three-by-two-foot cases where dealers display their most valuable coins. Some dealers had a single table and some had as many as eight, depending on the quantity of coins being displayed. The cases (like the one shown in Figure 16.1) are two to three inches deep and covered with glass to protect high dollar value coins, a combination mostly of modern and numismatic gold and silver collectibles.

The less costly products are left outside cases on the table for potential customers to buy and for children to look at and handle. (See Figure 16.2.) I have often seen "Treasure Chests" or "Fun Buckets" from which children can pick coins (mostly made of copper or cupronickel, the material dimes, quarters, and nickels are presently made of) for 50 cents each—and often free. These, the coins of countless countries whose currencies have collapsed in value over time, are just for fun, a poor illustration of the financial catastrophes endured by the great many nations that have mismanaged their economies over time. Most of the coins are from Eastern European, Latin American, and African countries. I recently saw a number of coins from Mexico, a country I have lived in. One Mexican coin from the seventies I found in a bucket reminded me how much an ounce of gold, the material found in the coins securely kept in the cases, has risen in peso terms due to fiscal

Figure 16.1   Open Coin Case Displayed at a Coin Show
SOURCE: Photo by author.

mismanagement and consequent inflation since the 1970s: around 5 million percent.

New buyers at coin shows are generally looking for basic investment precious metals in the form of coins or small bars, though some buy jewelry, which at coin shows is generally sold near metallic value (without the retail mark-up). But this is a market, so all prices are negotiable and haggling is common. Better prices requested are often provided.

I see more and more people taking their children to coin shows, and newcomers are surprised at how much kids enjoy the events. The magic age for my kids was probably when they were between six and eight. Not only is the experience tactile: Children get to touch and compare a

Figure 16.2   Silver Coins Outside Cases at a Coin Show
SOURCE: Photo by author.

great number of colorful items and take home a few prizes—and there are
plenty for all price levels; it is also a basic lesson in comparative value for
many, the easiest one being that gold is more valuable than silver per
ounce. Beyond that, they can compare the currencies and coins of many
countries and learn about their different values. They also find that subtle
differences between almost identical coins can mark the difference of tens
of thousands of dollars, much as two seemingly identical cars are separated
dramatically in value by a 100,000-mile odometer difference. A worn
silver coin minted in 1898 could be worth $35; a similar coin in superb
condition is worth in excess of $50,000.

Most of the products bought and sold in volume are bullion, which is
to say non-numismatic silver and gold coins as well as a very small amount
of newly minted—and increasingly popular, I'm told—platinum and
palladium coins. The least expensive silver and gold products are those
closest to their "melt" value, which in the case of gold and silver is the
spot price listed on the international market, which was $1,770 for
gold and $34.66 while I was at the Cowtown event. Some examples of
close-to-melt-value products would be *rounds*, which look like coins but
were minted by a private company (often a refiner) independent of

the government and for this reason trade at a discount to more respectable American Eagles, silver and gold coins issued by the U.S. Mint. These generally are the most desirable bullion coins judging by the premium they command over most other coins. Gold Eagles can trade at 5 percent over the spot price of gold and I have seen silver Eagles trading at 10 percent over spot silver.

Thanks to the trust investors have in American Eagles, the U.S. Mint must be making a mint. I say this because of the large number of "monster boxes" that it has been selling to coin dealers, an event that transformed the scale of the physical precious metals business in the United States. A monster box contains five hundred freshly minted coins and the color of the box marks the difference between a used Honda and a limited edition Ferrari Enzo: Green boxes contain silver, making a box worth $18,500, as I write in October 2012. Red boxes are serious business: 500 gold bullion American Eagle coins are yours for $925,000. Any distrust of government felt by coin dealers does not extend to the U.S. Mint: Monster boxes are often bought and sold without either side in a transaction breaking the U.S. Mint seals to inspect their contents. (See Figure 16.3.) But I suspect that would only apply to green boxes!

Among silver options, aside from American Eagles the most popular modern bullion coins (minted, say, in the last 10 years) are Canadian

Figure 16.3 U.S. Mint-issued "Monster Box" Containing 500 One-Ounce Silver Coins

SOURCE: Austin Rare Coins & Bullion.

Maple Leafs, Australian Kookaburras, and Austrian Philharmonics. (See Chapter 15 for descriptions of investment coins.) Many antique U.S. silver coins, ironically, can be found at cheaper prices than modern coins. There are two reasons for this: First, although Morgan and Peace silver dollars (minted between 1878 and 1928) are roughly the same size as a modern one-ounce silver coin, they only contain 90 percent silver (the remaining metal is copper), so their metallic content is slightly less valuable. (The silver in each coin is roughly 0.77 ounces.) The second reason is that the least expensive "common date" (as they are called) silver coins are not rare— millions were minted and thousands survive—and thus less desirable as collectible items. This is why these "junk" Morgan and Peace dollars are generally found on open table outside cases, as seen in Figure 16.2.

However, there are also Morgan and Peace silver dollars in the cases that are generally in better condition. Here is where the numismatic silver coins are kept and they can range in price from the value of their silver content, say 35 dollars, to hundreds of thousands of dollars per coin based on their condition and rarity. They also vary in value based on the mint mark shown on each coin, which determines where the coin was made. For example, one of the pennies in your pocket might have a "D" under the year in which it was minted, which would tell you it was made at the Denver, Colorado mint. Table 16.1 shows all the American mints and mint marks.

Table 16.1   American Mints and Mint Marks

Mint marks are letters found on coins that show where they were minted. You will find them on many of the coins in your pockets on the "heads" side.

C	Charlotte, North Carolina (gold coins only; 1838–1861)
CC	Carson City, Nevada (1870–1893)
D	Dahlonega, Georgia (gold coins only; 1838–1861)
D	Denver, Colorado (1906 to date)
O	New Orleans, Louisiana (1838–1861; 1879–1909)
P	Philadelphia, Pennsylvania (1793 to date; P absent in early years)
S	San Francisco, California (1854 to date)
W	West Point, New York (1984 to date)

As you might expect, some of the most valuable rare coins were minted in Carson City, Charlotte, and Dahlonega, where coin production ended more than a century ago.
SOURCE: R.S. Yeoman, *A Guide Book to United States Coins 2007* (Atlanta: Whitman Publishing, 2006).

Figure 16.4   Peace Silver Dollars for Sale at the Cowtown Coin Show
SOURCE: Photo by author.

I mention the Morgan and Peace dollars as they are among the
most liquid (easy to buy and sell) investment coins on the market simply
because so many of them were minted and remain in circulation. The
lower quality ones sold in bulk are shown in one of the coin stacks of
Figure 16.2. Figure 16.4 shows a closer look at how the lowest quality
Peace silver dollars were displayed at the Cowtown coin show.

Notice how they were priced at $30, a deep 13 percent discount to
the market price of a silver ounce at the time. Once again, this reflects the
lower silver content, but it is also a way for the dealer to attract interest to
his or her table. But I have often found that dealers at times haven't
noticed that silver may have climbed in value more quickly than they
knew. Figure 16.5 is a picture of lower quality Morgan silver dollars.
Notice that they are closer to the market price of silver (only an 8 percent
discount at the time). These generally trade at a premium to Peace dollars,
which were minted years after Morgan dollars and are therefore less rare
and, in many eyes, less attractive.

There are a number of other silver coins, such as the nickels, dimes,
and quarters from the years before 1964, when the government was

Figure 16.5   Morgan Silver Dollars for Sale at the Cowtown Coin Show
SOURCE: Photo by author.

forced to remove silver from American coins due to the metal's fast-rising price. (You can read about this in Chapter 10.) Although an uncountable number of these coins were ultimately hoarded and melted down in clandestine smelters in the 1960s and 1970s, a great number of them survive in collections. The ones in poor condition are bought and sold in bulk at coin shows such as Cowtown. (See Figure 16.6.)

Higher quality coins, which are obviously rarer, are often set in small cardboard frames and filed in boxes for people to search mostly for inclusion in collections. These collections can also include more modern coins that might not have silver in them. For example, there might be

Figure 16.6   Dimes Minted Before 1964 Sold in Bulk
SOURCE: Photo by author.

someone looking to complete a collection of the highest quality Mercury dimes from each year since they began to be minted in 1916. That person could look through a Mercury dime collection for sale at a coin show. (See Figure 16.7.)

While there are innumerable types of coins for sale, including ones used in ancient Rome and Greece more than a thousand years ago, the coin show business is really driven by investors in precious metals. On the surface, surveying the floor and watching the activity, one would find that a typical transaction would be the purchase of 5 to 10 silver bullion coins, a one-ounce gold coin, or some other item set that would add up to less than $2,000. But more often, dealers tell me, doctors and architects are making the occasional $50,000 purchase in gold and silver. There are transactions between dealers that could be in the tens of thousands, but there are also buyers sent by larger national coin dealers—some that might advertise on television or radio—who may be searching for special rare coins valued at between $20,000 and $50,000 each. Rare coins in the $100,000-plus range—and there are some that are worth millions—are

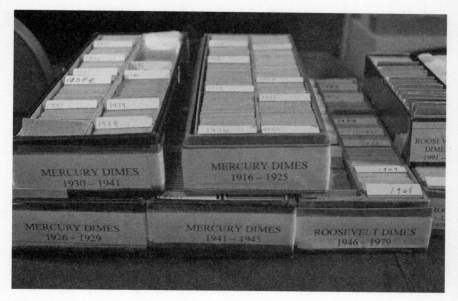

Figure 16.7 Mercury Dimes from Multiple Years on Display at a Coin Show
SOURCE: Photo by author.

sold in private transactions or at auctions: You would likely never see a transaction this large at a coin show.

The world of coin collecting, as well as that of investing in physical gold and silver coins, is an extremely small one. As a financial professional, I often scan the floor and make a rough estimate of the total value of coins on the floor, the size of the market. Let's say there are 40 dealers, each with an average of 50 ounces of gold and 1,000 ounces of silver (though most would be happy to have anywhere near that much). Then let's say everything else they have—the collectible coins from many years and countries—is worth $20,000 each. This is being extremely conservative, but it gives me an inventory value of $143,000 each for a total of $6 million in merchandise on the floor.

Now, let's say there are an average 100 coin dealers in each state of the country, a very conservative estimate considering the diminutive size of the coin world and the fact that each dealer goes to many shows. (You often see the same persons at multiple venues.) That would mean all the coin dealers at coin shows in the United States have around $715 million in gold and silver coins, though the number might be half that amount. This amount, $715 million—the rough value of all the coins at the nation's coin shows (not including ultra-rare coins)—is about what trades in shares of McDonalds in a day and a half.

This is such a small market that it makes no sense for financial institutions—like the pension fund I work for—to even consider investing in it. One reason why the market is small is the absence of credit. Buying stocks, bonds and innumerable financial products on credit has long been easy on Wall Street. But this is strictly a cash-only market, making it all but inaccessible for many, particularly gold buyers. Your local coin show is a diminutive marketplace that is best suited for people with middle class incomes, or those who want their children to learn from the experience and have a good time. High net worth individuals investing in precious metals coins generally deal directly with dealers, who specialize in higher value transactions—like ones involving silver and gold monster boxes.

If you are considering investing in physical precious metals, I think you will find a coin show well worth the visit. Coinshows.com is a good place to find one near you.

Chapter 17

Silver Mining Stocks*

A s of this writing, silver stocks are recovering from one of the steepest downswings in years. 2011 had begun as a great year for silver and other precious metal mining stocks, as the Philadelphia Gold & Silver Index had risen a sharp 20 percent from June through early September. Gold and silver were up 27 percent and 20 percent, respectively, from the low points of the summer and the sun was shining in the precious metals mining world. I had recently chaired a gold mining panel discussion in Colorado between two leading figures in the industry. The panel discussion was called "The Running of the Bulls," which spoke to the optimism in air at the time. But after September 5th, with gold and silver selling off sharply the index suffered a sharp decline, falling 37 percent over the following months until bottoming in May of 2012. (See Figure 17.1.)

---

*Some parts of this chapter were taken from my book *Hard Money: Taking Gold to a Higher Investment Level* (which was published in 2010), with permission from John Wiley & Sons.

Figure 17.1 Performance of Philadelphia Gold & Silver Index (Symbol: XAU)
SOURCE: Bloomberg.

But that was just the index, which reflects the performance of a group of equities dominated by gold stocks. Consider how a few silver mining stocks traded. Figure 17.2 is a chart of Pan American Silver, one of the world's largest silver mining companies.

Now consider the performance of a slightly smaller silver stock, that of First Majestic Silver, a Canadian-based silver mining company. (See Figure 17.3.)

If silver is gold on steroids, the stocks of companies mining the metal can at times behave like *silver* on steroids. As you can see in these charts, silver stocks like First Majestic can surge far more than silver during upswings: First Majestic almost doubled in value from May through September. Obviously, this was a rare event and downswings can also be sharp, as Figure 17.3 clearly shows. But these extreme price swings are something to keep in mind if you are considering investing in silver stocks, which can be a profitable way to invest in silver. But they are a highly volatile play on a volatile asset, so it is not something to consider if you would simply like to have an investment in silver. And, as mentioned

Figure 17.2 Stock Performance of Pan American Silver (Symbol: PAAS)
SOURCE: Bloomberg.

in Chapter 6, you always need to consider the right amount of silver (including silver stocks) to own as a percentage of your total wealth.

If you would like to invest in precious metals stocks but not deal with the difficulties inherent in stock selection, it would make sense to consider some of the top notch precious metals funds on the market. The three funds I respect the most are the Tocqueville Gold Fund, the Van Eck Gold Fund, and the Gabelli Gold Fund. Each of the funds have extensive (more than a decade) and strong performance track records and are managed by three of the most respected precious metals fund managers in the world today—Caesar Bryan, Joe Foster, and John Hathaway.

During some periods, silver stocks can underperform the price of silver even if the metal's price is rising. This is counterintuitive. Silver stocks provide leverage to the price of silver because their earnings can rise faster in percentage terms than the metal. And higher earnings are the primary driver of higher stock prices. But while share prices climb with

Figure 17.3   Performance of First Majestic Silver (ADR symbol: AG)
SOURCE: Bloomberg.

earnings over time—and there are a number of silver stocks that have surged in value over the past decade—there are periods during which a number of factors can drive silver stocks lower despite rising metal prices. It's just a fact that one has to face when considering taking a dive into the world of silver stocks.

One initial thought is that one should maintain a healthy degree of skepticism when approaching mining stocks, because something a beginning precious metals mining investor faces when examining the investment landscape is the abundance of promise. There is a sense that silver and gold are being discovered or are about to be discovered everywhere, that new resources and reserves are on the verge of being announced by a great many mining companies. While annual global silver production has been rising at a good pace, having increased 35 percent over the last decade to 750 million ounces produced during 2011, gold production remains near its peak reached in 2001, when a little over 85 million ounces of gold were produced.

A study conducted in the early 1990s by Cominco, a mining company, found that out of over 2,000 projects on which it had spent at least $1 million each, the company had only made six or seven mines. So less than half of 1 percent of promising projects (after all, at least 1 million dollars was spent on each one) actually proved to be successful! Considering that it takes years to determine, once gold or silver has been found at a given location, if extracting the metal profitably is possible, there are opportunities for dishonesty and financial fraud that investors always need to be alert to, especially if we are going into a protracted precious metals boom. Gold and silver have a way of attracting swindlers, who prey on investors' ever-present desire for fast profits, and even the smartest mining analysts and investors have been deceived. I wrote about an example of this in my first book:

> That the history of gold mining is replete with stories of deception is evident in Mark Twain's cynical observation that "A gold mine is a hole in the ground with a liar on top." Twain would have laughed at the story of Bre-X, a corporate scandal that rocked the gold mining world in the 1990s. For the sake of brevity, let me give you the highlights of this cautionary tale. Bre-X began as an obscure Calgary gold exploration company with no revenues or earnings. Its executives, having searched for gold unsuccessfully in the far-off jungles of Kalimantan, Indonesia, decided to say that they had actually found rich deposits. In time, providing false earth samples that gullible analysts trusted, Bre-X went from estimating deposits of three million ounces of gold to *200 million*, which at the time amounted to 70 billion dollars for an asset the company didn't even have a clear title to. Wall Street ate this up—salivating for each of the many lies Bre-X management continually fed it—and a great many analysts promoted the stock relentlessly, some saying they "had seen the gold" with their own eyes. In what we might call its Microsoft phase, Bre-X went from trading at pennies per share to a peak of $286.50 in 1996 to reach a stunning market capitalization of $6 billion. Its Enron phase— during which a Bre-X executive en route to explain why there was no gold dove to his death from a helicopter—ended with the stock recording a final trade at 7 cents a share.[1]

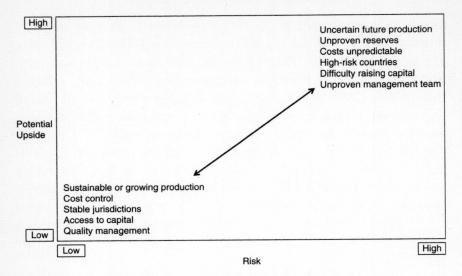

Figure 17.4   Risk/Reward Trade-Off for Precious Metals Stock

Fortunately, there are multiple silver and gold stocks listed on world markets that can promise and deliver. And notwithstanding the low-odds possibility of picking the next Bre-X bomb, there is also the low-odds potential for picking the next jackpot stock, like Silver Wheaton, which rocketed from a tiny company in 2006—just 6 years ago—to become the second biggest silver stock in the world, with an impressive market value of $13 billion: the share price has risen by roughly 1,000 percent. Silver Wheaton, though deriving all its revenue and profits from the silver mining industry, is a royalty company. (There is a section that discusses Silver Wheaton and royalty companies at the end of this chapter.) Considering its multiple sources of revenue at present, it is no longer the riskier play on silver that it used to be and consequently, though it is certainly a promising stock, it does not provide the same potential for explosive growth that it once did. So the precious metals stocks' investment challenge is to find the proper balance between risk and reward, a trade-off that is represented in the key fundamental drivers of precious metals stocks shown in Figure 17.4.

Intuitively, each of these factors makes sense and they all point to the potential for increasing earnings, the prime determinant of a given's stock's appreciation in any industry, from mining to dental implants. For example, investing in a mining company that has access to abundant capital for exploration is less risky than buying a stock that doesn't, and the former likely trades at a premium (offers potentially less upside) than the latter, all other factors being equal. But it will be useful to consider a few of the points separately, as all are major considerations when approaching mining stocks. All of them are reflected in the valuation that we consider in a few pages that follow.

Sustainable or Growing Production

Mines are depleting assets with a finite life. Some can be productive for many decades and new veins can be discovered, but any given mine has a finite number of ounces that can be extracted profitably at current market prices. (However, a rising silver or gold price can make mines with declining grades profitable to operate again, and many sites abandoned many years ago are being reopened.) As such, for a producing company to maintain or grow beyond a given production level—like the 73 million ounces of silver that Fresnillo, the world's largest silver company, is expected to produce in 2012[2]—it will always need the reserves to be mined next, much like a supermarket needs to be continually stocked to continue operating. Table 17.1 shows the world's largest operating silver mines.

However, Fresnillo differs from Safeway, the supermarket operator, in that the miner's goods are nonperishable and rapidly rising inventories (reserves) is a good thing—actually, a great thing!—which would not be the case for Safeway. (Reserves, a precious metals miner's inventory, are not to be confused with resources that have not been proven to be economically viable. See the definitions in the next section.) To replace the reserves that are being depleted by production, a mining company will need to incur costs to make further exploration at existing sites, find new reserves on its own land, or acquire other properties or existing mining companies. (The never-ending search for new reserves is the main driver of mergers and acquisitions activity in the mining sector.) Not surprisingly, companies that have the highest reserves, as well as a good history of reserve replacement (either via their own properties or through good acquisitions) trade at higher multiples. But not all reserves are the same, as the following terms explain.

Table 17.1   World's Leading Silver Mines

(millions of ounces)

Rank	Mine/Country	Operating Company	2011 Production
1	Cannington,[1] Australia	BHP Billiton plc.	32.17
2	Fresnillo, Mexico	Fresnillo plc.	30.30
3	Dukat,[2] Russia	Polymetal International plc.	13.60
4	Uchucchacua, Peru	Compañia de Minas Buenaventura S.A.A.	10.09
5	Palmarejo, Mexico	Coeur d'Alene Mines Corp.	9.04
6	Pallancata, Peru	Hochschild Mining plc./ International Minerals Corp.	8.77
7	Gümüsköy, Turkey	Eti Gümüş A.Ş.	8.37
8	San Bartolomé, Bolivia	Coeur d'Alene Mines Corp.	7.50
9	Pirquitas, Argentina	Silver Standard Resources Inc.	7.06
10	Greens Creek, United States	Hecla Mining Company	6.50
11	Arcata, Peru	Hochschild Mining plc.	6.08
12	Saucito, Mexico	Fresnillo plc.	5.90
13	San José, Argentina	Hochschild Mining plc./ McEwen Mining Inc.	5.87
14	Imiter,[3] Morocco	Société Métallurgique d'Imiter	5.48
15	Alamo Dorado, Mexico	Pan American Silver Corp.	5.30

[1]Reported payable metal in concentrate.
[2]Including Gotsovoye.
[3]Estimate.
Material and statistics in this section were adapted in part from the Silver Institute's World Silver Survey 2012 publication.
SOURCE: The Silver Institute.

Definitions[3]

Proven Mineral Reserve—is the economically mineable part of a measured mineral resource demonstrated by at least a preliminary feasibility study. This study must include adequate information on mining, processing, metallurgical, economic, and other relevant factors that demonstrate, at the time of reporting, that economic extraction is justified.

Probable Mineral Reserve—is the economically mineable part of an indicated and, in some circumstances, a measured mineral resource demonstrated by at least a preliminary feasibility study. This study must include adequate information on mining, processing, metallurgical, economic, and other relevant factors that demonstrate, at the time of reporting, that economic extraction can be justified.

Measured Mineral Resource—is that part of a mineral resource for which quantity, grade or quality, densities, shape, and physical characteristics are so well established that they can be estimated with confidence sufficient to allow the appropriate application of technical and economic parameters, to support production planning and evaluation of the economic viability of the deposit. The estimate is based on detailed and reliable exploration, sampling and testing information gathered through appropriate techniques from locations such as outcrops, trenches, pits, workings, and drill holes that are spaced closely enough to confirm both geological and grade continuity.

Indicated Mineral Resource—is that part of a mineral resource for which quantity, grade or quality, densities, shape, and physical characteristics, can be estimated with a level of confidence sufficient to allow the appropriate application of technical and economic parameters, to support mine planning and evaluation of the economic viability of the deposit. The estimate is based on detailed and reliable exploration and testing information gathered through appropriate techniques from locations such as outcrops, trenches, pits, workings, and drill holes that are spaced closely enough for geological and grade continuity to be reasonably assumed.

Inferred Mineral Resource—is that part of a mineral resource for which quantity and grade or quality can be estimated on the basis of geological evidence and limited sampling, and reasonably assumed, but not verified, geological and grade continuity. The estimate is based on limited information and sampling gathered through appropriate techniques from locations such as outcrops, trenches, pits, workings, and drill holes.

Hedging

Given any mining company's significant dependence on metal prices to determine its level of revenues—which affects its profitability and ultimately the wealth of its shareholders—during periods of metal price weakness, such as the 1990s, a great many miners protected themselves using hedging mechanisms. Essentially, hedging means *selling forward* production (typically to a bullion bank) at prices often near today's to insure revenues against a potential future decline in metal prices. The problem with hedging, as a great many companies proved during the 2000s, is that it also limits revenue upside since part of future production will have been sold at a (potentially lower) set price. Hedging made sense for precious metals miners and worked during the 1990s, when the price of gold fell all the way below $300 an ounce, and silver was never able to regain $10 an ounce. But with rising prices, investors have sought completely unhedged companies that offer greater leverage to higher prices. As a result, most miners today have limited or no hedges, although this could change in the future, so it's something to keep in the back of your mind as an investor.

Cost Control

Cost control is evidently a key determinant of profits, as companies with a low cost of production are able to obtain the highest profits from each ounce of silver or gold produced. Companies that experience significant volatility in per-ounce cost of production often trade at a discount as investors worry about management discipline or they are concerned that unforeseen production difficulties are arising. Some South African miners (mostly gold producers) have faced significant challenges in recent years due to energy costs—a major detractor from mining stock profits during the 2000s—and interruptions. This becomes vital for mining companies extracting low-grade ore—from which less silver can be extracted and hence lower revenues—which is increasingly the case today, especially for gold miners: Decades ago there were many mines that produced 30 grams of gold per ton of ore extracted. Today, there are profitable *one-gram-per-ton* mines in operation, but evidently they are only profitable because of the lower relative cost base needed to obtain each refined ounce of gold. Ironically, the greatest leverage to rising silver or gold prices can be found in companies with higher costs—that is, the riskier ones! Table 17.2 shows a simple example of how this is the case: Despite having a higher cost base

Table 17.2   Example of Operational Leverage Performance

	Company X		Company Y	
	Period 1	**Period 2**	**Period 1**	**Period 2**
Silver Sales (oz.)	$1,000,000	1,000,000	1,000,000	$1,000,000
Price	$30	$40	$30	$40
Revenue	$30,000,000	$40,000,000	$30,000,000	$40,000,000
Cash Costs per oz.	$15	$15	$8	$8
Cost Base	$15,000,000	$15,000,000	$8,000,000	$8,000,000
Profit	$15,000,000	$25,000,000	$22,000,000	$32,000,000

	Company X	**Company Y**
% Change in Profit	66.7%	45.5%

($15/ounce), Company X enjoys higher profit *growth* than Company Y (which has a lower cost base of $8/ounce) when silver prices rise: it has higher operating leverage.

That being said, if silver prices decline, Company X will see a far more severe profit decline than the company with a lower cost of production. In fact, it has a higher potential of actually having to *shut down* operations if prices fall below $15/ounce while Company Y could remain in operation. The important thing to keep in mind is that a company with a high per-ounce cost of production will have higher earnings volatility.

Stable Jurisdictions

Mining companies in a productive stage cannot leave the site they are mining at, and if they happen to be operating in a region where laws can be changed easily, this can become a major concern. There are countless instances of governments demanding higher royalty payments and/or different working conditions for workers. It is well known that mining is perceived as a dirty, nasty, dangerous business that can be detrimental to the natural environment, and some governments will change standards as they see fit. Hence, mining companies that operate in countries where political stability is questionable trade at a discount to those with mines in stable jurisdictions, which include countries like Canada, the United States, Australia, and Mexico, among others that have a relatively benign and predictable regulatory and tax environment. One important fact to consider regarding jurisdictions is that due to the weak economic environment in a number of countries and need for employment opportunities, governments anxious for job creation have been more open to consider new mining ventures than they were a few years ago.

Quality of Management

This may seem obvious, but having sharp management is more important in the mining industry than it is for many other types of companies. Consider that most of mining activity occurs away from the eyes of investors, unlike what is the case with, say, a media company: Any investor can turn on a television and get a sense of how good the programming is on a given channel. But compare this to a new mining company, which, despite the increasing costs and expenses—negative cash flow—being incurred to build a new mine, will not be producing anything until several years in the future. Once again, keep in mind that mining is a complex and dangerous business. Miners use explosives extensively, are often exposed to harsh temperatures and environments in which it can be difficult to breathe properly, and most of them work for hours in the dark. A great many of them are injured and dozens die each year, which makes management that can provide for safety and proper operating standards vital.

There have been significant instances of management corruption, and problems can be hidden for years. (Refer to the Bre-X incident mentioned before to see the potential downside of having a management problem!) Hence, trust that management is taking the proper and necessary steps to develop a mine on time and under the conditions set at the outset is something that takes a great deal of time to prove. Companies that trade at rich valuations, as we will see, tend to do so in part because their managements have garnered the trust of the investment community, who believes that a given miner will meet its cost and production targets and will often provide positive surprises in terms of new deposit discoveries and the continual expansion of reserves.

Valuation

Obviously, a company with rapidly growing silver production and fantastic cost control, operating multiple mines distributed among stable jurisdictions like Canada and Australia under impeccable management, sounds great. But that doesn't mean its stock will be a great investment. Few would deny that Microsoft is an amazing story, which grew from an idea into one of the largest companies in the world, but its stock price has been stuck in a trading range for the last decade. And there are similar situations in the precious metals mining industry: There are companies with high, often well-deserved valuation levels, whose performance might be capped, at least for some time, due to their lofty price relative to earnings. Let's take a look at its valuation compared with the precious metals mining industry.

Table 17.3, based on estimates provided by BMO Capital Markets, divides the industry into senior, intermediate, and emerging companies based on their level of production. Seniors are established high-volume producers while emerging producers are usually just beginning or about to produce their first ounces of silver. There is another category altogether commonly regarded as junior stocks, which focus on the vital mining stage of exploration, an exciting investment arena that can produce stocks that either surge like Apple Computer or fall to zero. There are hundreds of juniors listed on exchanges around the world, mostly in Canada and Australia, and *some* of them will eventually become spectacular winners. Just keep in mind that juniors are invariably stuck at a money-absorbing stage, as they require investment capital to acquire properties and carry out exploration. Virtually all of them will never move on to the final stage of developing a project that ultimately produces refined silver or gold; successful explorers often define success as selling a promising asset to a precious metals miner that can fully take advantage of a given deposit's potential. To closely examine the potential of junior stocks requires a level of detail beyond the scope of this book, as well as an ability and desire to

Table 17.3   Silver Company Valuation Table
As of October 15, 2012

Company	Ticker	Market Cap USD mm	Price to NPV BMO Assumpt. (1)		Net Asset Value Premium/ (Discount) US$33.52/oz.	
			0%	10%	0%	10%
Senior Producers						
Coeur D'Alene Mining	**CDE**	2,609	0.78x	1.62x	(33.0%)	47.0%
Fresnillo	**FRES**	22,485	1.28x	2.57x	1.0%	117.0%
Hochschild Mining	**HOC**	2,747	0.92x	1.57x	(26.0%)	34.0%
Pan American Silver	**PAAS**	3,256	1.09x	1.35x	(7.0%)	21.0%
Silver Wheaton	**SLW**	13,941	0.86x	2.34x	(35.0%)	65.0%
Senior Producers Total/Average		45,037	1.08x	2.29x	(7.0%)	84.0%
Intermediate Producers						
First Majestic	**FR**	2,731	1.14x	1.91x	(6.0%)	65.0%
Hecla Mining	**HL**	1,985	0.69x	1.26x	(42.0%)	11.0%
Silver Standard	**SSRI**	1,171	0.34x	0.65x	(73.0%)	(46.0%)
Silvercorp	**SVM**	1,023	0.59x	1.13x	(50.0%)	(1.0%)
Intermediate Producers Total/Average		6,911	0.80x	1.39x	(44.0%)	7.0%
Emerging Producers						
Bear Creek Mining	**BCM**	344	0.27x	0.66x	(80.0%)	(48.0%)
Endeavour Silver	**EDR**	854	0.80x	1.45x	(36.0%)	26.0%
Fortuna Silver	**FVI**	654	0.78x	1.29x	(34.0%)	15.0%
MAG Silver	**MAG**	694	0.71x	1.49x	(52.0%)	8.0%
Mandalay Resources Corp.	**MND**	321	0.66x	0.99x	(41.0%)	(8.0%)
Minco Silver	**MSV**	108	0.17x	0.37x	(89.0%)	(74.0%)
Orko Silver	**OK**	213	0.56x	1.30x	(68.0%)	(20.0%)
Tahoe Resources	**THO**	2,999	0.52x	1.13x	(62.0%)	(9.0%)
Emerging Producers Total/Average		6,187	0.59x	1.19x	(61.0%)	(15.0%)

NOTES:
(1) Price to NPV: The current share price divided by BMO NPV per share calculated using a 10% discount rate. Value greater than 100% is a premium (trading above its respective NPV per share), and value less than 100% is a discount (trading below its respective NPV per share).
(2) Price to Earnings (x): The current share price divided by adjusted earnings per share. *For values of more than 50, the P/E multiple is capped at 50.0 and negative P/E values are displayed as "na."*
(3) EV/EBITDA (x): Enterprise Value divided by EBITDA forecast. *For values of more than 50, the EV/EBITDA multiple is capped at 50.0 and negative EV/EBITDA values are displayed as "na."*
(4) Dividend Yield: Estimated common dividend divided by the current share price.
(5) Net Debt To Equity: The ratio of Net Debt (long-term debt + short-term debt – cash) to total shareholders equity.
SOURCE: BMO Capital Markets, Bloomberg, Thomson Reuters Corp.

Adj. Market Cap. Per Rec. Oz. (US$)	Price to Earnings (x) BMO Assumpt. (2)		EV/EBITDA (x) BMO Assumpt. (3)		Dividend Yield (4)	Net Debt to Equity (5) %
	2012E	2013E	2012E	2013E	2012E	
$11.6	16.38x	6.60x	5.1x	2.4x	0.0%	−11.1%
$14.6	29.60x	17.04x	15.1x	9.4x	3.1%	−38.5%
$11.6	35.73x	15.39x	7.5x	4.5x	2.7%	−27.8%
$14.9	15.59x	8.57x	6.0x	3.1x	0.5%	−18.6%
$18.4	21.17x	15.80x	17.9x	12.7x	0.5%	−15.4%
$14.0	25.59x	15.34x	14.2x	9.3x	1.9%	−27.7%
$11.7	23.58x	10.58x	16.4x	6.1x	0.0%	−9.9%
$8.9	37.23x	9.39x	11.6x	4.0x	0.0%	−17.3%
$5.3	>50	17.07x	14.1x	5.5x	0.0%	−27.5%
$5.8	13.74x	19.85x	5.6x	6.8x	1.4%	−35.6%
$11.4	26.55x	12.71x	13.0x	5.5x	0.2%	−18.8%
$3.1	>50	>50	nap	nap	0.0%	−51.9%
$8.0	13.06x	7.27x	6.8x	2.8x	0.0%	−22.2%
$8.7	14.57x	8.40x	6.5x	3.4x	0.0%	−22.6%
$7.3	nap	nap	nap	nap	0.0%	−37.1%
$8.3	4.60x	2.96x	3.0x	1.1x	0.0%	−20.2%
$3.2	>50	>50	nap	nap	0.0%	−18.5%
$2.9	>50	>50	nap	nap	0.0%	−87.1%
$8.3	>50	17.02x	nap	13.2x	0.0%	−22.0%
$4.9	12.12x	13.19x	6.1x	9.3x	0.0%	−27.5%

take on investment volatility to an even higher level than producing mining stocks already have. In the risk/reward chart in Figure 17.4, junior stocks are way into the top right-hand corner!

As you can see in Table 17.3, Fresnillo has a market cap per recoverable silver ounce of $14.60 and it trades at a significant premium to the silver mining sector in terms of price-to-net present value (P/NPV). There are a great many more valuation metrics that mining analysts and portfolio managers use, but this one can offer a snapshot of the company's short-term and long-term valuation based on analyst estimates: The P/NPV compares the current share price with the present value of all net future cash flows derived from the entire life of all its mining operations (typically using a discount rate of 10 percent). In layman's terms, NPV tries to place a value on all the ounces a company will ever produce at its mines based on what we know today. Obviously, unlike estimated earnings, which are unlikely to vary substantially over the short term (absent some major event), NPV can change dramatically based on changes in things like reserves, cost estimates, and projected silver prices. Net present value is the hardest thing to estimate, and yet its importance is made evident in that most of Fresnillo's value is beyond what it will produce over the next two years. Table 17.3 shows that virtually all precious metals miners trade at a premium to their NPV, which JPMorgan Chase analyst John Bridges attributes to three factors: the expected value of new discoveries; the potential value from additions to new mines; and *optionality*, the potential for higher precious metals prices, which would immediately impact any miner's NPV.

Another important metric is market capitalization per recoverable ounce. This multiple places a value of all the reserves of a mining company on a per-ounce basis, which essentially tells an investor how much he is paying for each ounce the miner has in the ground. By buying Fresnillo, one is paying $14.60 per ounce (compared with the price of silver as I am writing, $32.72), but one could buy Bear Creek Mining at less than *a quarter* of that price. The tremendous variation is due to the market's perception of likelihood that Bear Creek will have the silver at its mining operations in the quantities expected, and that it *will* be extracted—and *profitably*. A significant portion of Fresnillo's incremental production will come from mines that are already in operation, and as such are proven, viable assets. But as you can see in Table 17.4, Bear Creek will not be producing any gold until 2015, and before then there

Table 17.4 Silver Company Production

Latest Silver Price: US$33.52/oz.

October 12, 2012

Senior Producers

Company	Ticker	Silver Equivalent Production (Moz) (1)						Growth in Silver Equiv. Production (2)			
		2010A	2011A	2012E	2013E	2014E	2015E	2010A to 2013E	2010A to 2014E	2010A to 2015E	Compound Annual
Coeur D'Alene Mining	CDE	27.3	29.0	31.9	31.4	32.6	26.6	15%	19%	19%	–1%
Fresnillo	FRES	70.1	68.3	72.8	79.5	90.1	103.0	13%	29%	29%	8%
Hochschild Mining	HOC	25.9	21.0	18.7	18.7	22.6	26.5	–28%	–13%	–13%	0%
Pan American Silver	PAAS	32.9	25.9	30.6	31.7	34.7	43.9	–4%	5%	33%	6%
Silver Wheaton	SLW	20.5	21.1	28.3	29.5	34.7	38.4	44%	69%	69%	13%
Senior Producer Total		156.1	144.2	154.0	161.3	180.0	200.0	3%	15%	28%	5%
Intermediate Producers											
First Majestic	FR	6.7	7.4	9.1	15.1	21.0	25.1	125%	213%	273%	30%
Hecla Mining	HL	22.1	16.1	12.1	17.5	18.6	20.7	–21%	–16%	–16%	–1%
Silver Standard	SSRI	5.9	5.2	9.0	10.4	13.3	25.0	75%	124%	124%	33%
Silvercorp	SVM	9.1	9.2	8.4	8.1	11.3	15.0	–11%	24%	65%	11%
Intermediate Producer Total		43.8	38.0	38.6	51.1	64.2	85.6	17%	46%	95%	14%

(continued)

227

Table 17.4 *(Continued)*

Latest Silver Price: US$33.52/oz.

October 12, 2012

Senior Producers

Company	Ticker	Silver Equivalent Production (Moz) (1)						Growth in Silver Equiv. Production (2)			
		2010A	2011A	2012E	2013E	2014E	2015E	2010A to 2013E	2010A to 2014E	2010A to 2015E	Compound Annual
Emerging Producers											
Bear Creek Mining	BCM	0.0	0.0	0.0	0.0	0.0	9.4	nap	nap	nap	nap
Endeavour Silver	EDR	4.4	4.8	7.1	8.9	9.9	10.1	102%	125%	130%	18%
Fortuna Silver	FVI	4.5	3.8	6.1	6.2	6.4	7.0	37%	43%	55%	9%
MAG Silver	MAG	0.0	0.0	0.0	0.0	0.0	0.0	nap	nap	nap	nap
Mandalay Resources Corp.	MND	1.0	2.7	4.9	5.8	6.6	7.3	461%	500%	500%	48%
Minco Silver	MSV	0.0	0.0	0.0	0.0	0.5	5.5	nap	nap	nap	nap
Orko Silver	OK	0.0	0.0	0.0	0.0	0.0	0.0	nap	nap	nap	nap
Tahoe Resources	THO	0.0	0.0	0.0	8.7	19.6	20.5	nap	nap	nap	nap
Junior Producer Total		5.4	7.5	12.1	14.7	16.9	32.2	171%	212%	493%	43%
Sector Averages											
Sr./Int. Producer Total		200.0	182.2	192.6	212.4	244.1	285.6	6%	22%	43%	7%
Overall Total		205.4	189.7	204.7	227.1	261.1	317.8	11%	27%	55%	9%

NOTES:

1) Silver Equivalent Production: Silver production plus silver production as a Silver equivalent. Silver production that is treated as a credit to costs is not included. Also does not include any ounces accrued from royalties except for royalty companies.

A Growth in Silver Equivalent Production: The percentage growth in production between the stated years. For averages, the growth in Silver Equivalent Production is capped at 100% and the compound annual growth rate is capped at 25%.

2) Growth in Silver Equivalent Production: The percentage growth in production between the stated years. For averages, the growth in Silver Equivalent Production is capped at 100% and the compound annual growth rate is capped at 25%.

SOURCE: BMO Capital Markets, Bloomberg.

are a great many obstacles the company's management needs to overcome to reach its goal—and reach it on time.

The market, by which I mean the ocean of global investors voraciously reading up on mining stats and watching computer screens across the world, generally determines the valuation of all stocks in a rational way. That Minco Silver, which (as you can see in Table 17.4) will not be producing silver for a number of years, is trading at a fraction of what Coeur D'Alene (CDE) does has a logical reason. CDE, guided by a reputable management team, is an established miner that produces millions of ounces of silver each year at its mining installations. The upside potential for Minco, which is certainly far cheaper than CDE on a market cap/ounce basis, is substantial—but so is the risk of failure. Hence, unless the market has completely missed something (which is a rare occurrence, but can happen), the discovery of any cheap stock really means uncovering the reason for a discount, which one may or may not agree is valid. If you buy a cheap stock (a stock trading at a discount based on P/NPV), you're essentially betting that the market will be proven wrong in time. For example, you may think that Minco's discount is excessive considering the probability that it will deliver as promised.

Royalty Companies: A Different Play on Silver and Other Precious Metals

The trade-off between risk (operational problems at mines, political risk, reserve, and production growth disappointments) and reward (higher leverage to a climbing gold price, potential for new discoveries, and expanded production) that mining companies present as an investment can be extreme, a fact reflected in trading volatility for the sector. But royalty companies, which are less exposed to many of the miners' operational challenges, can offer a middle ground between the low volatility/low reward of a precious metal ETF or purchase of a precious metal coin and the high volatility/higher potential reward of mining stocks. And over the last year, investors have preferred that trade-off, as royalty companies have substantially outperformed mining stocks.

Royalty companies, of which there are really only a handful listed on stock exchanges (see Table 17.5), derive most of their revenues from royalty streams provided by mining companies. In a typical transaction, a

Table 17.5 Precious Metals Royalty Companies

Ticker	Name	Market Cap (Local)	Country of Domicile	2012 Price to Earnings	2013 Price to Earnings	Dividend Yield	Price to Cash Flow
FNV CN	FRANCO-NEVADA CO	8,460,249,023	CANADA	47.5x	34.9x	0.93%	27.1x
RGLD	ROYAL GOLD INC	5,326,127,441	UNITED STATES	42.6x	28.4x	0.81%	28.6x
SLW CN	SILVER WHEATON	12,977,245,117	CANADA	22.5x	16.7x	1.03%	20.9x
SSL CN	SANDSTORM GOLD	1,032,022,705	CANADA	41.7x	24.7x	nap	21.7x

SOURCE: BMO Capital Markets.

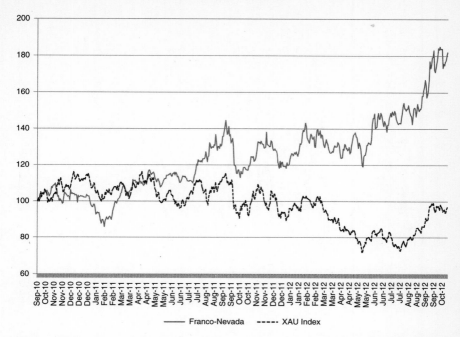

Figure 17.5   Price Performance of Franco Nevada versus the Philadelphia Gold &
Silver Index (Indexed to Start at 100)
SOURCE: Bloomberg.

company like Silver Wheaton will provide a mining company with an
up-front cash payment to help finance a specific mining operation, say a
new gold mine in Peru. In return, the mining company will pay the
royalty company a specific percentage of the silver tonnage produced at
the mine each year. However, the royalty percentage doesn't have to be
derived from the primary metal extracted at a mine; for example, the
royalty company could receive the gold or silver by-product streams of a
copper mine. And typically, these payments will be made during the
entire life of the mine, even if this is decades longer than expected.

The royalty percentage is paid regardless of the costs the miner will
need to incur to produce the metal. As such, the royalty company is not
exposed to a sudden increase in capital or operating costs—all such risks
remain with the mining company. However, despite being insulated
from higher operating costs, royalty companies *do* share the miners'
political and operating risks that could lead to shutdowns and lower
production. Although most royalty agreements for a company like
Silver Wheaton are revenue-based, there are other royalty agreements

Figure 17.6   Price Performance of Silver Wheaton versus Silver (Indexed to Start at 100)

SOURCE: Bloomberg.

(a minority) that do expose the company to operating costs—and leverage to precious metals prices.

Since royalty companies are essentially financial companies (which can be seen as providing the third leg in the financial structure of mining operations that includes debt and equity), their costs related to any project are almost negligible. They are remarkable cash-flow machines that enjoy the highest margins in the precious metals industry—or just about any other industry you can imagine. Consider that Franco-Nevada, another royalty company, has a staff of fewer than 25 people and revenues approaching $200 million, and yet the whole company could almost be run out of a park via laptops. The result is an $8 billion company with an operating cash flow exceeding 80 percent of revenues.

Although royalty companies are seen as providing less leverage to precious metals prices than mining companies (since they are insulated from many operating risks), they have performed very well in recent years, as shown in Figures 17.5 and 17.6.

Chapter 18

Platinum and Palladium: Alternative Metals as Old as the World, but as New as the Internet, as Investments*

U nlike gold and silver, which—with the brief exception of the past four decades—were regarded as money around the globe for thousands of years, platinum and palladium are as new as the iPhone in the investment and monetary world. Since the technology

---

*This chapter is an updated version of one that appeared in my book *Hard Money: Taking Gold to a Higher Investment Level*, which was published in 2010, with permission from John Wiley & Sons.

needed to smelt the metals had yet to be developed, Benjamin Franklin surely did not pull out a platinum coin to pay for his famous kite nor get change in palladium in the eighteenth century. Besides, for millennia the metals were regarded simply as undesirable impurities in the refining process of other metals. For practical purposes platinum and palladium, which are as old as the world, went public a few years after Google's stock was listed.

In 2007, two financial firms launched exchange-traded funds (ETFs) for each metal and as a result it finally became practical for mainstream funds to invest in them and for individuals to buy shares for their 401(K)s. Before then, any person wanting to own one of the two P's had to buy coins issued by the Bank of Canada or the few other central banks that mint them, or invest in the metals via the futures market, an investment arena mainly used by professional traders or industrial hedgers. Showing how new these metals are as investments, the Sprott Physical Platinum and Palladium Trust (symbol: SPPP), which allows for the conversion of the ETF into the actual metals, went public in late 2012.

Platinum and palladium are two of the six platinum group metals, commonly referred to as PGMs. There are no practical vehicles for investing in the other four—osmium, iridium, ruthenium, and rhodium—for the time being and their markets are far smaller, so they are not explored in this book. The six metals share important chemical and physical properties that make them useful in industrial applications, and the beauty of at least two of the metals makes them popular in jewelry. Platinum and palladium have catalytic properties, which means they accelerate certain chemical reactions, are good electrical conductors, and perform well in high-temperature applications. Most significantly, these two PGMs are vital inputs in antipollutant catalytic converters in the world's automobiles, which can convert up to 90 percent of the gases produced by cars into less harmful emissions. But they are also used in dentistry, medicine, computers and other electronics, groundwater treatment, and a great many chemical applications.

The investment potential of platinum and palladium is being driven, as with gold and silver, by dramatic changes in the supply and demand dynamics for the metals. Naïve as it sounds to even state the obvious, it is important to keep this in mind: Platinum and palladium prices will only rise if demand is greater than supply. When you think about industrial demand for platinum and palladium, think cars—as both metals are primarily used in autocatalytic applications in the automobile industry, which accounts for around half of total demand for the two metals. However, an ounce of platinum costs more than twice as much as a palladium ounce. This difference is partially explained by the fact that twice the amount of palladium is needed to substitute for platinum in the production of auto catalysts. Also, only platinum is used at present in the fabrication of diesel catalytic converters. Another 29 percent of demand comes from the jewelry industry—where platinum is in greater demand—and most of the rest is used in a variety of chemical, electronic, petroleum, and other industrial applications. The minuscule remainder of demand, around 5 percent, is from financial investors in the metals.

The combined value of all platinum and palladium supplied to the market each year by the mining industry (71 percent), along with the remaining autocatalyst and jewelry scrap is $18 billion, as shown in Figures 18.1 to 18.4. It's a tiny fraction of the silver and gold that are produced each year. To put the amount into investment perspective, the money traded in shares of Google in a week could buy the world's entire annual production of platinum and palladium.

Such a tiny market has tremendous risks and volatility. Since the prices of platinum and palladium are influenced by such factors as demand for automobiles and supply from South African mines—which produce half

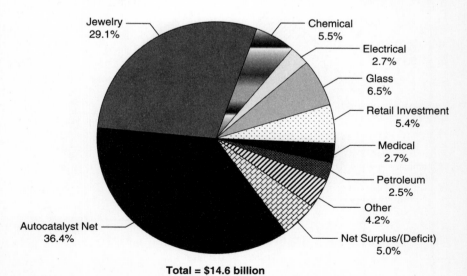

Total = $14.6 billion

Figure 18.1   Sources of Platinum Demand
SOURCE: Johnson Matthey.

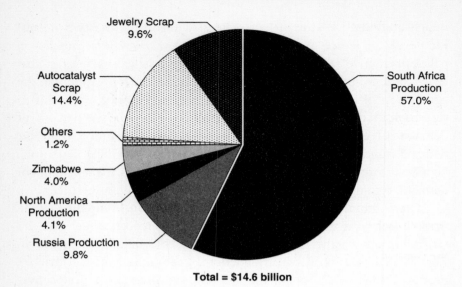

Total = $14.6 billion

Figure 18.2   Sources of Platinum Supply
SOURCE: Johnson Matthey.

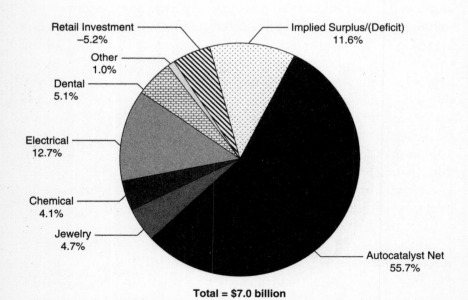

Total = $7.0 billion

Figure 18.3   Sources of Palladium Demand
SOURCE: Johnson Matthey.

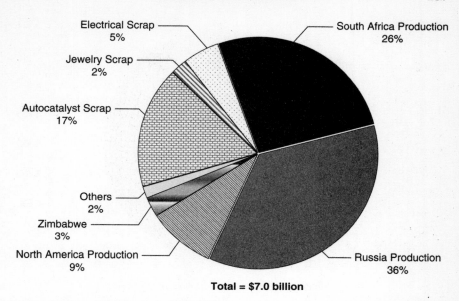

Figure 18.4   Sources of Palladium Supply
SOURCE: Johnson Matthey.

the world's platinum and more than a third of all palladium—a decline in car purchases or an energy crisis in South Africa can have a deep effect on the market. In fact, this is exactly what happened during 2008: The world experienced one of the worst years in the auto industry's history, with global output plunging by almost a third, and South African mining production was repeatedly interrupted by power outages. Consequently, the small number of investors in the metals, which at this point make up less than 10 percent of demand, were rocked in an amazingly volatile year: Platinum prices swung between a high of $2,273 an ounce and $763. In one of the worst years in stock market history, platinum was significantly more volatile than equities during 2008. Figures 18.5 to 18.7 point to these metals' volatility. This is not a market for investors with weak stomachs.

Glancing at these charts, one notices that the price of platinum has surged while that palladium has struggled. Intuitively, considering the fact that most of the demand for both metals comes from the auto industry (as shown in Figures 18.1 and 18.3), one would have thought that their prices would have moved in lockstep, or at least in a similar direction, over the past 10 years. Perhaps that will happen in the future, but the supply/demand

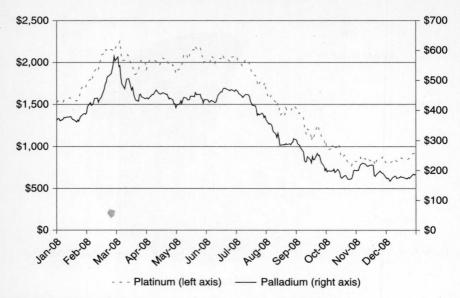

Figure 18.5 2008 Price Chart for Platinum and Palladium
SOURCE: Bloomberg.

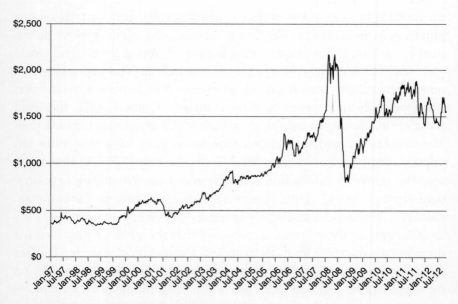

Figure 18.6 10-Year Platinum Price Chart
SOURCE: Bloomberg.

Figure 18.7   10-Year Palladium Price Chart

SOURCE: Bloomberg.

balance for palladium was deeply affected by a supply disruption in the late 1990s, when Russian shipments were delayed partly for political reasons. Considering that Russia is the largest producer of palladium, the market imbalance caused a panic that eventually drove the price of palladium over $1,100 in 2001. (See Figure 18.7.) Some of the major users at the time began to assume that the Russian supply problem would continue for years, most notably Ford Motor Company, which accumulated a massive stockpile of the metal. But the end result was an excess supply of palladium on the market (and a huge loss for Ford) that has kept the metal's price well below its 2001 peak. However, the palladium market finally appears to be closer to balance, implying that the metal may start behaving like platinum, whose demand has outstripped supply year after year. The metal's price was rising sharply into late 2012, though jewelry demand has not recovered, as had been expected. (See Figure 18.8.)

Investors in these metals should always keep in mind that platinum and palladium are significantly more sensitive to the economic environment than silver—and certainly gold. Though investment demand for the metals is rising, they are still not broadly perceived as having the same investment characteristics as gold, the only precious metal to rise in 2008.

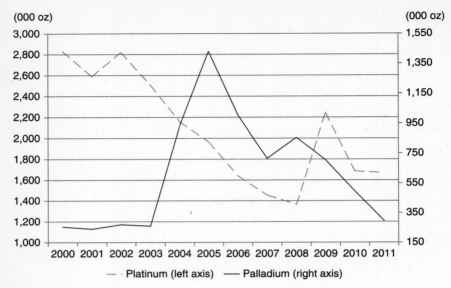

Figure 18.8 Jewelry Demand
SOURCE: Johnson Matthey.

In that year, as a result of collapsing auto demand and weaker industrial production, PGM prices fell very sharply, with platinum losing over 40 percent and palladium close to 50 percent, as shown in Figure 18.5. They fell substantially more than silver. Platinum and palladium are vital inputs in a great many applications, from cell phones to anticancer drugs, but when economic growth falters, demand for PGMs will falter as well; that's an inescapable fact. Only gold has a proven record of being reliable investment insurance, and silver, though far more volatile, is more of a safe haven asset than the two P's.

That being said, considering that the recent recession became the worst since the Great Depression and that the recovery has been very weak so far, it is remarkable that both metals have recovered ground lost as a result of the recession. And despite the price volatility, these PGMs have surged in value; platinum, in particular, has tripled over the past decade. Although the sharp recovery in metals prices is partly explained by the economic rebound, they were also influenced by a new rise in investment demand: The substantial increases in platinum and palladium

ETF purchases, respectively, partly compensated for weakness in demand from any particular industrial source.

The essential theme and investment concept of my books is that gold is recovering its position as a core asset in investment portfolios and that silver will move with its sister metal. This should have a significant effect on metals prices because the market is so small and the potential investment so large: A mere 2 percent shift from global equity and bond holdings into precious metals could make prices double and triple. Considering that prices of other precious metals—silver, platinum, and palladium—tend to move in the same direction as gold, a gold bull market implies a bull market for all, but in varying degrees. Although palladium was being held back, to some degree, by the supply overhang from 2001, both it and platinum have been reacting to the increase in investment demand in a very different way because their markets are so very small. If a relatively small $10 billion (a few days of trading in Exxon shares) were to move into the combined palladium and platinum markets, the effect would be hard to visualize.

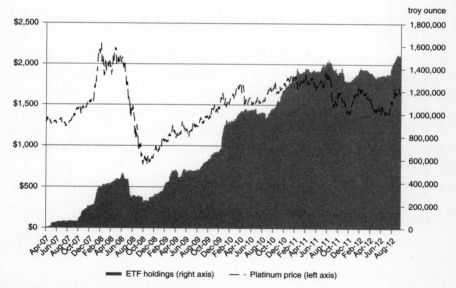

Figure 18.9   Platinum ETF Holdings
SOURCE: Bloomberg.

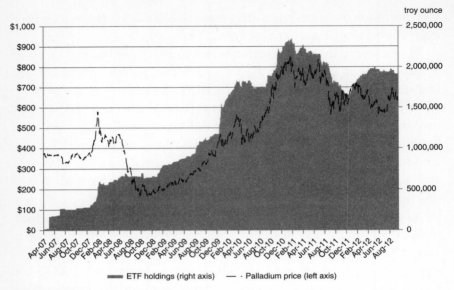

Figure 18.10 Palladium ETF Holdings

SOURCE: Bloomberg.

What differentiates platinum and palladium from gold and silver is the low starting point for investment. Though forgotten over the past 40 years, gold has always been an integral part of the global financial system. Silver was pushed out of the financial system long ago, but it has begun trading closely with gold in recent decades. But, although one could have invested in platinum and palladium mining companies, the two P's only became truly investable *for anybody* as pure metals in the past few years thanks to the listing, in London and Zurich by ETF Securities and the Swiss Zürcher Kantonalbank (ZKB), of exchange-traded funds, whose inflows have risen sharply since they began trading. And in January 2010 two new platinum and palladium ETF funds were listed for the first time in the United States by ETF Securities, which opened investment in the metals to the largest investor base in the world. (See Figures 18.9 and 18.10.) The exchange-traded funds, which effectively remove platinum and palladium supply from the market as shares are completely backed by physical deposits of the metals in vaults, have become a major driver of demand for the metals.

Conclusion

The other principal precious metal—silver—has also been used from time immemorial as a metallic base for currencies as well as for actual currency itself. It is used by probably half the population of the world. It constitutes a very important part of our own monetary structure. It is such a crucial factor in much of the world's international trade that it cannot be neglected.
—President Franklin D. Roosevelt, 1934[1]

Considering the run the metal has enjoyed, is silver about to explode substantially higher in price or will it burn out like other high-performing investments in the years ahead? There are a number of historical precedents pointed to in this book that could make you as an investor cautious about investing in the metal—or at least making silver a major part of your investment portfolio. The disappointing performance the metal displayed in the early years of the Great Depression, when silver fell to an all-time-low of 25 cents per ounce, is an important negative mark on its investment track record. Also, though due to an extraordinary situation—a conspiracy by two wealthy families to corner to market—it is a fact that silver lost half its value in a single day during 1980. The metal has a history of investment setbacks that tended to arrive very rapidly, a fact that is important to keep in mind always. Why is today different?

Although I mentioned a number of investment drivers in this book, I could condense them all into three major considerations that I believe make the case for silver compelling today. The first is, to put it simply, the multiple challenges that traditional investments face in today's financial environment, factors that are pushing more and more investors into real assets. Having concluded a decades-long expansion in American debt as a driver of economic growth—what some regard as the "debt supercycle"—in 2008 the economy went into reverse, unable to continue growing based on debt. Consider that in 2007, $5 in new debt were needed to produce one dollar of gross domestic product. To replace the debt-driven demand that collapsed in that year, governments around the world picked up the borrowing baton and ran with trillions of dollars in deficit-spending that pushed federal balance sheets into unsustainable conditions. Furthermore, a number of countries were forced to provide various forms of insurance for a large portion of the financial system, which makes their debt situation more alarming than it would appear on paper. To point to just one example, the vast majority of American residential mortgages being issued at present are insured in one way or another by the U.S. government. Although American debt has started to decline, the chart below would suggest we are in the early stages of debt reduction (see Figure C.1).

Traditional investments—stocks, bonds, real estate—thrive in a healthy financial environment based on a steadily growing economy encouraged by stable government finances. Today, a number of governments in the developed world face fiscal cliffs of varying steepness, but the conundrum is not only the difficult choices that need to be made between increased taxation and spending cuts; it is that growth-inhibiting decisions need to be made in an economic environment that is *already* extremely weak. And the record-low level of interest rates seen around the world only emphasizes the risk that eventually they will need to rise in the future, as there is not much further they can decline.

Consider a number of metrics comparing today's financial situation with that of three decades ago in Table C.1. The year 1980 is important because it marked the end of the previous rally in precious metals, a time at which the bond market, in particular, offered tremendous compensation for risk with extremely high interest rates. The eventual decline in interest rates provided a tailwind for all major asset markets, as stocks and real estate soared in value thanks to falling borrowing costs. And the attractiveness of these traditional investments encouraged investors to leave precious metals behind after the rally of the 1970s. But today, the situation is almost the inverse, particularly considering the extremely low

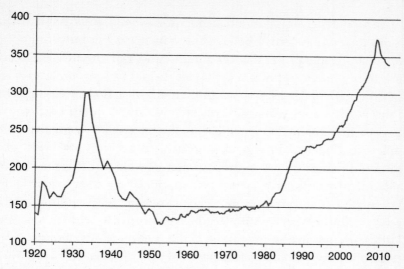

Figure C.1 U.S. Total Debt to Gross Domestic Product
SOURCE: Morgan Stanley.

interest rates in the bond market, as you can see in Table C.1. And a rise in interest rates would not necessarily indicate the return of positive investment dynamics, but rather, the threat of inflation, which encourages investment in silver and gold.

Table C.1 Comparing Economic and Financial Levels from 1980 and Today

	1980	2011	Comparison
S&P 500 Earnings Yield	10.9%	7.1%	Higher
S&P 500 Dividend Yield	4.6%	2.2%	Double
10-year Treasury yield	12.4%	1.6%	6x
Fed Funds Rate	22.0%	0.17%	n/a
Prime Rate	21.5%	3.3%	7x
30-year mortgage rate	13.8%	3.4%	Triple
Inflation rate	13.5%	2.0%	Peaking vs. troughing?
U.S. federal debt/GDP	41.0%	93.6%	Half
U.S. federal deficit/GDP	(2.7%)	(6.9%)	A third
Gold as % of Global Fin. Assets	2.8%	0.8%	3x

SOURCE: Bloomberg, Morgan Stanley, CPM Group.

The second driver is the reincorporation of gold, silver's sister metal into the financial system. I believe this concept is the most important driver of both metals for the years ahead and I discussed it at greater length in my previous book, *Hard Money*. Gold was pushed out of the financial system in the 1990s because central banks, financial executives, and the world's asset managers collectively came to believe it was no longer an investment asset needed in the financial system thanks to complete confidence in the U.S. dollar. As recently as 1980, gold represented half of global monetary reserves—that is, it remained the foundation of the global monetary system. But over a 20-year period that ended in 2008, central banks dumped an average of 10 million ounces of gold on the market and replaced them primarily with U.S. dollars and dollar-denominated investments, like U.S. Treasury bonds. Gold, always a minority holding by fiduciaries of many stripes, was also pushed out of diversified portfolios almost completely after years of poor performance. And the combination of central bank and investor selling pushed the metal down well into the 1990s, when the Bank of England governor told a European parliamentary committee: "Whereas gold used to be seen as a good asset, it is now seen as the bottom of the pile" (see Figure C.2).[2]

Today, following the worst financial crash since the Great Depression and a surge in U.S. federal debt, gold is reclaiming its position as the only safe asset that is not another entity's liability. In 2011, central banks accumulated more gold than in any of the past 40 years. Pension funds and diversified portfolios of many kinds have been accumulating gold, and yet a typical pension fund today still holds a minimal investment in the metal. In both Europe and the United States, banking regulators are considering allowing gold to be regarded as a "zero-weight" asset on institutional balance sheets, one holding the same risk requirements as the safest of assets.[3] If banks began to accumulate gold to hold as assets on their balance sheets—a return to historical banking tradition—they would be starting practically from zero: Since the 1930s, banks essentially were not allowed to hold gold. The implications of gold's return to the financial system as the viable investment asset it was for thousands of years are hard to measure with precision. Perhaps most striking is the reality that the bulk of so-called "safe assets" in the world are bonds, loans to governments that must be trusted to make payments of principal and

(Million ounces)

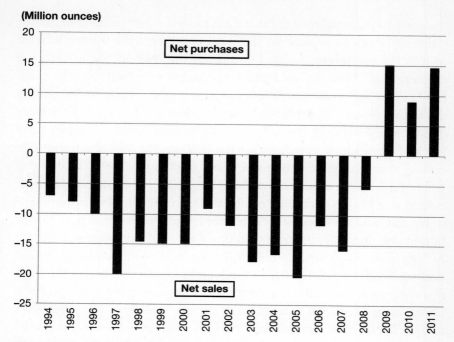

Figure C.2   Central Bank Sales of Gold
SOURCE: CPM Group.

interest with money the world believes in. Gold stands in stark contrast with bonds and fiat currency, as I wrote in 2010:

> Gold is the only currency, the only credible store of value whose quantity cannot be expanded to meet the spending needs of governments in distress. By its very nature, it remains scarce and rises in value as the quantity of paper money grows.[4]

The rise in gold driven by multiple sources of demand has prompted a reevaluation of silver's position alongside gold. By virtue of silver's outperformance of gold—as well as of all major commodities—over the last decade, the market has judged that silver is more a precious metal than an industrial one. Silver has moved more closely with gold than with "Dr. Copper," whose price is widely regarded as a barometer of the world economy's health. Though silver has traded in a turbulent way for the century following the end of bimetallism and rise of the gold standard, in recent history the metal has moved closely with gold, which reflects a return to normal: As the late Economics Nobel Prize laureate Milton Friedman once pointed out, for 3,000 years ending in 1873 the exchange rate between gold and silver traded in a fairly narrow range for 3,000 years.[5] Following a lengthy adjustment period, as discussed in the historical section of this book, the metals began to move in the same direction beginning in the early 1970s. Considering their similar nature and high correlation, it makes sense to think that the metals will continue trading closely together: the rise of gold implies the rise of silver.

A final driver of silver is rather simple, a change in our financial culture that I believe is occurring and will gain strength. It is the desire to move and hold a portion of wealth outside the financial system of stocks, bonds, and financial instruments in physical form, assets that can be held in the palm of your hand. When the largest bank in the world, the Royal Bank of Scotland, and the largest insurer, AIG, collapsed during the 2008 financial crisis, this marked a deep change in our understanding of just how safe the economic foundation of the world really is. Gold and silver initially fell in 2008, but although many commodities investors expected the metals to follow other collapsing commodities, both snapped back rapidly driven primarily by surging physical demand. This reflects the ongoing return of precious metals back to their historical place as a basic alternative form of savings. Considering that the present generation holds a lower portion of wealth in precious metals than ever before, I believe the investment future for gold and silver, sister metals with different personalities, remains promising.

Notes

Preface

1. In *Buy Gold Now* (Hoboken, NJ: John Wiley & Sons, 2008) and *Hard Money* (Hoboken, NJ: John Wiley & Sons, 2010), I wrote chapters entitled "Why Silver Might Rise More Than Gold" and "Silver: Poor Man's Gold May Offer the Richest Returns," respectively.

Introduction

1. This is not a reference to the wealth Buffett has accumulated, which has been exceeded by others, but rather to his track record as an equity market investor over multiple decades spanning bear and bull markets. Consider one of his early investment decisions. In 1969, concerned about the market's overvaluation, Buffett sold virtually his entire portfolio. The sage of Omaha liquidated Buffett Partnership and returned money to investors after a 1,100 percent return over the previous 10 years—five times better than the Dow Jones Industrial Average had returned. In 1970, the market promptly lost roughly half its value and in time Buffett warmed up to stocks again but after having saved his investors substantial wealth. That was long before he became a legendary investor. (Source for performance: Roger Lowenstein, *Buffett: The Making of An American Capitalist* (New York: Random House, 1995), 114–115.)

2. Warrenbuffett.com.

3. Margo Beller, "Civilized People Don't Buy Gold," cnbc.com, May 4, 2012. Munger said: "Gold is a great thing to sew into your garments if you're a Jewish family in Vienna in 1939, but I think civilized people don't buy gold, they invest in productive businesses."

4. Laurence Siegel, "A Riskless Society Is 'Unattainable and Infinitely Expensive,'" in *Insights into the Global Financial Crisis,* ed. Laurence Siegel (CFA Institute, 2009), 12.

5. John Acher, "Soros Warns Euro Crisis Could Destroy the EU," reuters.com, April 16, 2012.

6. Stephen Cecchetti, Madhusudan Mohanty and Fabrizio Zapolli, "The Future of Public Debt: Prospects and Implications," Working Paper 300, Bank for International Settlements, March 2010.

7. Susanne Walker, "'Budgetary Crystal Meth' Risks U.S. Haven Status, Gross Says," *Bloomberg,* October 2, 2012.

8. In 2011, the Fed bought more than half of the net new debt issued by the government. Source: Lawrence Goodman, "Demand for U.S. Debt Is Not Limitless," *Wall Street Journal,* March 28, 2012.

9. Noah Rayman, "Manhattan's 15 Central Park West Fuels Ultra-Luxury Condo Surge," *Bloomberg,* August 17, 2012.

10. Scott Reyburn, "Ford GT40 Sells for $11 Million, Auction Record for a U.S. Car," *Bloomberg,* August 19, 2012.

11. "Lee Man Fong Sets New Record for South East Asian Artists," artron.net, October 22, 2012; Frederick Balfour, "Chinese Stamps Sell for Record $709,000 at Hong Kong Auction," *Bloomberg,* October 13, 2012.

12. "Safe Assets: Financial Market Cornerstone?" International Monetary Fund, April 2012.

13. Those knowing the history of silver in the United States might question this assertion, given the large silver purchases carried out during the Franklin D. Roosevelt (FDR) administration. While this is discussed in Chapter 9, for now I'd ask the reader to acknowledge that for practical purposes the United States remained on a gold standard and that silver had lost much of its monetary importance, no matter what the "silver interests" said.

14. Shayne McGuire, *Hard Money: Taking Gold to a Higher Investment Level* (Hoboken, NJ: John Wiley & Sons, 2010), 5.

15. Collectors have always been able to buy rare silver coins, many in poor condition, but they are not the same as the new bullion coins that are widely available and which do not require any expertise to buy them confidently.

16. In this book I will not elaborate on how astonishing this fact is. Just 78 years ago, China, the most populous nation in the world, was on a silver standard, and

today the metal has no significance in the financial system. The nation was forced to abandon silver as a direct result of the U.S. government's silver purchase program in the 1930s, which drove up the metal's price, and for Chinese reserves to leave the country to be sold in the United States. Eventually, China was forced off silver and in time would go into an inflationary crisis that would lead to Mao Zedong's rise to power under a new form of government.

17. As in previous books, I regard gold as a commodity here simply because it is widely viewed as such in the financial community. It was only recently that a number of financial professionals, noting that gold was outperforming all other commodities significantly, began regarding it as a currency, which it always has been. Silver has not been a currency since China, the last major economy on a silver standard, opted for paper money in 1934.

18. Jeremy Siegel, *Stocks for the Long Run* (New York: McGraw-Hill, 2008), 13–15.

19. Fifty-two percent are in equities and 35 percent in bonds. Nick Rockel, "An Equities Comeback Would Take Decades," *Institutional Investor*, October 18, 2012.

20. While funds invest in commodities (baskets giving them exposure to price movements in things like crude oil, natural gas, and copper), gold represents less than 5 percent of a typical commodities portfolio, which forces the metal to be almost completely lost in the overall asset allocation math dominated by stocks and bonds at pension funds. Here's why: If commodities represent 3 percent of a given pension fund's assets (a typical level these days), this would mean gold probably represents 0.15 percent of a total fund's assets (5 percent of 3 percent is 0.15 percent, as shown by example of a hypothetical $10 billion fund in Figure I.4). So, including whatever it may hold in gold mining stocks and ETFs (maybe another 0.15 percent of total assets, but unlikely more than that), a typical pension fund holds less than a third of 1 percent in gold—that is to say, virtually nothing. McGuire, *Hard Money*, 11.

21. This is public information available on Bloomberg.

22. Gold is money, by strict monetary definition, but it will remain an *investment* comparable with stocks and bonds in our present monetary system so long as currencies remain unlinked with the precious metal. (The expansion of currency in circulation faster than the amount of gold production makes the value of gold rise; in other words, it becomes an "investment" whose price increases.) If we were to return to a gold standard, under which the money supply would only increase in line with gold entering central bank vaults, then gold would essentially be "cash" once again and offer no investment return. Gold has really only been an investment since 1971. McGuire, *Hard Money*, 16.

23. Ben Bernanke at the Economic Club of Indiana, Indianapolis, Indiana, October 1, 2012.

24. Lawrence Goodman, "Demand for U.S. Debt Is Not Limitless," *Wall Street Journal*, March 28, 2012.

25. "Safe Assets: Financial System Cornerstone?" International Monetary Fund, April 2012.

26. Ibid., 1.

Chapter 2

1. The period between 1933 and 1971 when gold was frozen at $35 an ounce is also cited, but gold's price adjustment was merely delayed. The U.S. government sold thousands of tons of gold over this period to preserve the mirage that the dollar was strong. But what was happening is that leaders were rapidly depleting the American gold base as foreign governments, observant of accelerating U.S. deficit spending, cashed in their dollars for gold. The adjustment came in the 1970s, when gold rocketed up 2,300 percent in nine short years (double the speed of the 1990s Nasdaq as an investment), making up for lost ground.

2. Milton Friedman, "The Cause and Cure of Inflation," in *Money Mischief* (Orlando, FL: Harcourt Brace Jovanovich, 1992), 193. The italics are Friedman's.

3. Quoted from John K. Galbraith, *The Affluent Society* (Cambridge, MA: Riverside Press, 1958), 17.

4. Studs Terkel, *Hard Times: An Oral History of the Great Depression* (New York: Pantheon Books, 1970), 245.

5. Gerard Minack, "Downunder Daily: It's Simple: Too Much Debt," Morgan Stanley report, February 17, 2010.

6. Steve H. Hanke and Nicholas Krus, "World Hyperinflations," in *The Routledge Handbook of Major Events in Economic History*, ed. Randall Parker and Robert Whaples (London: Routledge Publishing, 2013).

7. Peter Bernholz, *Monetary Regimes and Inflation: History, Economic and Political Relationships* (Northampton, MA: Edward Elgar Publishing, 2003), 69.

8. Ibid., 71.

9. Goodman, "Demand for U.S. Debt Is Not Limitless." *Wall Street Journal*.

Chapter 3

1. While we have fairly reliable estimates for total aboveground gold, it is difficult to find a good source for silver. The Silver Institute, the best source of information on the metal, produced a report in 1992 providing an estimate of total silver that had been mined and refined, as well as one for the metal that remained. Their estimate for silver produced from 4,000 B.C. through 1991 was

37.5 billion ounces. Due primarily to industrial use, they estimated that by 1991 only 19.1 billion ounces still existed in the form of bullion, coins, and other forms of the metal. My estimate for present amounts is based on this initial study and subsequent reports produced by the Silver Institute, which include annual supply and demand statistics. See Charles River Associates, *Stocks of Silver Around the World* (Washington, D.C.: The Silver Institute, 1992).

2. Ibid.

3. Roy Jastram, *Silver: The Restless Metal* (New York: John Wiley & Sons, 1981), 106.

Chapter 4

1. Michael Cembalest in "Eye on the Market: Outlook 2013," J.P. Morgan report, January 2, 2013.

2. McGuire, *Hard Money*, 6.

3. Mohamed El-Erian, "How to Handle the Sovereign Debt Explosion," *Financial Times*, March 11, 2010.

Chapter 5

1. For this simple example, I have excluded transaction costs.

2. I'm using 14 for simplicity in this example, considering it is the rough average over time, as the ratio varied and was much lower in pre-Roman Empire years.

3. Dickson Leavens, *Silver Money* (Bloomington, IN: Principia Press, 1939), 1.

4. Information about the silver ratio throughout history is from Leavens, *Silver Money*, 243 and Milton Friedman, "FDR, Silver and China" in *Monetary Mischief* (Orlando, FL: Harcourt Brace Jovanovich, 1992), 167.

5. Jastram, *Silver*, 62–64.

Chapter 6

1. Jastram, *Silver*, 157.

2. Ibid., 119.

3. Siegel, *Stocks for the Long Run*.

4. Fracis Fukuyama, *The End of History and the Last Man* (New York: Free Press, 1992).

Chapter 7

1. From interview with James Blanchard, New Orleans Investment Conference, November 7, 1993. Quoted in James Blanchard, *Silver Bonanza: How to*

Profit from the Coming Bull Market in Silver (New York: Simon & Schuster, 1993), 19.

2. You can find a longer discussion about this in *Hard Money*, 67–70.

3. You can find a lengthy discussion of the rare coin market in Chapter 15 of McGuire, *Hard Money*.

4. Jastram, *Silver*, 65.

5. Stephen Mihm, *A Nation of Counterfeiters: Capitalists, Con Men, and the Making of the United States* (Boston: Harvard University Press, 2007), 3.

6. Leavens, *Silver Money*, 3.

7. Mihm, *A Nation of Counterfeiters*, 211.

8. Jastram, *Silver*, 65.

Chapter 8

1. Jastram, *Silver*, 72.

2. Milton Friedman, "The Crime of 1873" in *Money Mischief* (Orlando, FL: Harcourt Brace Jovanovich, 1992), 57.

3. Leavens, *Silver*, 36.

4. Milton Friedman, "The Crime of 1873," 63.

Chapter 9

1. Terkel, *Hard Times*, 245.

2. The pre-1940 silver price movements are explored in great detail in Leavens *Silver Money*, 141.

3. Ibid., 141.

4. Jastram, *Silver*, 53.

5. Leavens, *Silver*, 345.

6. Allan Seymour Everest, *Morgenthau, The New Deal and Silver: A Story of Pressure Politics* (New York: King's Crown Press, 1950), 43.

7. Stephen Fay, *Beyond Greed: How the Two Richest Families in the World, the Hunts of Texas and the House of Saud, Tried to Corner the Silver Market—How They Failed, Who Stopped Them, and Why It Could Happen Again* (New York: Viking Press, 1982), 38.

8. Jastram, *Silver*, 93.

9. Friedman, "FDR, Silver and China," 166.

10. Leavens, *Silver Money*, 273.

11. Jastram, *Silver*, 53.

12. Friedman, "FDR, Silver and China," 178.

13. Ibid., 174.

14. Jastram, *Silver*, 98.

15. Friedman, "FDR, Silver and China," 167.

Chapter 10

1. Jastram, *Silver,* 106.

2. Ibid.

3. William Burke and Yvonne Levy, *Silver: End of an Era* (Federal Reserve Bank of San Francisco, 1969), 11.

4. Burke and Levy, *Silver*, 11.

5. Jastram, *Silver,* 107.

6. Ibid.

7. Burke and Levy, *Silver*, 13.

8. Henry Merton, *The Big Silver Melt* (New York: MacMillan Publishing Co., 1983), 4.

9. Jastram, *Silver,* 108.

10. Burke and Levy, *Silver*, 15.

11. Ibid., 13.

Chapter 11

1. Quoted in Fay, *Beyond Greed*, 32.

2. This passage, explaining monetary developments in the 1970s, is taken from my first book, *Buy Gold Now*, 28–29.

3. Burke and Levy, *Silver*, 25.

4. Quoted in Fay, *Beyond Greed*, 103.

5. Ibid.

6. Ibid.

7. Ibid., 59.

8. Blanchard, *Silver Bonanza*, 122.

9. Ibid., 123.

10. Ibid., 33.

Chapter 12

1. John Hathaway, "A Contrarian's Dilemma," letter written to investors, December 2009. The first gold ETF was launched by Gold Bullion Securities in

Australia in 2003, but what has become the most important one is the SPDR Gold Trust (GLD), launched in November 2004.

2. McGuire, *Hard Money*, 147.

Chapter 13

1. Safety box rental is more affordable than you might think. Though obviously availability and price is dependent on the supply and demand of boxes where you live; in Austin, Texas, the price range is between $50 and $200 per year for small to very large boxes.

2. The Neil/Carter/Contursi specimen 1794 Flowing Hair Silver Dollar sold for $7,850,000 in May of 2010, setting a new record as the world's most valuable rare coin. Graded PCGS Specimen-66, it is the finest known 1794 dollar and believed by several prominent experts to be the first silver dollar ever struck by the United States Mint. (Source: "1794 Silver Dollar Sold for World Record Price," coinupdate.com, May 20, 2010).

3. If you would like to read more about the rare coin market, see "Rare Coins: An Attractive Market Unreachable to Fund Managers" in McGuire, *Hard Money*.

Chapter 14

1. In my conversations about GATA I've found that most professionals in the gold mining and financial industries have not taken the organization seriously over the years due to what they see as its penchant for hyperbolic descriptions of alleged manipulation of the precious metals market. But I've also realized that, despite this widespread view, a great many investors receive and read GATA emails pointing to relevant facts and periodicals discussing precious metals!

2. Joe Weisenthal, "Everyone's Buzzing About Bernanke's Controversial Comments About Gold," businessinsider.com, July 13, 2011.

3. Jack Farchy, "Four-Year Silver Probe Set to be Dropped," *Financial Times*, August 5, 2012.

4. Jordan Schwarz, *1933: Roosevelt's Decision: The United States Leaves the Gold Standard* (New York: Chelsea House Publishers, 1969), 106.

Chapter 15

1. McGuire, *Buy Gold Now*, 154.

Chapter 16

1. At the Inside Commodities Conference held at the New York Stock Exchange on November 4, 2011, I made a presentation about gold at global pension funds.

Chapter 17

1. McGuire, *Buy Gold Now*, 160.

2. These are estimated "silver equivalent" ounces that include the benefits ("credits") from by-product minerals, like gold, that typically result from the same silver mining activity. Ore is always a combination of minerals and a number of combinations can come out of the ground, often very profitable ones holding more than one valuable mineral.

3. Canadian Institute of Mining, Metallurgy, and Petroleum.

Conclusion

1. Franklin D. Roosevelt, *On Our Way* (New York: The John Day Company, 1934), 219–220.

2. Kenneth Gooding, "Death of Gold," *Financial Times*, December 13, 1997.

3. See Natalie Dempster, "Current State of Play of Basel III Implementation in the EU", lbma.org and "Regulatory Capital Rules: Standardized Approach for Risk-Weighted Assets," FDIC Financial Institution Letter, June 18, 2012.

4. McGuire, *Hard Money*, 6.

5. Friedman, "FDR, Silver and China," 167.

Further Reading
about Silver

If you share my view that silver is being reincorporated into the financial system as an investment asset, you may want to learn more about the metal and its history. Unfortunately, in my opinion very little serious work has been produced on the subject of silver in recent decades, the most recent writing being Nobel Prize Laureate Milton Friedman's "FDR, Silver and China", published in 1992 and Roy Jastram's *Silver: The Restless Metal*, published more than 30 years ago. Furthermore, while there are a great number of books dealing with monetary history, as well as a surge in new writing about gold, few books or periodicals focus specifically on silver as an investment. Below I provide references for the publications about silver that I believe provide useful information about the metal.

Sources of Information on Present Silver
Supply and Demand

The Silver Institute. The best source of information regarding changes in the demand and supply of silver is the Silver Institute, whose most important publication is the annual *World Silver Survey,* which unfortunately is far more expensive than several ounces of silver. (The steep price reflects the cost of producing the valuable resource, which is then sold to the relatively small number of serious readers who need it, mostly investment professionals and mining industry executives.) The survey is produced on behalf of the institute by GFMS, one of the world's most reputable sources on precious metals supply and demand statistics. (The other one is CPM Group, which produces top notch statistics and publications on precious metals and commodities markets.) It not only details global production and demand for silver, it provides ample detail on market conditions around the world. Aside from this publication, the institute's website (www.silverinstitute.org) is a great resource for abundant information about silver and all is free.

Precious Metal and Mining Company Websites. It is also possible to read about the present silver market on the websites of some of the world's largest silver producers, like that of Endeavour Silver. Many companies provide information about their most recent activities and production along with their views on the supply and demand for silver. Consider that what you might find on these websites is information provided by the persons that watch the supply and demand of silver most closely since they depend on it. Other useful websites are kitco.com, mineweb.com, and bloomberg.com.

Books and Articles

Unfortunately, many of these books are out of print although there have been reprintings of some of them.

James Blanchard, *Silver Bonanza: How to Profit from the Coming Bull Market in Silver* (New York: Simon & Schuster, 1993). Mr. Blanchard, one of the most influential precious metals dealers in the United States when this was published, presented the bull case for silver in the 1990s and offered useful information regarding ways of investing in the metal. Unfortunately, Blanchard could not foresee the rise of digital photography and the significant negative impact this would have over the next decade on silver demand as the film developing industry changed dramatically.

William Burke and Yvonne Levy, "Silver: End of an Era," Federal Reserve Bank of San Francisco, October 1974. This is a good, though brief, source of events in the 1960s and early 1970s.

Stephen Fay, *Beyond Greed: How the Two Richest Families in the World, the Hunts of Texas and the House of Saud, Tried to Corner the Silver Market—How They Failed, Who Stopped Them, and Why It Could Happen Again* (New York: Viking Press, 1982). This is the best book on one of the most amazing episodes in silver history—the attempt by billionaires to corner a small market, their spectacular failure, and what it meant for the silver industry.

Milton Friedman, *Monetary Mischief* (Orlando, FL: Harcourt Brace Jovanovich, 1992). Nobel Laureate Milton Friedman wrote a few chapters in this book discussing important chapters in the history of silver, like President Franklin D. Roosevelt's intervention in the metals market during his first administration and the currency crisis this indirectly caused in China.

Roy Jastram, *Silver: The Restless Metal* (New York: John Wiley & Sons, 1981). In my opinion, this is the most important book ever written for silver investors. Though primarily an academic work, as it provides a well-documented history of silver supply and demand dynamics throughout recent history. Its information is vital to understand the present silver market. Jastram also wrote an influential book about gold that has become a gold investment classic, *The Golden Constant: The English and American Experience, 1560–2007* (Northampton, MA: Edward Elgar, 1977).

Dickson Leavens, *Silver Money* (Bloomington, IN: Principia Press, 1939). Published in the late 1930s, this is one of the most important sources for researching silver because it had fresh information from a pivotal point in the metal's history: its nadir as an investment metal. The Great Depression is the only period in the millennial history of finance in which gold and silver went separate ways: Gold demand surged, while that of silver collapsed. Leavens discusses the drivers leading silver to fall sharply before its surge in the late 1930s.

Laurence Laughlin, *The History of Bimetallism in the United States* (New York: Appleton and Co., 1892). The name says it all, though the ultimate effects of the end of bimetallism are best understood after reading Friedman, Paris, Leavens, and Jastram.

James D. Paris, *Monetary Policies of the United States, 1932–1938* (New York: Columbia University Press, 1938). This provides abundant detail on the politics of silver during this vital period of monetary turmoil.

Hugo Salinas Price, *La Plata: El Camino para Mexico* (Mexico City: Editorial Diana, 1996). This is one of several books by Mr. Salinas in which he discusses the desirability of remonetizing silver in Mexico, one of the world's largest producers.

Allan Seymour Everest, *Morgenthau, The New Deal and Silver: A Story of Pressure Politics* (New York: Columbia University Press, 1950). Another useful tome taking a deep dive into the politics behind the government's silver purchase in the 1930s.

About the Author

Shayne McGuire manages the $850 million GBI Gold Fund and is the head of Global Research at Teacher Retirement System of Texas, one of the world's largest pension funds. Prior to holding these positions, Mr. McGuire managed a $2 billion European stock portfolio and in 1995 and 1996 he was ranked among the best Latin American analysts by *Institutional Investor*. In addition to launching the first dedicated gold fund within the U.S. pension system, he has written two books on gold investing, including *Hard Money: Taking Gold to a Higher Investment Level* (John Wiley & Sons, 2010). Mr. McGuire graduated from Fordham University and holds a Masters in History and an MBA from the University of Texas at Austin.

Index